RED DIRT GIRL
ESSAYS AND STORIES

KATIE LAUR

Orange *frazer* Press
Wilmington, Ohio

ISBN 978-1949248-593
Copyright ©2022 Nancy Catherine Laur
All Rights Reserved

No part of this publication may be reproduced in any material form (including photocopying or storing in any medium by electronic means and whether or not transiently or incidentally to some other use of this publication) without the written permission of the copyright holder except in accordance with the provisions of Title 17 of the United States Code.

Published for the copyright holder by:
Orange Frazer Press
37½ West Main St.
P.O. Box 214
Wilmington, OH 45177

For price and shipping information, call: 937.382.3196
Or visit: www.orangefrazer.com

Cover design:
Oakley Scot with Catie South and Orange Frazer Press

Book design:
Orange Frazer Press with Catie South
Pattern from www.vecteezy.com

"The studio moon," from *Prairie Fires and Paper Moons, the American Photographic Postcard: 1900-1920*, David R. Godine Publisher, 1981; Photography by Marty Godbey, courtesy Frank Godbey; Center for Folklore Studies, The Ohio State University; Image on page 128 courtesy of Cal Kowal from his book, *Spoons*, 1975; The author has sought to identify all credits for photographs—the majority which came from her private collection—but if one has been inadvertently omitted, please make notification so any emendations may be made in future editions. Some of these essays have previously appeared in *Cincinnati* magazine, *CityBeat*, *OHIO* magazine, and *Country Journal*.

Library of Congress Control Number: 2022902591

First Printing

To Becky and Sam Hudnall—
Friendship is a collaboration from
which all blessings flow.

Make this night lovable,
Moon, and with eye single
Looking down from up there.
Bless me, One especial
And friends everywhere.

—W.H. Auden, Five Songs

ACKNOWLEDGMENTS

A couple of years ago, I sent my laptop to San Francisco to my friends, Sam and Becky Hudnall. Sam overhauled it and did a tune-up and found over 650 pages I had saved in the wrong place. I said, out loud, that I should write a book.

With the help of many, it is done!

Thanks to preliminary readers, Ian Fraser, Marcia Philipps, and Bob Lee, who provided helpful comments regarding the stories; and to Jeff Terflinger, Wayne Clyburn, Frank and Marty Godbey, Rich Flaig and Lou Ann Reese, Cal Kowal, and Michael Wilson, who supplied photographs. Thanks as well to Bob Flischel, master photographer and friend, for his photographs.

Special thanks to Oakley Scot, a friend for years, who did his usual fine job of designing and pulling together the graphics. And for being a great guy to work with.

A huge thank you to editor John Baskin who has been after me to write a book since he was the editor of *OHIO* magazine. I appreciate the encouragement, John.

And to Danute Miskinis and Lib Stone, without whom this book would not have been possible, I am eternally grateful.

CONTENTS

Foreword	IX
Introduction	XI

1 MEMORIES — 1
Leaving Tennessee — 3

2 FAMILY — 29
Aunt Dot's Scrambled Eggs — 31
Confessions of a Yellow-Dog Democrat — 35
Plain and Fancy — 38
Moving On — 45
In the Garden — 48

3 BLUEGRASS — 55
Pickers and Grinners — 57
Curly Ray Cline — 64
Walking the Hills — 70
Bluegrass Royalty — 73
Fox on the Run — 80
Harry Sparks, Guitar Master — 82
Voices From the Mountains — 89

4 ON THE ROAD — 93
On the Road Again — 95
Burnin' Up the Road — 102
Queen City Cowboy — 109
Rabbit Hash — 116
Playing Through — 122
A Prairie Home Companion (1980) — 124

5 OVER-THE-RHINE — 127
Saturday Night and Sunday Morning — 129
A Good Neighbor — 137
Breaking the Mold — 140
Street of Dreams — 145
Our Lady of Court Street (2010) — 153

6 NOSTALGIA — 161
How High the Moon — 163
Apothecary — 165
Blue Christmas — 167
Urban Legends: The Dark Side — 174

7 GREAT BARS — 177
Arnold's Courtyard — 179
Blue Nights — 181
A Comet Over Northside — 188
The Queen of Dixie's — 194
Salute To a Bass Player — 198
Swingin' at the Dee Felice Café — 200
He's Funny That Way — 203
John Von Ohlen: He's Got Rhythm — 209
Stop Time — 215

8 RADIO: "MASH THE BUTTONS, WAYNE" — 223
Radio Days — 225
Accidental Deejay — 230
Cornbread Nation — 238
A Dulcimer Scandal — 240
Where the Holler Meets the Hardtop — 243
Pester Flatt and the Magic of Good Writing — 248
O Pester, Who Art Thou? — 251
Letter to Pester — 258

9 FRIENDS — 261
Afternoons with Irma — 263
Cruisin' Down the River — 270
The Funeral of John Hartford (2001) — 276
Sister: Digging Up Bones — 284
A Sophisticated Lady (2012) — 292
Curtain Call (2011) — 299

"Oh, Sweet Mama" (for Katie Laur) — 307

FOREWORD

For many years Jackie Demaline, the intrepid theater reviewer for the *Enquirer*, invited a group of interesting women to get together during the dreary month of January. She named the event "Soup's On." Jackie loved soup! We would gather at Lib Stone's home contributing soup, freshly baked breads, and desserts. During our gathering, we would go around the table for a quick update of everyone's activities. In 2018, Katie Laur said that she had been encouraged to write a book, and when it was my turn, I said, "Katie, I would love to help you with your book."

So began the serendipitous alliance of Katie, Lib, and Danute. We met to discuss how to proceed and collect Katie's literary works into a manageable file. As Lib put it, "Katie's the author, Danute's the director, and I am the stage manager." As weekly meetings were held and themes discovered, I put the stories into chapters. During two years of work we continued to talk and laugh as we read excerpts aloud, enjoying the flow of Katie's words, the humor behind her insights, memories and travails.

Passion for the project kept us going, inviting others to read the stories, and seeking advice since none of us knew the first thing about publishing a book.

So here we are ready to let go of our baby—a package created in the time of Covid—and put it to the test of public exposure.

We are proud of our accomplishment and delight in the friendship of hard work, respect and admiration for each other. We hope you will find the sense of heartfelt adventure, the love of family, music, and friends, the labors and humor of a musician's life on the road all wrapped up in Katie's great stories.

Enjoy!

—*Danuté Miskinis*

INTRODUCTION

Nancy Catherine Laur: a Southern girl raised on the red dirt of middle Tennessee. This is where she began to fashion for herself a different kind of American Dream. If this compilation of her stories rings true, it's because Katie is a keen observer of the human condition and her writing reveals a thread in the fabric of life that holds us all together.

She writes about human frailty and successes, and celebrates the lives of ordinary people with great compassion. She'll remind you of your own experiences, and she is as fascinated with people who might wander into a country bar at midnight to people attending an event hosted by the symphony.

You'll discover her appreciation for country people, street characters, and those who live below the radar. She is fond, bordering on reverent, of Appalachian folks—those who had found their way out of the coal mines and hollers to travel up Highway 23 (known as the "hillbilly highway"), where they found work in places like Cincinnati, Detroit, and Cleveland, far enough north to get a good paycheck but not far enough that they were unable to go home on weekends to family. Her own history was similar in that her father moved the family to Detroit where cultural differences played a role in shaping her young life.

It has been said that if you haven't lived it, you haven't learned it. Katie's life in music has provided many unusual experiences, from performing bluegrass to singing for sophisticated audiences in New York City. She writes of family and friends, of relatives she hasn't seen in years, and of characters as different as riverboat captains and women who are her heroes.

Reading these stories is like being guided through a museum filled with paintings of interesting people, each presented in a way that allows us to walk arm in arm with Katie as our docent. A docent with a quick wit and a smooth Southern accent … you'll see.

—*Bill LaWarre*

1
MEMORIES

THE HALEY SISTERS IN DETROIT IN BACK.
FROM LEFT: SANDRA, JACKIE, AND KATIE.
LINDA AND PATTI IN FRONT.

LEAVING TENNESSEE

My earliest memories are dark, like under-developed film: reaching for a flower, my mother's smell, the sound of music. It floated out of the radio like magic. When the theme music came on for *Noon-Time Neighbors* I got on Fancy, the wooden rocking horse my grandfather made for me, and began to ride. At night, the radio told the war news, Roosevelt's hearty voice buoying all the grown-ups gathered around as if it were the beating heart of the house. For me, the memories are fusty and old, as gauzy as cobwebs—you could dissolve them with your hand.

Yet the isolation of those World War II years in the rural South, the love and the warmth, the anxiety over those who were far away, the tears when no letters came, and always the laughter, marked me and taught me to live with contrast. I learned to need loneliness and to cry out for company, to act out the sadness of their lives, yet not take myself too seriously. My family was my first audience.

"How does the rooster go?" my grandmother Kate would say at the General Store, and I would flap my arms and cry, "Cockadoodle doo!"

"How do you spell 'cat?'" she'd ask, and I'd say, "C-A-T."

Then one day, I pointed to the wall and said to my Aunt Dot, "See dat bug," and I had discovered the miracle of language. I would lie on my stomach under the ironing board while my mother pressed the sheets and say, "Read to me." I'd hold the book where she could see it and turn the pages when she told me.

She suspected I could already read when I began to turn the pages for her without prompting. It was a blessed liberation for my family. No more tales of Spot or Fluffy. No more Ned and Nancy. Later, when someone did something she didn't like, my Aunt Dot would giggle and say, "He's dumber than Ned in the first reader." It had never occurred to me that anyone might judge Ned and find him wanting. He and Nancy and Spot lived in a perfect fictional world of green lawns and painted houses.

At night, my mother put me in a washtub of warm water for my bath. At eighteen or nineteen, she was a girl herself with lovely olive skin and deep brown eyes and the gentlest touch. She sluiced the warm water over me with a cloth. I had played barefoot all day in the red dirt, and my feet and ankles were the color of rust. I could hear the music of the cicadas outside the window. From the pond, came the singing of the bullfrogs, and the overpowering sweetness of honeysuckle. In the country, there was no noise at all, just an occasional train whistle. The hugeness of it was overwhelming: I was the center of the universe; I was nothing at all.

Sometimes we'd spend the day with Grandaddy while he delivered the mail. Mother would drive her old Model T, Daisy May, and stop at each mailbox if there was a red flag up. The red flag meant there was a letter to be picked up. Grandaddy was very good at delivering the mail, probably because he knew all the families in that small community. He hoed in the garden or milked the cows, grew vegetables which the women cooked and canned, but mostly he carried the mail. His hair was gray, and he wore small glasses which slid down his nose.

"Let's go, Suzie," he'd say, and Mother would step on the gas and head for the first mailbox, the red gravel kicking up a cloud of dust. Everybody wrote on post cards during the war, because the postage was cheaper, so Grandaddy read their mail and knew before anybody else who had been sent to the front or who was sick or seeing another woman. In fact, he got so absorbed in reading the postcards that he'd forget to tell my mother when to stop. Then he'd look up, sheepishly, and ask her to back up. She had to work hard to keep her old Model T from going in the ditch. The roads were not paved or graded. When he had delivered all the letters in his bag and picked up all the cards in the mailboxes with their red flags sticking up, he'd take everything back to Mary Francis at the General Store P.O.

MEMORIES

While we were at the store, he would buy me a Coca-Cola from the red box near the counter. I wasn't supposed to drink it because it spoiled my appetite for supper, but he got it for me anyway. When we got home, he'd tell Aunt Dot all the news he'd gathered carrying the mail. Joe Neese's son was wounded in Okinawa, he'd say, and Aunt Dot would cry and get the "sick" headache. Everybody made a beeline for Aunt Dot when they had bad news because she was quick to cry with you. She'd validate your sadness, make it real. But if you told her something good, she'd laugh the biggest of anybody. I watched the grown-ups, and it seemed like they wanted to tell her things before they told anybody else. My grandmother clucked and said it was why she had the "sick" headache.

When I was just starting to walk, my mother took me on a long train trip all the way to California so that we could visit Daddy. The train was full of Army men, but they gave my mother and me their seats, and we rode a long, long way to California. During the war, the servicemen got the first of everything—the first train tickets, things like that, and everybody in the family was nervous about us going clear across the country, but the soldiers were nice to Mother and me. At stops, a soldier would take my bottle into the station for my mother and heat it up. My mother told me we were going to San Francisco to a place called the Presidio. I wore a handmade dress with rosebuds sewn on the bodice and high-topped white baby shoes. My hair was in short dark curls because I would be meeting Daddy for the first time.

When we got to California, my mother got us off the train. It was so foggy it was scary; and California looked different from Tennessee and smelled different too, like eucalyptus. We looked everywhere, but there was no Daddy waiting for us. We had never seen so many people. Everywhere the throngs crowded around, getting on or off the train. It was hard to move. Soldiers kissed girls, and there was shouting and talking and pushing.

Mother turned around to look for Daddy, the train pulled out, and suddenly she lost her bearings and didn't know where she was. A woman reached out to her and caught her just as she was about to faint. A kind voice spoke and asked us if we needed to rest, and we went with the woman to a room close by. My mother and I took a nap, and when we woke Daddy was there, and everything was all right.

We rented a room on Fell Street in San Francisco, and we lived there while Daddy spent his days learning to fight in the Army. Mother got a job as a waitress in a Chinese restaurant. Neither one of us had ever seen a Chinese person before, but San Francisco had a lot of Chinese people. Of course, my mother couldn't understand Chinese, and the Chinese couldn't understand her, but at the restaurant they worked out an arrangement where she could write out her orders, copy them from the menu, and the cooks could fill them and, with many hand signals, get them delivered to the right tables. She had pretty brown eyes, she smiled a lot, and she found people smiled back at her.

In the afternoons, we'd walk in Golden Gate Park and see old Chinese men with beards and fingernails so long they hung down the arms of their chairs like talons. Someone told us the long nails meant they were rich and didn't have to work. It meant they could afford to hire servants. They looked far away into the distance; maybe they were looking out towards China, just like we looked towards Tennessee. I didn't know what to think of the Chinese men, but I never forgot them.

Daddy's unit went to war eventually, and we went back to Tennessee. When the radio said that the war was finally over, everyone laughed and then cried, especially my Aunt Dot. She cried for a long time and began to get another headache. My daddy and my uncle had been to the concentration camps with their units, but they never talked about it. Aunt Dot said not to ask them. Uncle Fred had been fighting the Japanese, and our cousin Bob had been on the Bataan Death March and came home with no hair and a nervous tic. Uncle Clarence had nightmares and began to drink heavily. Death had hovered over our house, Aunt Dot said, but now we were safe.

It was as if we had gone through a long, dark tunnel and come out the other side into a different kind of light. We were all happy, of course, but we struggled to find new ways to be with each other, new parts to play. Daddy and Uncle Clarence enrolled in Murray State University in Kentucky, spending two years studying accounting. My little sister Jackie was born when we lived at Murray, and sucked her milk out of a Coke bottle with a nipple on it. She had blue eyes and cornsilk hair, as utterly unlike me as she could be. She used to stare straight at me, sucking her thumb, blinking her blue eyes. From a distance, I watched my star fade. Mother said I once tried to kill her, but those years are only vague memories.

My father yelled that I was spoiled, and it seemed I was always crying. He tried to force me to eat. He chased me around the kitchen table with a scrap of bread left from my plate, dropped it in the dishwater, and still he tried to make me eat it. Aunt Dot would say, "This isn't the way," but Daddy was angry because we had made a unit without him.

There was not much time to brood because Grandaddy was sick, and the doctor came a lot—Dr. Horace McSwain—but there was nothing they could do for Grandaddy. He had a liver disease, and Aunt Dot explained that his days were numbered.

One day I went in the living room and looked at everybody. Nobody was missing, and I got a bad feeling. "Who is taking care of Grandaddy?" I asked. My mother took me in the bathroom. It was a hot day, and she bathed me in the tub. She pursed her lips together and sighed and petted me. "Let's get quiet," she said. She told me that Grandaddy had died and, little as I was, I reached my skinny arms up to the ceiling and screamed and screamed.

The house was already beginning to fill with neighbors bringing platters of cold fried chicken, but nobody said a word, just sat with silent tears running down their faces, listening to the sound of my screams bouncing off the walls. Then *they* began to cry. They were afraid, and because of the fear that gripped them, they began to be closer than ever, to do everything together.

When the farm was sold and the belongings of a lifetime packed and sorted, we moved to Detroit where Daddy and the other men hoped to find work in the automobile factories. We left Tennessee on a hot, sunny day in 1950, singing songs and playing games where you had to remember things you packed in a trunk and then add something to the list. By the time we got to the Ohio River, my sister and I were fighting. We sat in the back seat with Grandmother Kate in between us. We used her as our fort and hit at each other from the cover of her ample bosom. A lot of times we missed and hit her. Daddy had to use his "Don't-make-me-have-to-stop-this-car" voice until we were crying and ill and cranky.

My mother had that faraway look she used to get when she was troubled. Her eyebrows knit together until she looked cross. "Let's have quiet time," she'd say, and for fifteen minutes we were all required to be totally quiet, even Daddy. I could tell she felt sad about leaving her parents back in Tennessee.

It came to me in a flash that grandmother and grandfather were *her* mother and father just as she and Daddy were my parents, and though it was a stretch of the imagination I could see that one day I would be somebody's mother, too.

"When am I going to be a mommy?" I asked her.

Jackie and Katie at their grandparents' house in the country.

"Oh," Mother said, "I don't know," and she began to cry.

Nobody said anything. There was just the radio, the station playing country music full of static, the signal coming in and then going out again. You could hear Bill Monroe or Hank Williams on the radio. Daddy liked Flatt and Scruggs singing "Maple on the Hill," and he could usually divert us all with a little singing, but the night was falling fast. At home, in Tennessee, the chickens would be roosting. It would be time to milk the cows. I wanted to ask questions about all these things, but I felt like I had pushed my luck as far as it would go, so I leaned my head into my grandmother's side and fell asleep.

When I woke up next, Mother was driving and Daddy had dropped off to sleep. We were headed for Lansing, Michigan, which would take us to Detroit. We got lost somewhere around Lansing, and everybody got out to look at the map. I didn't think grown-ups got lost, and I was a little scared. My Aunt Olyne had the best sense of direction of any of us, and she took the map and traced the right route with her pointed fingernail. Her family car took the lead as she fed directions to Uncle Clarence and, finally, we got through Lansing. Daddy sat lower in his seat and scowled. "Olyne is a smart aleck," he said, but I didn't know what that was, and Jackie wasn't talking.

In Detroit, everything around us was new, the way things were new right after World War II—the smell of raw lumber and sawdust hung in the air. Even the light looked new, so thin it was the color of skim milk. We lived in a house on Glastonbury Drive, all of us together, like thousands of other immigrants. I can barely remember anything about it, but we marveled at the noise: horns blared, sirens were frightening, and loud radios blasted rhythm and blues. We held hands everywhere we went, as if in solidarity. Our fathers had been to Europe in World War II, fighting the Germans, so they had seen things we couldn't have dreamed of: big cities, bombed out buildings, people walking aimlessly with vacant eyes. We had seen nothing much except the red dirt of Henry County, Tennessee.

My sisters and my cousins and I were used to country ways, to small truck gardens, to milk cows, and to bacon stored in our own smokehouse.

All we knew of violence was when the hogs were butchered on the first cold day of autumn and hung from sharp hooks in the yard. All we knew of commerce was when we had a nickel to take to the General Store for a Coca-Cola. And the world beyond our family consisted mostly of the old farmers and their wives sitting on the bench outside the clapboard store, the men in overalls, frayed serge jackets, and brogan shoes; the women in faded rayon dresses, hairnets knotted at the temples.

On one of our first forays into the city, we saw country boys in rhinestones and cheap silk shirts lying in the gutters along Woodward Avenue, sleeping where they fell. Most of them had grown up in an agrarian economy; they had never had money before, and now they were paid cash on a weekly basis for working in the automobile factories. They spent their pay in a weekend-long orgy of beer, women, and flashy clothes.

Mother said that the country people in Detroit had so much cash they thought they were rock stars. When you farm you don't ever see the money. You eat off the garden you plant and your livestock, and what money you get goes right back into seeds for next year's crop. She said it was scary that money could change those people like that, but we weren't so different. When we got a place to live and some money coming in, the first thing we had to do was buy clothes, cheap dresses from chain stores like "Monkey" Ward's—that's what they called Montgomery Ward's. Daddy bought his first guitar there, a Kay archtop with great big f-holes in it. Daddy wore it over his neck with a tassel strap that went from the neck to the bottom of the guitar. He never changed that strap, either. The one he had when he got the guitar was the same one on the guitar when he died.

Daddy and Uncle Clarence bought little box houses on the same street. My mother worked at a bakery, standing on the assembly line all night packaging coffee cakes until the veins in her legs were broken. Our grandmother fed us breakfast and got us off to school while my mother slept until her next shift. One summer night we ate dinner hurriedly and walked outside with both our parents. When we got to the big tree in the middle of the block, we met our aunt and uncle and our two cousins, and they began to walk with us.

I don't remember any tension, just curiosity. The furrows on my mother's brow were knit tightly together. My father kept his hand in his pocket, jiggling his keys nervously. We, the children, were small, and thin as storks. Our knock-knees stuck out from our short dresses, along with the edges of our big-girl panties.

My cousin Sandra wore her blonde hair in a perfect pageboy, cut just to her jawline. Her bangs were partially pulled back off her pretty face and fastened with a barrette. I was taller and even skinnier, with thick curly black hair and a sunny grin, so habitual I even squinted after dark. Our parents told us to hold hands, so we squeezed tight and pinched each other, impatiently. The first signs of a crowd appeared ahead of us, an undertone of noise drifting back to where we walked.

The crowd began to grow as we approached the next block, and we could hear an undercurrent of anger. "Stay together," my mother told us, "and stay with us." The sound of voices grew louder, but our parents were as quiet as we'd ever heard them. We tried to find out what was going on, but no one said anything except, "Be quiet," and for some unknown reason we decided we should. There was smoke coming from across the street, and a cross was burning in the front yard of a small house, which was much like ours.

It was eerie, then people began to throw rocks at the house and scream names we couldn't understand. There was a moving van in the driveway. Had someone just moved in? The crowd of people obviously didn't like the new neighbors, and that was what this was about: to get them to leave again. Eventually the police showed up, and the crowd dispersed. We walked home the way we had come, Sandra and I still holding hands, and none of us said a word.

We got home, washed our hands, and went to bed. When I was drifting off to sleep I heard snatches of conversation between my mother and father: " … just people like anybody else … " " … I'd a' been too scared to do it … " my mother said. " … more trouble coming … " my father said.

I drifted off with my own thoughts. There were no Black children in my school, but city-wide junior orchestra and city-wide choir were integrated. A week after that incident, at our choir performance downtown, I asked a little girl to be quiet. I must have been a little prissy, because she turned around in her seat and looked at me. "You tryin' to jump bad at me, little pink cheeks?"

When we got a television set my father and my uncles gathered to watch the McCarthy hearings, stunned. Aunt Dot said, "There are Communists in Hollywood!" with an air of incredulity. Over glasses of Canadian whiskey (another new thing they'd developed a taste for), they'd talk about Communists in Hollywood (it amounted to nothing, my father said), while the women grew bored and drifted into quieter rooms. My father and my uncle worked on the assembly lines with rough union men and people they had no experience with. Blacks wanted to work there, too. The men didn't hate that as much as they were puzzled by it. As far as they were concerned it was a lousy job. Equal wages was not something anyone thought about.

"They're just not the same as us," Daddy would say.

"They sure can play ball," my uncle would counter.

I'm sure it was his idea of a compliment, although how he knew that was a mystery. Integrated sports teams were as scarce as hens' teeth in those days.

At the House of Un-American Activities hearings, Blacks and whites appeared to be friends, not like the Blacks in Tennessee to whom we'd distributed watermelons on the Fourth of July. It was more like they were equals, and that troubled my family.

"It's because they're from Africa," my father said, musing almost to himself. It was a new issue for us. Back in Tennessee, everyone had been so poor. The effects of the Depression on the rural south had been so profound that whites competed with each other for the menial jobs. There were few jobs, anyway. Daddy had worked in the General Store in rural Tennessee. One of my aunts had worked at the shirt factory in a nearby town. They were poor people, living on the edge of despair when they picked up and moved north.

Of course World War II had changed things. Why *not* leave home? There was nothing to keep the men in Tennessee, plowing hardscrabble farms, or driving twenty miles one way for a little job. The Depression was still fresh; my family was too young to know what they were facing and too fearless to care.

It had not yet occurred to them—if it would—that poverty and despair didn't discriminate; white or Black, we were all driven by the same desire for something better, and we all had the same dream of honest work and fair wages. Almost a half million Southerners, both Black and white, made the exodus from the south to the north. Suddenly, we were all tossed in the pot and stirred.

On most weekends, we gathered in the basements of our new houses and played music. The basements were concrete with poles which ran from floor to ceiling. Mother wrapped crepe paper around the poles, set up soft drinks and pretzels and potato chips in the corner, and by the time it was dark, everybody was headed for our basement to listen to music and dance. The first song was always Bob Wills singing, "Stay All Night, Stay a Little Longer," and even hearing it all these many years later makes me feel just as cheerful as it used to in those early days in Detroit, surrounded by my family: Aunt Dot on the piano, Uncle Fred on the fiddle, and Daddy on the guitar, doing a little western swing.

"Bob Wills was so big during the war," Daddy told us, more than once, "that when he came to the Cow Palace in San Francisco, people lined up clear around the block to hear him play. He had that beat. That's what music is all about," Daddy said. "It's all about the *timing*. If you ain't got that, you ain't got nothin'." I was little still, but I heard him and absorbed his words into my own consciousness as indelibly as the Ten Commandments were inscribed on the stone tablets. *It's all in the beat*, I said to myself.

The men set up a bar area in one corner of the basement where they mixed Canadian Club with 7-Up or ginger ale and ice. Their smiles would get just a little bigger, their faces would get a little redder. Later on, they'd be almost scary and mother would shoo us up to bed, though we snuck back down to sit on the top basement steps and watch the singing and dancing.

On Sunday mornings everybody slept late, except my sister and my cousins and me. We'd get up and sneak out on our bikes, meeting in the middle of our block, under the sheltering branches of a big tree. We rode our bikes through the campus of the high school across the street, closed for the summer, which made it ours.

By the time I made it to second grade, the world began to open for me. There was an auditorium for our plays and talent shows which was where our teacher, Miss Moran, showed us movies of what to do if we were hit by The Bomb: we were to go backstage in the auditorium and follow the heavy velvet curtains into the darkness. We were to walk a certain distance, then take a black rubber gas mask from the cabinet and put it on. That way, we were told, we could breathe safely and survive the onslaught of atomic warfare. If a bomb were to be dropped without warning, we were to get under our desks on our knees, tucking everything under us like the lotus position in yoga. The Bomb seemed to come with a stringent list of requirements.

Our teachers were not the kind of women we understood. They were sophisticated— they wore dresses bought in stores, high heels, and costume jewelry. Their hair looked dyed, and modern, as if they visited the beauty parlor regularly. So strong was our faith in these well-dressed teachers that we believed everything they said. Possibly they believed it, too. They showed us short films about atomic bombs going off in the desert somewhere: flickering black and white pictures on a pull-up screen from the audio/visual department. America was atomic bomb crazy in those days, and at night, my sister and I would talk the whole thing over. We felt we had to convince our parents to put up a bomb shelter, but Daddy was cynical.

"Why do they do this to kids?" my father asked my mother.

"What did they do?" she asked. She seldom paid any attention to end-of-the-world scenarios. Instead, she worried about her blind father, her mother who swept the church steps for $3 a week, her Aunt Lilly who lived in a trailer attached to my grandmother's house. (When there was a rise in crime in the tiny town where they lived, Grandaddy installed a bell on a rope. Aunt Lilly walked the five steps to her trailer at night and rang the bell, and my grandmother would know she was safe.) No, my mother had bigger fish to fry.

There were moments of happiness, brief passages like a cardinal's quick show of red wing against the snow. I discovered the school library and couldn't believe my luck. Rooms full of books that could be taken home to read. I read right through them—one volume after another until I had read all they had to offer and then I got a library card at the big library on Fenkell Avenue. There I learned to love detective books. I had read all of Nancy Drew, of course, and from there I went to more adult fare: my mother caught me reading the Mickey Spillane thriller, *My Gun Is Quick*, and after that I had to keep it hidden under the mattress.

I took violin lessons from Mr. Ara Zerounian, who was perhaps the only male teacher in my school. He was young then, possibly Russian, possibly from the concentration camps. I had seen pictures of the bodies stacked up like cordwood in the bleak German landscape. We were just beginning to learn about the war. Mr. Zerounian was thin and had thick dark hair which he wore in an unruly mop of curls, one of which sprang out from the rest when he was angry.

I chose violin because I had one. My mother's father had played fiddle at square dances around the county, and before we left he had made a ceremony of giving me one of his favorite instruments. He turned it over to show me the mother of pearl inlay on the back of the fiddle. It was in the shape of a diamond, and the gaps in the design were filled in with a kind of red putty. Best of all, my grandfather had gotten two large rattlesnake rattles which he slipped into the "f" holes on the front of the fiddle. Years later someone told me that Bill Monroe kept them in his mandolin and that the old-time fiddle players thought they kept the instrument dry and seasoned.

When Mr. Zerounian put the fiddle under his chin he heard the rattlers rustling inside the body of the instrument.

"What ees thees?" Mr. Zerounian asked in his heavy accent.

I told him they were rattlesnake rattlers.

"Don't you have any?" I asked, prepared to offer him one of mine.

"Heelbeely children," he said. His curls were springing out all over the place, and he looked as if he might have apoplexy.

"I study and study, and thees is what I get to teach."

Needless to say, we had to go to Montgomery Ward's and pay $25 for a new unseasoned violin, with no ornamentation, cut out mechanically like a jigsaw puzzle.

Winter was cold in Detroit. Mother made us put on leggings then a sweater and a big heavy coat after that. Then we'd go out to the car, and the cold wind cut through us like a keen knife. My sister and I huddled together in the back seat waiting for the heat to come on. It seemed to take forever. By the time we'd get to Aunt Dot's in Hazel Park about a half hour later, the car was just beginning to warm up.

Aunt Dot would meet us at the door, her coppery curls brushed till they crackled with electricity from the hundred daily strokes she gave herself with the brush. On Saturdays in the cold time of the year, the women gathered in each other's kitchens, cooking navy beans and cornbread or making an endless supply of pies. The men worked most of the time or played poker and watched baseball on television. I preferred the company of my sister and girl cousins, anyway. I loved the music coming from the radio, the aroma of cooking, and the chatter of my aunts.

We were tempted by the forbidden nature of the older women's conversations: "Fred makes me so mad I could spit," I heard Aunt Dot say, and I was hooked. What could arouse such a violent response? "He gets up at six every morning," she said, "And fixes himself breakfast. Then he paddy-foots around or jingles his keys until I'm awake." She shook her hair around as if she were really going to leave him over such a thing as her interrupted sleep. "This morning, I jumped out of bed and just started following him, putting my feet where he put his." She demonstrated, imitating Uncle Fred's bow-legged walk so accurately that we laughed until we were sore, and then she started laughing.

"I ought to just kill him and put him out of his misery," she said, choking on her own laughter.

"You'd better be careful who you kill," my grandmother said. "Ruth Owens went to the pen that way ... "

"What's the pen?" I asked.

"Put your head back in the oven," my Aunt Olyne said. She saw a definite correlation between a wet head and a fatal disease. Hand-held hair dryers had not been invented and going outside with wet hair was tantamount to a death wish, so every Saturday afternoon we got our heads shoved in the stove. We had to be spit-shined and perfect for church on Sunday morning, and the idea of running around with our hair wet was simply too insane to be entertained. So we laid our tender heads on the baking racks in the oven and cooked at 350 degrees until done.

The next time the women were in the kitchen together I asked about us being different. "Why do they make fun of how we talk?" I asked. "And why do they make fun of our clothes?"

"Put your head back in the oven," my mother said firmly.

"You'll get pneumonia," my aunt added.

"Ask 'em what banana boat *they* came over on," my grandmother piped in.

"No," Aunt Dot said, "Tell them you come from Tennessee, and act like you're proud of it."

On Saturday night, we usually went to Aunt Dot's because she had a spinet piano. We stayed up as late as the grown-ups, playing music and then wandered into the bedroom and fell asleep on Aunt Dot's bed. Sometimes, we'd get up after Aunt Dot and Uncle Fred were asleep and watch *Shock Theater*. Our favorites were *Frankenstein* and Bella Lugosi's *Dracula*. "Use the silver bullet," we screamed when it looked like Dracula was going to kill again.

Back home we had to put Jackie through the milk chute to unlock the back door for us. Daddy was not used to locking up a house, and if he did do it, he was sure to misplace the key. "I'll be damned," he'd snort, as if it were a surprise. "I forgot the key. Must have left it on the shelf," and then: "Jackspot, we need your services."

Spring means a bonnet—That's Katie at right and Sandra beside her, all dressed up for Easter.

Jackie looked mad and stood off by herself but eventually she let Daddy slide her through the chute where the milkman left the quarts of milk. Then she'd stumble around inside the house until she remembered to unlock the door.

Daddy watched her with growing despair. "She's the only one little enough to slide through," he said. "When she gets bigger, we're sunk."

∼

Summer was traveling time and Memorial Day was the start of summer holidays that stretched luxuriantly before us. On those potentially four-day weekends—the Fourth of July, Labor Day—we piled in two cars and drove for fourteen or fifteen hours straight. We'd usually get into Henry County about three or four a.m. the next morning. My eyes were gritty with sleeplessness, and all of us were a little slaphappy.

I sat straight up in the front seat talking to Daddy so he'd stay awake. We tried to get WSM, the station that broadcast *The Grand Ole Opry*, and then we'd feel like we were really close to home. Mother ended up in the back seat asleep with Jackie, and Daddy and I were listening to Hank Williams. The announcer sounded friendly and cheerful. "It's *The Martha White Show*," he'd say. "Make welcome Lester Flatt and Earl Scruggs," or "Goodness gracious, it's good."

Daddy smiled really big. Then we'd take a curve in the road and lose the station. "Damn a'mighty," Daddy would shout, his good mood forgotten. But it was okay. We fiddled with the dialing knob and it might come back in right away or maybe not, but we knew it was out there, like a big star, guiding us back to Tennessee in the cool dark night.

When we drove through Buchanan, the little country town where we were from, Daddy would laugh and say, "Ida Cannon will be on the phone all night tellin' that a car went through Buchanan at three in the morning." By the time we got to Puryear, where my mother's parents lived and where we'd spend the night, even I was asleep. The back porch light was on, and our grandparents were up, anyway. I heard the crickets chirping loudly and I could see the stars as if they were right in front of my nose. It looked like someone had scattered them across the fabric of the night sky, millions of them.

"Now there's the Big Dipper," Daddy said, and we looked, but we lost it. We just couldn't focus anymore. My sister and I slept in the same bed, a great big featherbed my grandmother made, and we rolled towards the middle all night and woke each other up fighting for space.

The next day we drove to the lake and went out on boats. Mother came home holding her string of crappie victoriously above her head but Daddy didn't catch anything. That night I drove with Aunt Dot to pick up the cook, a large Black woman named Viola, and all I knew of Viola was that Aunt Dot said her son was "in the pen," and that sounded alluring and exotic to us as children, although we still did not know what it meant. Viola fried the fish and hushpuppies and cut up the cole slaw, and everybody raved and said nobody could do it like Viola. Then she was gone, somewhere into the invisible divide between the races.

I looked out the window at the scrubby pine trees while the women talked. I didn't listen to them. I just drifted, my mind darting from one thing to the next. We were going to play music after supper, and I wondered who would come. Summer stretched out before me like another country. Except for the long weekend trips to Tennessee, we were free until school started in the fall. We could ride our bikes and play pioneer women in the backyard. In our game, we were women lost in the wilderness, like the *Little House on the Prairie* books we read. Our husbands had all been killed by Indians, and we had to care for our babies and wash our clothes in imaginary mountain streams, scrubbing them on the rocks. We had to find our own food, make a camp, and keep watch for hostile Indians.

We had no company in those years, and every weekend, every vacation, every holiday was spent together. Sometimes the grown-ups got dressed and went out for dinner to someplace elegant. Aunt Dot had a box of face powder in bronze colors and a puff like a rabbit's foot, which she used to powder her nose. "Don't use powder after you're forty," she told me sternly. "It'll settle in your wrinkles and make you look old."

In the mornings, Aunt Dot watched Jack LaLanne, who was something of a fitness guru in the 1950s. If I spent the night, I'd be up in time to watch her do her exercises with the television set. One morning, she was doing a bicycle pedaling exercise, her legs in the air moving in a circle, her left hand supporting her hip, and her right hand was dipping into a box of Sanders chocolates. She averaged about three circles per chocolate. It was too much for Kakie, our father's mother. She lived with me and Jackie as a rule, but sometimes she stayed with Aunt Dot, her daughter. She could really raise Aunt Dot's blood pressure. She sat down in the chair, holding her apron up over her mouth as if she could hide her laughter, but it burst out like champagne from a bottle.

"What the hell's the matter, Mother," Aunt Dot said, mad as a red rooster.

Kakie tried to get control of herself but did not succeed. "Well, you're exercisin' real good, but you're eatin' chocolate candy. Seems sorta, I don't know what," and then she shook all over with her laughter.

In any case, Kakie was our champion. She may have been the mother to the grown-ups, but we knew absolutely that she was on our side. When everybody left that night, we decided to fix her hair and put some powder and lipstick on her like we'd seen our own mothers do, and she was completely content with that. We were smoothing on a little rouge and watching *Shock Theater* when the knock came at the door. Kakie made a sound like a frightened elephant, opened the door and flew out into the night, leaving us children to face whatever intruder was there alone.

"I'm just deliverin' a script from Sam's drugstore," the boy said, apologetically. "It'll be $3.99, please."

One of us paid him and another went after Kakie, who all her life would be subject to sudden frights and starts. "It was just the drugstore," we told her when we finally found her at Daddy's house down the street. She had the best sheepish smile. We didn't tell anybody she'd run off and left us, but they found out anyway.

So our lives, which were poor in material goods, were rich in stories, and while Mother made our dresses out of what looked like flour sacks when we were little, things got better as we got older. My life was all ahead of me, like the intervals between notes, and I recognized the map of it. Somewhere, we outgrew our tomboy ways, and we organized ourselves into the singing Haley Sisters. We were mainly cousins, but that was close enough for show business. I played the piano and, looking back, I realize I was a bossypants leader. Each page of music would have commands set off by my exclamation points. "Don't forget to breathe here," I had written. "Don't forget to smile between verses."

The women stitched dresses stolen from fairy tales: blue organza with crinoline petticoats starched into voluminous shapes; yellow satin dresses with cummerbunds and corsages. Our youngest cousin, Patti, had long red hair and her mother draped ribbons in it to match our wardrobe. The men got us our gigs, drove the cars, and learned how to cram crinoline petticoats into the trunk and how to close the lids without crushing them.

If instrumental recitals made us physically sick with nerves, singing was something different. We got a little nervous, that was natural, but it was nothing like a recital. Singing was a joyous kind of tension and release we experienced that grew out of something we'd been doing all our lives, and we knew we did well. We entered a contest, and met Hank Williams's widow and Hank Williams, Jr., who was just a boy about our age. Audrey Williams sat in a framed compartment with purple drapes hanging artfully from the top. The purple meant she was in mourning, Aunt Dot said. On the stage, her son, Hank Junior, was playing the guitar and singing his father's songs: "Your Cheatin' Heart" and "Lovesick Blues," in Hank Senior's voice and style. I remember watching him and worrying about him: his father was dead, yet he had to stand up and try to sing and play the guitar just like him.

Thanks to Audrey, we won the contest, which included an appearance with members of the Grand Ole Opry. We met Minnie Pearl in the dressing room and hit the stage singing "Tumbling Tumbleweeds." After that, we began to get paid for our appearances.

In 1959, my father's job transferred him to Huntsville, Alabama, to work on the space program. We cried and begged and refused to eat, but the grown-ups were adamant. We had to go. So we took ourselves, bag and baggage to Huntsville, in the middle of a record hot summer.

Flying for the first time to Alabama would normally have been exciting, but the farewell scene at the airport was a soggy mess of tears and tissue. Our cousins were just as shattered as we were. As we boarded the plane that would take us away forever, we vowed to remain best friends, but it was never the same; it never is. It occurred to me that we were now playing a particularly intense game of "Pioneer Women," faced with breaking up the campsite and losing our cousins in one fell swoop. It was if the elevator we were on fell two floors and left us with our hearts in our throats.

In Alabama, the heat was so bad we could barely breathe, much less come up with any games or activities. We had no air conditioning and when we stood up from the leather furniture, our sweaty bodies made a plopping sound. We put in a powerful fan, but it couldn't chase the humidity away. All of us were soaked with salty sweat all day.

MEMORIES

The Haley family ready to perform. Sandra, Aunt Olyne, and Katie in back, then Linda and Jackie, and Patti in front.

"There's nothing to do," we whined.

"I hate people who say that," my father shouted, slapping the side of his recliner chair with a rolled-up newspaper. "Go learn," he said. "Figure out how to ride the bus, join the library."

It was easier said than done. Huntsville was a sleepy southern town with one dentist, a couple of limited department stores, and an old-fashioned courthouse with its statue devoted to the Beloved Confederate Dead. Long-time residents were aghast at the changes the missile program brought to Huntsville: suddenly Redstone Arsenal, a small military outpost in north Alabama, was booming with soldiers, pilots, and worse yet, Yankees.

In addition, we arrived in June or July of 1959, and the school year would not start until September. We found the library and a bus that traveled back and forth a couple of times a day. My sister became the belle of the local skating rink, and I think we may have found a municipal swimming pool that first summer. I leaned towards reading, so I went to the library, which was air conditioned, unlike our little boxy house on Oakwood Drive, and started reading English romantic novels that led me to focus on King Henry VIII and his wives. Like a contestant on *Jeopardy* I could recite their names and their fates at the drop of a hat: "Catherine of Aragon—divorced; Anne Boleyn, beheaded … "

Because of the space program, Huntsville had a lot of German scientists living side by side with the hard-core Southerners. Many of Hitler's scientists, who had been working on rocket missiles up until the end of the war, were reassigned to Huntsville to develop President Kennedy's space program. Russia had launched Sputnik, and we were behind. It took awhile, but when the first missile was launched successfully from Cape Canaveral, all the citizens of Huntsville danced in the streets all night, and businesses were closed the next day in honor of this achievement. We had been at the mercy of rocket sonic testing on any given day of the week; now it seemed it had increased, and when you were least expecting it, the china cabinet would rattle and the boom of the explosion deafened you.

This was the internationally flavored atmosphere we moved into. Werner von Braun could be seen at the local horseshows with his little daughter. Many streets in the residential neighborhoods had German names printed below the English names, and once we got to school, the German children really skewed the curve in math and science classes.

My family eventually met the German couple who lived next door to us: Bernie and Teresa. I always assumed Bernie had been a party member in Germany during the war, but now he was needed by the American scientific community, so like half of the scientists at Peenemünde, he was pardoned and brought to America afterwards. I was curious, but Daddy said it was none of our business.

They spoke little English, but I was fascinated with Teresa's cooking, especially her pie crusts. She made a nest of white flour on the cabinet and broke an egg into the center of it. She worked butter through the whole mixture with her hands, and she used sugar in the crust. In fact, she didn't use sugar in the filling but only in the crust. She kneaded and rolled out her dough, picking up every last scrap of sticky mixture as she rolled. When she finished, the countertop was as clean as a whistle. Daddy said it was because they were Germans, their being so neat and tidy and all.

We were unable to close the language gap between us and Bernie and Teresa, though, so the friendship died on the vine, and eventually I got tired of waiting for Henry VIII to lop off another head. By the time December came, reading about English kings and watching Theresa make pie dough had worn thin. I'd had enough of my sister's company, my mother's distracted looks, enough of my father's forced good nature. Nobody was coming to see us, and Christmas loomed over our heads like a mushroom cloud.

Huntsville didn't have snow for Christmas; that year a dark rain began to fall and showed no signs of stopping. The shopping center north of town had one meager string of Christmas lights. It looked barren and bleak and not the least bit festive. We bought a Christmas tree there, a scrawny live tree that was slightly crooked. Daddy put all the energy into picking out Christmas trees as he put into other areas of home decoration—none—so we were stuck with it and worked hard to decorate it. Mother tried to remain cheerful.

"Christmas is a spirit," she'd say.

"Oh, hush up, Suzie," Daddy said.

He tried to keep up a hearty facade which we could tell wasn't real. He had lost the most. His beloved brother was still in Detroit, as well as his sister and his mother, and he must have ached for them and for the lively Christmases we had enjoyed when we were all together. By Christmas Eve, even Daddy's hearty laugh had given way, and we sank into a miasma of gloom. You could hear the clock ticking, and by noon, Daddy had had enough.

"Come on," he ordered us. "Pack a bag and throw the presents in the trunk. Hell, throw the tree in there, too." Daddy always tended to extravagant gestures.

Mother made pimento cheese sandwiches for a lunch, and we were on the road by late afternoon, headed for Tennessee, where at least we had family. The rain stopped after an hour or so, and we drove north on Highway 431 towards the mountains and Tennessee.

We felt better the minute the wheels were moving. There was a slight crust of frost on the hard, red Alabama dirt and a sprinkling of snow—a little "skift" is how my grandmother would have said it. The road was a dark, two-lane country highway with no signs and a small town every twenty miles or so.

We stopped at a neglected little service station just across the Tennessee border, for gas and some of the rag bologna Daddy loved so well. It came wrapped in thin, gauzy cloths shaped like a cylinder, and you sliced it with a pocketknife and ate it on saltine crackers with cheddar cheese.

We stopped again in Dover, Tennessee, at another little service station that was giving away free glasses with every fill-up. Three men in grimy overalls sat on a wooden bench inside the door, drinking Coca-Cola and Orange Nehi and staring at us. Their faces were narrow and mean, like men on a Most Wanted poster. They did not smile.

"This used to be bad moonshine country," Daddy said in a candid man-to-man way when we were safely back on the road. "It was the kind of place you wouldn't want to get stuck in after dark." A shiver ran down my spine.

The moon was full, heavy and yellow, and Daddy began to sing softly in the dark car, which cheered us as we traveled through miles of country with no lights or people as far as we could see.

"Good-bye, my Coney Island Baby," he sang, waving his right hand in a conductor's pose. Our harmony was sweet and perfect from years of practice. We sang the "Tennessee Waltz," and as we harmonized, our heads were so close we could have kissed.

We were going to see our grandparents, my mother's mother and father. "I'll bet they'll be surprised to see us," I said.

My mother just smiled. "They'll be in bed," she said, but my sister and I were having none of it.

"They won't be asleep on Christmas Eve," we said.

When we pulled up the long gravel driveway and got out of the car, we scrambled to the trees outside their window and sang, "O Little Town of Bethlehem." Our voices matched each other's perfectly, as if we had been given a kind of grace for the night. I don't think we ever sang so well again.

From inside, I heard my grandfather say, "I hope that's not them durn church people," and he and my grandmother came to the window. My grandfather had on a long white cotton gown and a nightcap. My grandmother's thin hair was piled into a bun on her head. Then somehow they knew it was us, even though my grandfather was blind and both of them were sleepy. When we went close to hug them, they were crying.

Things got better after that. My sister and I got involved in our own lives—at Daddy's prompting, of course—and we all grew to love Huntsville. I worked on the school newspaper and sang in a madrigal chorus, and by senior year, I was voted most talented in my class and had to pose for the *Pierian*, the school yearbook, in a caveman's suit complete with a club and a bearskin, the whole thing taken straight from *The Flintstones*. That was the theme for our class that year, *The Flintstones*. Pam Eddins was voted Cutest Girl, and her male partner was pictured dragging her by the hair towards their cave.

Somehow I got into the University of Missouri, primarily because of my high verbal scores on the SAT tests. I decided on a career in journalism, but my professors discouraged me. Journalism, they assured me, was no place for me, and they pointed me in the direction of an English major. The past five years had been a strain for me, though. I was tired of making my way in the world, tired of saying goodbye to old friends and learning how to make new ones, tired of adjusting. After my first year, I packed my bags and rode home on the bus and said goodbye to school for awhile.

*

Perhaps I came to Cincinnati because my grandmother thought it was so pretty, and she liked it being set on hills. She was terrified of floods, and Cincinnati looked safe to her. "I'd love to have a little place there with just a few chickens," she said.

I remembered it because of how hard it was to get across the bridge. The I-75 bridge hadn't been completed then, and the lanes on the expressway had to merge into one to cross the Ohio River. On the south side of the river, huge signs advertised "Fireworks, cherry bombs, rockets." We were wild with excitement for fireworks, but our parents, finding us incendiary enough, said, "No."

I gradually learned to adjust to Cincinnati. I began to make a few friends; I learned to play guitar and took lessons from Jose Madrigal who played in the basement of the Maisonette. He managed to teach me several chords, and I learned to play them on a gut-string classical guitar with a neck that was too wide. Sometimes I played at parties. Singing came naturally to me; I had always done that. And I seemed to know when to change the chords at the right time and how to keep time.

In the early seventies I took a course at the University of Cincinnati, on country music, old-time southern music, and what I learned to call "bluegrass." I had always heard it, of course, on the radio in Alabama, on the television on Saturday afternoons. You could see Flatt and Scruggs every week, an impossible luxury. And Dolly Parton appeared in the same block of programming, singing in her pure mountain soprano, songs about coats sewn from scraps and women who were trying to take her man. In between, she sold boxes of Breeze detergent with towels or washcloths inside them.

When I heard this music again, so far from home, so needy, I was hooked. I couldn't find anywhere to hear it live, and it never occurred to me that I could hear the country music I longed for, in bars, mostly downtown in Over-the-Rhine. So, for a time, I played at what we called "hootenannies" at Christ Church. Churches were reaching out to appeal to younger, potential members, and I was part of that. I sang folk songs like "Stewball" and "Turn, Turn, Turn."

Then one night some friends dragged me to a bar called Aunt Maudie's, on Main Street in Over-the-Rhine. I was utterly mesmerized. The metallic rhythm of the banjo supported by the huge, rhythm guitar was exactly what I had wanted to hear.

I had finally found a home.

2
FAMILY

AUNT DOT SANG LEAD BACKED UP BY UNCLE FRED, DRUMMER
ROY WISE, AND KATIE'S DAD, JACK HALEY.

AUNT DOT'S SCRAMBLED EGGS

It rained all the way to Mississippi that Thanksgiving. It pelted against the windshield of the car and the sound of it, like a quiet roar, was enough to drown out the radio. Eventually I gave up on the radio anyway; the rain took all my concentration. Around Nashville the water was ponded over the road so deep my tires lost traction for minutes at a time. I had to slow down drastically to keep from hydroplaning. The exits off I-40 were closed. Flashing signs above the highway announced that none of us could get on or off of the interstate. I couldn't remember ever having seen a storm like it, and I realized it was a southern storm, torrential, angry, swollen.

By the time I got to the state line, the storm had blown itself out. In another half hour it was over, and the stars came out like diamonds strewn across the sky. I finished the last leg of my trip and pulled into the driveway, got out and stretched. My parents lived in a colonial style ranch house surrounded by pine trees and honeysuckle. My sister called it "Tara," but she was being sarcastic.

My mother was outside running to hug me before I could even grab my suitcase, and then I was in the middle of a cluster hug. I felt uncles and aunts and in-laws, nieces and nephews all around me until I had to come up for air.

"Welcome home," my father said and wiped a touch of moisture out of his eyes. As we came nearer to the front door I could hear a football game blaring out over the television set in the den. Once I was in the house, the tension in my shoulders from the long drive dissolved. Inside there were cake stands with Lady Baltimore cake, jam cake, a German chocolate cake and pies from my aunt. A turkey and a ham sat out on the dining room table next to a platter of fried chicken. I reached for a drumstick but my sister was there in an instant. "Don't pick," she said. "I'll make you a plate."

She looked at me and laughed, that mix of giggle and full throated laughter that was so endearing.

Daddy sat down in his recliner, a can of beer in his hand. "How was the traffic?" he asked.

I sighed and let go of more tension. I was home; my nightmarish journey was over and forgotten.

I wanted to sleep late the next morning, but at 8 a.m. I woke up on the lumpy old sofa bed. Smelling the aroma of fresh coffee, I heard a mix of voices, male and female. I jumped out of bed and ran into the kitchen, reluctant to miss anything.

"Well, good morning, honey," my mother said, her brown eyes dancing. "I'm glad you're up. They're just fixin' to go see the coon hound cemetery."

"A graveyard for dogs? Isn't there a nice museum somewhere? Some place with a lunch counter?"

Mother always liked for us to do something educational on our visits, but the coon hound cemetery was a desperate stretch. She just smiled. "They have the coon dog museum right on the grounds of the cemetery."

My uncle turned around to face us. "You've got your fox hounds, your bird dogs, and your coon hounds," he said solemnly. "The coon hound tracks raccoons and trees them. They're fierce creatures, the raccoons I mean."

"Get dressed," Daddy said. "I think we can all fit in one car. We'll get breakfast when we get back. Aunt Dot is frying quail in lard, the way we used to do before ever'body got high cholesterol."

Even though it was the end of November, the weather was pleasantly warm; and the air smelled clean after the rain.

"Have you ever heard a dog tree a raccoon?" my uncle asked. "It's a real hair-raisin' experience. The dog howls way on up in high falsetto, and pretty soon the other ones hear him and join in until it's like a choir of voices." My uncle lit a cigarette and went on. "It's called 'giving throat,'" he said.

Daddy managed to get us across the state line into Alabama with a minimum of cussing, and miraculously we found the turn-off dirt road to the cemetery. Daddy had no sense of direction normally, but now he looked a lot like a picture I saw of President Roosevelt, with his hat pulled down and a victorious smile on his face.

We parked and went in, and the first thing we saw was a large statue of a coon hound. The dog was black and tan with big ears, and the sign on the statue said, "Tecumseh, A Fine Dog." Behind the statue was a long, low building, probably kennels. Other marked graves lay under ancient magnolia trees, and a pile of leaves, brown and dried, swirled in the soft wind.

We walked aimlessly for a while, reading the obituaries of the dogs. "People spend more money on dogs in this place than they would spend on their wives," Daddy said, snorting a little.

Uncle Clarence was still thinking about dogs. "It says here that the pointer is the Cadillac of hounds."

"Is that right?" Daddy said, but I knew he was not paying attention. He was over the coon hound cemetery, and I was hungry. On our way home we passed a generic gas station, poor and run down.

"Stop here, Daddy," my sister said suddenly. "I've got to get a Coke."

Daddy looked around at us and arched his eyebrows. Look at those men working on that old car over there," he said. It was an old '80s model, rusted out, with blankets on the seats in place of upholstery. "You don't ever want to stop at a place like that, especially not alone."

We were silent for a beat. One of the men who had been hidden by the hood of the car straightened up and looked directly at us. His eyes were little and mean. I shuddered. I had almost stopped at just such a place on my trip down. "Mississippi is dangerous," I said.

"You need to have a dog," my uncle said and laughed at himself.

Daddy tuned the car radio to a country station. Soon we were rolling along to the music of the pedal steel guitar and a smooth, swinging fiddle. Daddy began singing the lead, and Jackie and I grabbed a harmony part and sang along.

Anytime you're feelin' lonely
Anytime you're feelin' blue ...

The harmony was perfect, and we were swinging. We leaned our heads together for the last line: *That's the time I'll come back home to you.*

"We better get back," Daddy said. "We've got quail for breakfast."

"And scrambled eggs so light you have to hold them in the skillet," my sister said, laughing, and she added, "That's worth getting up for." My aunts and my mother would be in the kitchen now cooking, every pot and skillet pressed into service.

We piled into the kitchen laughing and hungry. Aunt Dot was in charge of the scrambled eggs and Daddy cut out the biscuits and arranged the freshly killed quail in a black iron skillet. Pans of fresh baked cornbread sat on the counter waiting to be mixed with the juices from the turkey into dressing for the evening feast.

"I swear," Aunt Dot said, "Every time I do this I miss Mother so bad." She paused and looked sad for a minute. "I believe I'm going to have to take a headache pill," she said. "Fred, get me one of my headache pills out of the train case."

Uncle Fred took his time getting up. He was bowlegged and solemn faced, and he looked a little like an adult toddler hurrying towards the bedroom. "God a'mighty," she said, watching him go. "Sitting Bull."

"You'd think I wouldn't have to suffer on Thanksgiving, as much as needs to be done. I better take that with milk," she said when Uncle Fred came back with the pill. "It'll start my ulcer up if I don't. I probably won't be able to eat."

Outside, a neighbor had started a bonfire. Inside, the men were pouring whiskey into shot glasses and drinking it down with a toss of their heads. Mother came through, her brow furrowed with disapproval. "Jack," she said, "there's children here."

"I'm well aware of that," he said, in a tight voice, and tension shot through the air like a bolt of lightning. Nevertheless, he put the whiskey away, and no more shots were poured until evening.

Everybody laughed when Daddy mentioned James Simmons. It was the signal that someone was going to tell a story, and James Simmons would be the star. He was a boy who lived somewhere in the woods around Henry County, Tennessee, where my family was from. "It was so far back that nobody knew exactly where they lived," Daddy said, "and they'd show up in Buchanan ever' now and then. Then you'd see them walking out of the woods, single file, like Indians. First Will, walkin' with a rifle over his arm, then Blanche, then James, bringing up the rear." Daddy paused. "Ever' now and then James would do a little dance step and squall. I swear it would raise the hair on the back of your head."

One time James walked up to Daddy real silently, scaring him half to death. They shared the same birthday, and James wanted Daddy to come over and have dinner. "We've killed ole Favver Duck," he said, "Now I reckon we'll kill ole Muvver Duck."

Daddy didn't answer; he just ran as hard as he could to the house and locked the door.

"How come you to run?" we'd ask, glued to the story.

"He could have been a murderer," Daddy said, laughing a little. "Turned out he wasn't, but what does a kid know?—'Gonna kill old Muuver Duck?'"

We sat in a circle around the living room listening; and the light made a halo around our heads. Whatever ties bound us, they pulled tighter at holidays. Whatever mysterious force drew us to each other on these occasions it was so compelling it was hopeless to fight it. It was blood; it had to be the blood that made us follow one another like neurotic lemmings marching into the sea for this food, these stories, these small unchanging rituals, and the music.

The songs my family sang wrapped themselves around my heart and soaked into my skin until I was as high and light as Aunt Dot's scrambled eggs.

CONFESSIONS OF A YELLOW-DOG DEMOCRAT

My grandparents got up early on Election Day. They lived in a small rural community in Tennessee, just ten miles south of Murray, Kentucky. They were country people; they dressed up to vote. My grandfather put on his Sunday pants and shirt, and my grandmother laced herself into a corset and a print dress. She wore her hat and carried her pocketbook.

Voting was a solemn, sometimes contentious event, especially the small countywide contests. That's why they got up early. If my grandfather was voting for his cousin for sheriff, my grandmother wanted to be right there to cancel out his vote with her own.

An election of national importance was different. On one such occasion, my great-aunt, Lilly, who had a sharp, pointed face and wore her hair parted in the middle and pulled straight back in a bun, gave my mother this advice: "Remember, honey," she'd say, in a chilling voice, "when you go in that voting booth, Franklin Delano Roosevelt will be looking over your shoulder."

Aunt Lilly took the long view.

The Democrats might produce a scoundrel here and there, but to her way of thinking things would right themselves as long as the party was in office. All of them knew it was Roosevelt who pulled them through the Great Depression. They were there. In that part of rural Tennessee, hard times had left an indelible mark on the people. (Hence the term "Yellow Dog Democrat," was someone who voted rigorously the Democratic ticket, or as was often said, would vote "for a yellow dog before any Republican.")

My mother's father, who had worked as far afield as Willow Run, in Michigan, after World War I, returned to Tennessee and married my grandmother. When no work could be found, he went to work on her father's farm. They grew their own food, kept cows and hogs and chickens. They even grew their own cotton—the children got the "third pick," which is to say after the crop had been gleaned twice by the men and the women, the children got the leftovers, the bolls of the white, white cotton left behind.

"Picking that left-over cotton was hard work," Mother said. At the end of the day her small fingers would be bloody from the oily seeds in the boll and the prickly plants. Still, they could buy horehound candy or a ribbon at the general store. I find it hard to believe there are jobs hungry people won't do, because my family did them.

My mother is convinced that country people had it easier in the Depression because they could at least eat. There just wasn't any money. They bought their seeds on credit and paid when the cotton and tobacco came in. They couldn't sell the produce because they didn't have a mule or a wagon, and the farm was fifteen miles from any kind of marketplace. Even if they could have driven the hogs or the cattle to market, no one had money to buy them.

They squirreled away egg money to buy needles and pins from the tinkers, who wandered the country sharpening knives. The women made quilts out of worn-out calico and stockpiled them against the cold winters. Mother's father was struck by a virulent strain of glaucoma when he was thirty-nine and lost his eyesight. His brother drove him in a buckboard wagon to Vanderbilt University in Nashville, but in those long-ago days they had no cure, and his blindness was a grave blow.

In spring he got a neighbor to help him plant. He hooked himself up in a mule's harness and pulled the hand-held plow the neighbor guided, and he still had spirit enough to play the fiddle at weekly square dances for a few dollars. My grandmother was paid for her cakes. She was a midwife before women went to hospitals for birthing. Later, she cleaned houses and swept the church steps. That ended when she fell through the attic floor and broke her back.

Their only son was killed in World War II, leaving them with nothing but a soldier's allotment. Without the Social Security disability for the blind that Roosevelt provided, what would have happened to my grandparents?

The land was thin and overworked in Tennessee after World War II, and, along with a half-million other southerners, my family moved north to work in the automobile factories. I was just four or five years old, but I remember the stories my father told, stories he heard from the older factory workers of the years before the unions.

They told stories of workers being forced to carry Model T engines on their backs from one side of the factory floor to the other. They said that you had to report to the factory at dawn and wait until there was work because you were paid only for what you did, not for the time you spent there.

Henry Ford did not revolutionize American industry by himself: Men worked like slaves, and they lay where they fell. There was no medical care, no pension, no fine mansions in Bloomfield Hills, Michigan.

I'm a Democrat because I value a government that values me. I want to be healthy and productive, and I want to make a contribution to my neighborhood, my city and my country. I want the freedom to express myself and to find spiritual energy where I can. I want to be stimulated, uplifted and entertained by artists and writers and to be enlightened by educators.

When we find those qualities in our leaders, then we have good government. And in my experience, the best government has been with the Democratic Party.

PLAIN AND FANCY

My grandmother was plump, like a proper grandmother. She had a disorderly bun at the back of her head with wisps of silver hair escaping in tendrils around her square face. Her older sister, my great-aunt Lilly, was just the opposite: thin and witch-like with a sharp nose and chin and shrewd black eyes. It was in the early 1960s, on one of my family's annual spring trips back to visit family in Puryear, Tennessee, that I got to see their differences close up. The first night we got there we obviously interrupted a quarrel.

"Nanny," Aunt Lilly said—for that was the name she had called my grandmother since they were children—"it wouldn't hurt a bit if you'd put a little more color in your quilts. The church quilt show is comin' up next month and with your stitches and my design we could take the prize."

My grandmother walked into the kitchen to get away from Lilly's scolding. True, all her quilts were pieced from plain squares cut from old dresses and shirts. But she was a practical woman with little time for frills.

The first morning of our visit, my grandmother—my mother's mother—woke up at 6 a.m. to get the cooking done while the kitchen was cool and sweet with morning air. She went out to the hen house and gathered the eggs, picked out a plump hen, wrung its neck, and put it in the pot to loosen the feathers. Then she baked biscuits and cornbread in black cast-iron pans in a wood stove, fried smoke-cured country ham, made red-eye gravy, and fried the morning's eggs and potatoes. Only after all this did she set her food down on the round kitchen table and call the family for breakfast.

Great Aunt Lilly, of course, was cooking, too, in the trailer where she lived just ten feet from my grandmother's house. As we sat down for breakfast, she strolled in with a platter in each hand and offered her own biscuits and homemade jelly. "Thought you might want to try this with your breakfast," she chuckled. " 'Course I like them better with bacon, but you be the judge of that. I just made the preserves yesterday—they're strawberry. I think they're about as good as any at the county fair. Just take a taste and tell me whether you like mine or Nanny's better."

At the stove, working on the sweetmilk white gravy, Granny gave us a hard look, as if to say, "Well … "

"I'll try one of each," my father said.

"You decided whether you're gonna bake a cake for the fair, Nanny?" my great-aunt asked casually. My grandmother's cakes were known far and wide for their light texture and the ambrosial frosting she spread between the layers.

"I thought I might do a German chocolate," my grandmother said with just a hint of hostility.

"Well," Aunt Lilly said, "don't nobody in town do a better German chocolate than you do." My grandmother's face relaxed for a minute.

" 'Course, I thought I'd do a jam cake myself," Aunt Lilly continued, her competitive spirit roused again. "And don't forget we've got to come up with a pattern for the quilt show, you know."

Every winter Aunt Lilly and Granny Ward got together with other women in the small village where they lived and made quilts. I remember the large wooden frame they used to stretch the quilts like drum heads when they stitched the borders to the edges. And I remember my aunt's relentless criticism. "They drove each other crazy," my cousin Sandra recently reminded me, chuckling over the old harsh words between the sisters.

My grandmother was a practical woman with a great deal of work to be done, and the last thing she had time for was making fancy quilts. If Aunt Lilly would peck at her about this thing or that, she'd simply wave her sister away like a mosquito and go on with her cleaning up. When the lines between her eyebrows tightened, though, Aunt Lilly knew she had got through.

Supper that night was a casual affair—mostly leftovers from dinner at midday with the addition of green beans she had brought in from the garden to "freshen things up." After dinner my grandmother had taken a white cotton cloth out of a drawer and spread it over the table of food like a shroud, to keep the flies away; when suppertime came the cloth was removed, and we ate the leftovers from the noon meal and anticipated what might be for dessert: one of my grandmother's German chocolate cakes, perhaps, or banana pudding at the very least. Everyone worked hard, and nobody quibbled over calories.

Aunt Lilly came in at suppertime with homemade yeast rolls, which she passed around in a basket. We were loyal to our grandmother, but homemade yeast rolls were a rare treat, and we didn't refuse them.

"Have you given any more thought to that quilt pattern, Nanny?" Aunt Lilly began.

"No, Sister, I haven't," Granny said, slowly and deliberately. "Have you?"

"Well," Aunt Lilly said, "I'm just sayin' if you're going to the trouble of making the quilt, why won't you put in some bright, pretty shapes? Cut a triangle instead of a square." (Aunt Lilly would probably have been happy working for Ralph Lauren.)

"I haven't had time to go through my scraps," my grandmother said, beginning to get a little heated, "and we don't have to start for another month."

"Planning is everything," Aunt Lilly nagged on. "The ones that wins the prize is the ones that plans."

My grandfather sensed a fight in the offing, so he got up and went outside. He had been blind since he was thirty-nine years old, but he could tell when things heated up between the sisters. He knew when it was best to clear out.

That usually meant going outside to play the fiddle, working on a tune like "Buffalo Gals" or "Washington and Lee Swing." He played for square dances on Saturday nights. They'd take two fiddlers and a guitar player, and when one fiddler tired out, he'd go out on the porch and have a little drink of brandy (for "medicinal purposes") until the muscles loosened up again and the arm was flowing smoothly.

My grandfather's vision hardly kept him homebound. Mornings, he walked into town to pick up the mail, his hearing acute enough to warn him of oncoming traffic. Of course, there wasn't much traffic to begin with. He carried a blind man's cane with a white stripe near the middle and another red stripe below it. The crook was curved to fit his hand—he had probably sanded and worked the wood himself. As he walked, he tapped it lightly ahead of him—one-two, one-two—and with this navigational system he got where he was going with ease and grace. To accommodate his blindness, nothing in the house was ever moved or changed lest he trip over an unexpected rug or knock his shins against a new footstool or stumble on a stack of books thoughtlessly left beside a chair.

Evenings, while my grandmother and her sister fussed, my grandfather and his best friend, Tommy, sat on cane-bottom chairs under the black walnut tree outside the house and listened to the St. Louis Cardinals on a small battery-powered Sears radio that cut in and out. They tuned in to every game, only missing the action when the radio briefly sputtered, leaving them with nothing but static.

My brother-in-law sat with them one summer evening and was puzzled by my grandfather's references to "Orlando Potatoes." *Which player was Orlando Potatoes?* John thought to himself, but he soon came up with the answer.

"Are you talking about Orlando Cepeda?" he asked my grandfather. My blind grandfather had never seen the name written in the newspaper, and he was parsing out the sound the best he could.

On rainy afternoons during our visits, my sister and cousin and I played in the huge trunks my grandmother kept in the smokehouse. They were full of letters, so dusty and old they nearly crumbled to the touch, the handwriting fine and spidery. "Dear Aunt Nanny," a postcard read. "Here we are at the beach in California." On the front of the card was a picture of one of my distant cousins with his head posed atop a muscled body—a painted prop made of heavy cardboard. In the bottom of the trunk we found a primer from 1832—a school book with the cover torn off. My grandmother's grandfather had worked as a tailor before moving to Tennessee territory, and we laughed over his meticulously drawn-up bills—$.25 for a yard of serge, $2 to sew a coat. We found Confederate money in the trunk and pretended it was real, and that we were rich and going to Hollywood.

Around us the smell of curing hams was everywhere, and smoked bacon, too. The fragrance permeated the wood, and the soft rustle of the rain on the asphalt roof felt cozy, as if we were behind a curtain in a faraway jungle in the rainy season.

The best pictures in the trunk were the ones of our parents and aunts and uncles—the men in Army uniforms with peaked caps and stripes sewn on the sleeves. Uncle Fred posed in an old-fashioned Naval uniform, the top of it shaped like a blue middy blouse with a white hat propped on the side of his head. Next to him, Aunt Dot was as slender as a model in a dress and high-heeled shoes, one of her little feet propped behind her on the side of an old Model T Ford. But there were older pictures, too, pictures which looked like wedding portraits, of women in long dresses which had been fashionable before we were born. There were pictures of my father's family, six of them posed in old-timey clothes beside a huge maple tree somewhere out in the country. It was such a small community that my mother's family and my father's family were close neighbors. Their lives and their mementos were intertwined.

Most of my grandmother's quilts were stored in trunks in the smokehouse, but I don't remember looking at them much. We spread them out to sit on while we went through the trunks looking at what we thought were more interesting items. The quilt I have on my bed now was probably in those trunks; I probably sat on it thoughtlessly a hundred times when I was a girl. Now I find myself studying it each evening, tracing the shapes of the patchwork, puzzling over the scraps of fabric, trying to unlock its mysteries.

It is thick and warm, practical you might say, but there are triangles inside of triangles stitched by hand, squares of bright red floral prints stitched beside coarse flour sack cotton. Striped squares are stitched next to circles, paisley next to polka dots, and there are pieces that look like they were cut from a red checked tablecloth. Was that the cloth my grandmother spread on the breakfast table? Were those careful, even stitches made by her hand? Were the bold fabrics and the intricate patterns my Aunt Lilly's doing? Is the quilt the result of their graceful collaboration, or a product of their colorful quarrels?

Either way, it seemed to me that it represented the best of both of them. I had admired this quilt on Mother's bed the last time I was visiting, and she insisted on giving it to me. How could I have even thought of passing it up?

Decoration Day, or Memorial Day as people call it now, was the real reason we went to Tennessee at the end of May—a chance to remember, to decorate the graves of the dead, to cry for them yet again. We took flowers to the cemetery and the men raked the dead grass away from where our ancestors lay, replacing stones that had blown over or been knocked over by high school kids. My mother and my grandmother cried for a little while over my Uncle Dempsey's grave. He had died in the Army and was buried in the Patterson Cemetery, way out in the country under old trees: sugar maple and pine and oak.

At the Buchanan Cemetery in Henry County, we tended the graves of my father's family. Someone brought a lunch and we ate the sandwiches and told stories of those who had died, laughing and crying all at once, the sad times overlaid by the funny times, patched together like my grandmother's quilts.

When Monday came, it was time to head back to Detroit—time for the sad leave-taking that always accompanied the end of our visits. My grandmother packed us a lunch of fried chicken, pimento cheese sandwiches, homemade pickles, cold biscuits, a jar of damson plum preserves, and a variety of cakes and pies just in case we needed to snack. Aunt Lilly followed with homemade cookies.

"God a'mighty," Daddy said when he put it in the trunk. "That's enough to feed an army."

Grandaddy made sure we hadn't left anything behind to trip him or interfere with his spartan lifestyle. Sometimes he even saw our departure as an opportunity to eliminate household items. If Mother admired one of my grandmother's baskets, he encouraged her to ask her mother for it. "She won't even know it's gone," he'd say.

Our car was already too full when my grandmother approached my mother with a homemade quilt.

"Why don't you just mail me that, Mama," my mother said. "We don't have any room for it."

"But don't you get cold up there in Michigan?" my grandmother asked, though it was almost June.

"Of course, I want the quilt, Mama, but it's summer in Detroit, too. There's plenty of time before winter."

My mother's eyes were beginning to fill with tears. "Please mail it," she said. "It's one of my favorites."

My grandmother's face softened and she too began to cry. Wrinkles formed in her forehead, and bright spots of color flushed her face. She stood there weeping, her only son dead, her husband blind, her daughter living in a northern climate, so far away she couldn't even understand where it was.

"Let's get going," Daddy said, looking at the clock, mentally calculating the time of the drive in holiday traffic. And suddenly we were all in the car, ready for last-minute kisses and hugs and waves.

"Be careful up there, honey," my grandmother said to my mother, and Daddy turned slightly in the front seat to back the car up. A rear door was not tightly shut; my grandfather felt it, and opened it.

"Everybody got their fingers out of the way?" he asked, and we did. He slammed the door, and we were off.

We pulled onto the highway and headed north. My mother put her head in my father's lap and cried as if she would never stop.

MOVING ON

I don't like change; I can see no virtue in it. The unavoidable changes, like growing old and dying, make me wonder why everyone isn't suspicious of words like "development" and "progress." The cheap little businessmen in Sinclair Lewis's novels are anathema to me, with their talk of "Onward and Upward" at their Boosters' Clubs. Yet, once again, I am faced with my old nemesis: moving. My beloved apartment building on Main Street is "going condo," as they say, and I must move so that the building can be gutted, rehabbed, and readied for the "YPs" or "Young Professionals" hoping to get a foothold in Over-the-Rhine.

"Just think of the fun of a new apartment," my friends say, but most of them own real estate and have lived where they live for over twenty years. Even my dog, Sister, looks glum about our prospects. She narrows her amber eyes at me as if we're checking into a houseful of cats in Northside. Somehow, I have let us both down, and I run around like a hillbilly Woody Allen, trying to make a decision.

When I was a child, we moved so many times that I made a promise to the adult me who lived somewhere in the future. "Never again," I vowed each time my parents started throwing furniture in U-Haul trucks, Daddy shouting orders at the top of his voice, gleeful at the opportunity to be "on the road again." Indeed, my family was at their best in stressful situations and always emerged laughing when they got to the new place. "Eat something," Daddy would say to me as the tears poured down my face, "It will cheer you up." To this day, the sight of dishes wrapped in newspapers is enough to send me to bed for days.

I have kept the promise I made to myself; and despite being part of a transient generation, I have not made many moves as an adult. My old friend, Amy Culbertson, moved into my house on Taft Road in 1975 while I was doing a ten-day gig on the Delta Queen with John Hartford and some other bluegrass pickers. When I got back, her possessions were already in place in the back bedroom, and she had accomplished the whole thing in one afternoon without a door key. "I just threw my sleeping bag in through the living-room window," she explained. "Then, I climbed in after it."

Moving was easier in those days; we were just starting out, emerging from blue jeans and poverty and dormitories. "I never want anything I can't pack in the trunk of my car," I was fond of saying. Oh, for the innocence of those years!

The next thing I knew, Amy and I had each bought "grown-up" beds, with box springs and headboards and had stopped "sleeping on the floor," as our mothers put it. "You'll get pneumonia if you keep sleeping on the floor," they said. We got color-coordinated sheets. Later, when I moved once again, to a small apartment on Dayton Street in Cincinnati's West End, my friend, Tom Cahall, helped me pack and carry. We spent a couple of afternoons trekking up and down stairs laden with lamps and tables and stereo equipment, but it wasn't so bad, really. Back then I didn't own much; but after I'd lived there for awhile, a friend lent me a charming white loveseat and various large items. Of course, I *had* to buy dishes, then a charming little rug or two and pretty blue towels. When it came time to move again, into a house on Bishop Street, I thought, "Great. The grand piano will look wonderful in the living room."

Day one of the "Removal to Clifton," as I called it, dawned clear and sunny and five degrees below zero. I packed three or four boxes, labeled them carefully and carried them to Bishop Street where we unpacked them and placed them in the proper rooms. "This is the only way to move," I said to Tom (who had remained a friend against all odds). "No trauma, no rush, no disorganization."

Tom looked doubtful and urged a faster pace. "It could take you twelve years to get done at this rate," he said. He looked at the job ahead of us and shook his head and chuckled "You've got about three times as much stuff as you had when you moved to Dayton Street."

"A steady drip fills the bucket," I said, quoting my great-aunt Lilly.

However, by the third day, I was beginning to get discouraged. I woke up feeling sick and achy. During the night the water pipes had frozen, and my landlord called to inform me that all the water in the house was off. I struggled into my blue jeans and took my temperature. It was 100 and climbing. At 101, I went back to bed and called Tom, but he had a gig, and it was my parents who came through for me once again. When I called my mother, she said, "We'll be there tomorrow, honey."

The next day they arrived in a rented pick-up truck and dismantled my apartment with that same manic energy I remembered from the old days. They threw furniture around, tossed pillows out the window, wrapped dishes in the classified section. They deconstructed my life, while I sat on the bed in a bathrobe with a thermometer stuck in my mouth. From time to time I whimpered.

"She always did hate being uprooted," my father said to my mother in a confidential tone of voice.

When it was done, my mother made pork chops and mashed potatoes and biscuits. I watched her spare, expert movements while she worked and listened to the slow sweetness of her voice. "Life goes on," she said, letting me know she was "Imparting Wisdom."

It was warm in the kitchen, and the windows were frosted with steam from the heat of the stove. My move was over, and I had lived through it, and it was getting dark outside, "gathering dark," as my grandmother used to say when she meant twilight.

My friend Barbara Sherman helped me move to Main Street ten years ago, when we were younger and stronger, but when she heard about this move she quickly scheduled a tour of the Amazon Rain Forest. "I'm dying to see the Brazilian rosewood trees," she told me and had her phone number changed.

This year I foresee that Melissa Mosby and I will be doing our Lucy and Ethel act, ineptly boxing up pictures and stories from pre-digital days. The entire Bible study group at Mt. Moriah Methodist Church will be praying for me. I hope David Peters will have some time to help, because he is soothing to be around, and he has a van. My old friend Sally, who is moving back to San Francisco in a week, is ministering to my psyche. (Talk about a cool customer: she's lived here a year, and the only marks she has from two bi-coastal moves in twelve months are blonder hair and better highlights.)

This time I want to get it right, so keep your fingers crossed for me; the next sound you hear might be the scraping of a new key in an old lock.

IN THE GARDEN

In the Dallas/Ft. Worth Airport, the pace was hurried—almost frenetic—on an early November night. Motorized carts wove in and out of crowds of pedestrians, their horns loud and blaring, peoples' voices raised in a polyglot of languages. The throng of travelers came from South America and Mexico. I had pictured cowboys in Dallas in ten-gallon Stetson hats, but no, these people were smaller, their clothing plain, their shoes, cracked and broken. The loudspeaker announced flights to places like Buenos Aires and Caracas. One man stopped his passenger cart to give me a ride through the terminal. He was singing and laughing. "I like to sing to my wife," he said. "I'm in good voice tonight."

I was flying to see my mother in South Alabama. She had been ill for some time and she had fallen and broken her hip, and I knew that was the death knell for this ninety-year-old woman who had sworn she'd live to be one hunderd. When she contracted pneumonia after her fall, I was anxious to get to her.

Lost in thought, I almost missed the gate to Raleigh, North Carolina, where I boarded an American Eagle for the next leg of my trip. My seat mate was a sweet woman who settled in for a chat. I didn't mind the intrusion; it kept my mind off Mother. I hoped she wasn't in pain or frightened, and that I'd get there in time to see her conscious.

My niece, Mother's granddaughter, was her executor, her power of attorney. She had decided not to authorize hip surgery, and had placed a "do not resuscitate" note on her chart. These decisions were straightforward, based on what Mother had requested years ago.

Since my sister lived in the same town as my mother, she was the original executor. I remembered the day they went to the lawyer's office to have the will drawn. Mother was giggling when they got back to the house.

"Now don't just pull the plug at the first sign of trouble," she warned my sister and laughed. My sister said, "You'd better be nice to me from now on." We all laughed when Mother pantomimed being extra nice to my sister. We were happy to be together. Pulling the plug was something far away, not even a reality to us then. Certainly, my sister's death in 2013 was not anywhere on our horizons either.

While the plane flew on in the dark, I thought about Mother's younger self. The most important thing in the world to her—after church—was music. She loved to listen to my radio show on WNKU, *Music from the Hills of Home,* but since she lived in Alabama it wasn't easily accessible. I made tapes and sent them home to her, but then my brother-in-law, John, who was our resident computer geek, fixed up the old machine in her den so that she could stream the radio show live. After that, as soon as she got in from church she could take off her shoes, lean back in her recliner, "mash" a button, and listen to three hours of bluegrass and old-time country music from five hundred miles away. It was a happy memory for me. I'd always get an e-mail from her saying, "Good show." Every week she wrote the same message: "Good show."

When we landed, I almost lost my way in the airport, but the crowd moved toward the baggage carousel and I followed. No one was waiting for me there, nor did I know how to reach anyone in my family. I had a cell phone with a weak battery and an old address book packed deep in the recesses of my suitcase, but I couldn't find either. I was about as prepared for this trip as a ten-year-old Girl Scout running away from home. It was totally dark outside at 9 o'clock, and I could feel the Gulf Shore warmth all around me and smell the sweet scent of the Southern air, but the airline workers were going home for the night, and it looked as though I might have to sleep on the floor.

My brother-in-law, John, strode in just as I was about to cry, and whisked me off to Fairhope, where my mother and my niece were waiting.

"She's had a turn for the worse," he said. "We have to hurry."

On the long drive, I talked to Mother twice on John's cell phone. Neither time made much sense. "This has been a bad day," she said to me, and I could see her long, thin face in my mind's eye.

"What's wrong?" I asked, but she really wasn't communicating any more.

Mother was a rock star in her old age, but she had not always been "cool." She had married when she was sixteen, and for the first part of her life she was in the shadow of my charismatic father. When he died, she fooled us all by coming up with a second act: taking a job in the public library. She learned the Dewey Decimal System, she stamped return dates on volumes of fiction, and was lenient with overdue fines. She visited the musical venues in Branson, Missouri, and Opryland in Nashville, and by the time she was able to apply for Social Security, she was ready to "roost." Her traveling days were done.

My sister wasted no time. Once the decision was made, she started packing boxes and house-hunting. My family drives me crazy that way. Instead of brooding, they *act*. I'm more like Hamlet: I can't make up my mind, can't commit easily. But I have learned from my family that by the time a situation reaches the discussion phase I had better be ready or my head will turn around three times on my neck, and I'll be left behind.

They found the perfect house, just what she wanted. It was a small blue cottage in Huntsville, Alabama, a little like an illustration from Beatrix Potter. It had a white fence and rabbits. You could see the bunnies emerging from the bushes like rabbits coming out of hats. Mother never had trouble luring her grandchildren or her great-grandchildren to come to see her; they adored visiting the bunnies.

It was a perfect storybook house for holidays, too. My sister had Christmas. It was sophisticated, glittering with LED lights and fabulous things to eat, but Thanksgiving belonged to Mother and tradition. She began cooking a week or so before the holiday. She preferred to be alone when she was making something tricky. When it was time to cook the boiled custard, for instance, she chased all of us out of the house so she could lay out the same utensils she'd been using for fifty years, which she regarded with something close to superstition. She came to her task concentrated and alone, like a wizard.

Boiled custard was similar to Floating Islands. The danger was that it could cook too fast and "fry" the eggs. So, Mother poured the milk and cream and eggs into the top of her ancient double boiler and simmered the mixture on low heat for a seemingly endless time. When it was done she poured it in her own mother's custard jar and stored it for a while on the fenced-in porch outside the kitchen. When it was sufficiently cooled, she put it in the refrigerator with stern admonitions about what would happen to anyone who might dare to sample it before Thanksgiving. But her mouth was curved in a half-smile, and her brown eyes twinkled.

When we pulled into the driveway of my niece's house, my brother-in-law got out and slammed the door. "Go, go," he said. "I'll get the suitcase."

Mother was still awake, and she smiled at me, the biggest smile, which grew bigger the closer I got. She knew me! She hid shyly behind my niece and smiled at me almost as if she were flirting. But it was hard to find traces of my lovely Mother in the face before me now. Her white hair was uncombed, there was no color in her face, and her nightgown was askew. The hospice nurse explained that her body was shutting down. She looked a little like a feral animal, wild, in pain, her eyes rolled back from time to time. I was stunned.

My niece, Rebecca, filled me in. Mother had been fine up until that day, and then she began to struggle to breathe. She had oxygen, but it didn't seem to help, and Rebecca had been left alone with morphine and Ativan to administer at her own discretion.

My niece hadn't slept the previous night. Someone had to sit with Mother because she insisted on trying to get out of bed. I immediately took over and sat until 3:30 a.m., recalling old times as I kept watch over the woman who had kept watch over me so many years ago. My niece tried to sleep but couldn't, and at 3:30 a.m. she stumbled back to sit beside me. I went to bed and slept for three hours in the same clothes I had worn when I arrived.

The next morning we were exhausted, but Mother was still panting, still trying to get out of bed, still fighting. My niece gave her morphine and she settled down for a while. We played music, hoping to ease her distress, and it actually worked for a couple of hours. We sat by the bedside, listening to old tapes of family reunions back in 1988.

We heard the tinkle of glasses, the sound of laughter, heard my father singing "Darkness on the Delta," playing a sock rhythm on the guitar. A year later, in 1989, he would be dead of cancer.

Mother was trying to get out of bed again, and suddenly there was no more time to indulge in memories. Rebecca tried more oxygen, more morphine, more Ativan. When she had charge of her own life she wouldn't take so much as an aspirin, so I was amazed to see her tolerating these drugs. Rebecca called the hospice nurse, and this at last produced some results. The nurse had been held over in her last assignment, but when she arrived around 1 p.m., in uniform, her long blonde hair loose in waves down the back, she was all action.

"The thing is to give her the morphine *before* she needs it," the nurse said. She showed us how to mix a morphine cocktail with Ativan. The Ativan, she explained, would quiet Mother in case she woke and didn't know where she was. It would also suppress her breathing.

Later my cousin, Patti, came by. We were all watching Mother, sleeping in her narrow bed, oxygen tubes in her nose, her mouth open, her neck attenuated (one of the seven signs of impending death, my niece informed me). My cousin, whom I've known since she was a newborn baby, looked up at me and wiped tears from her eyes. "I love your hair," she said.

"Thanks," I said. "I haven't combed it in two days."

"The sign of a good haircut," she said. And there it was, the compliment that made me know I was back in Alabama.

By afternoon I was so sleepy I couldn't keep my eyes open, so I passed out for a couple of hours in Rebecca's large, luxurious bed. I fell asleep and dreamed of visiting my mother when we were younger. I was sad about something and ended up crying on her couch. Then that image was gone, and all of them were in the kitchen. Daddy was playing the guitar, Uncle Fred the fiddle, and Aunt Dot played the piano. Everyone was singing, and their voices rose straight up as if carried by the air. I stood apart from them and longed to be one of them again. Then I saw Mother climbing the curved stairs up and up until she came to a door which opened for her as if they'd known she was there. She was young again, straight and pretty as she'd been when I was a toddler. I woke up then, and my niece came to tell me that she had died while I was asleep.

We had only a short time to prepare for a funeral. Mother had wanted to be buried out in the country in Buchanan, Tennessee. You couldn't fly there—the closest airport was Nashville, and the rest of the trip could only be completed by car.

The family gathered at the same Quality Inn where we always stayed when there was a family get-together. I had my own room, but I had a devil of a time getting on top of the bed. It was about four feet off the floor, and you couldn't just throw your leg over like you did in a normal bed. I tried scooting up on my derriere but I couldn't gain any purchase. I tried crawling up on my belly, but that didn't work either. When I finally got my pajama-clad leg on top, I slept like a baby.

Everyone was dressed in hiking clothes at breakfast, and we set out for the cemetery after we had consumed large quantities of coffee. John led the way. He knew this country well; he'd been coming here for more than forty years. I watched the trees, the maple, sycamore, and golden gingko floating past like splashes of oil paint splattered on a canvas, and the kudzu everywhere.

This part of Tennessee needed rain, and so the dust flew up when the cars pulled into the front of the old churchyard. The sky was gray and overcast. I had been feeling alright until then, but the lead-colored afternoon light brought me back to ground zero: Mother was dead. We were here to bury her.

"Look," someone said. "Look at the wooden signs."

"Cowpath Road," one read, and indeed, it looked like a rural intersection. My old fascination with roads came to mind. How did a path become a road? How many years did it take to wear the earth down? How many steps, one on top of the other, did it take to make a rut?

"What's the other one?" someone else asked.

"It's Dogwood Thicket."

There were half a dozen headstones in the old cemetery, most of them from the 1800s. Children had died of diphtheria in those years; whole families had been wiped out by the typhus or Spanish influenza soldiers brought home at the end of World War I.

We took large bags of Mother's ashes and poured them on the graves of her own mother, father, and brother. Everything was still and quiet.

My nephew began to play "Will the Circle Be Unbroken" on the guitar, then he played "In the Garden" and another old hymn she loved. We all sang and when it was time, each of us recited a poem. I read "After Great Pain, a Formal Feeling Comes ... " by Emily Dickinson, and my cousin Sandra read a poem my sister had written before her death—"She Bakes a Caramel Pie." It was about our mother, and it turned out to be the *pièce de résistance*. It honored Mother's resilience and her sense of celebration even in the wake of tragedy. It was a lovely poem. It had humor, family legend, and a story that was so true it went straight to the heart.

Finally, we drove across the road to my father's family cemetery and scattered the largest portion of ashes on his grave, and on the graves of the other family members buried there. I thought of a line from James Joyce. "They lived and laughed and loved and left ... " The joyous sounds of their voices, pianos, guitars, were silenced now. My world, my family, would never be the same again.

3
BLUEGRASS

THE KATIE LAUR BAND—IT WAS ONE OF THE BEST OF THE
BLUEGRASS BANDS. THE HARMONY WAS TERRIFIC
BOTH MUSICALLY AND PERSONALLY.

PICKERS AND GRINNERS

For some years in the 1970s and the early 1980s, I earned a living playing bluegrass festivals. Bluegrass festivals are weekend musical events mostly held in the spring and early summer, and I've always loved performing at them; it's a little like working for the circus.

All kinds of people attended. I'd see farmers wearing overalls so new the britches made a whipping sound when they walked, and city folk in expensive Nikes wearing aviator-style sunglasses and carrying mandolins or guitars worth a small fortune. One summer day when we pulled into Renfro Valley Bluegrass Festival, I saw a man who was a part-time musician leaning on a Porsche chopping chords on a mandolin, the cuffs of his white dress shirt rolled back precisely at the wrist. He was good, and my old friends from Louisville, Edna Mae and Cody Wolfe, were part of a small group of people gathered around to listen.

Edna Mae wore a house dress and a hairnet, and the corners of her thin mouth were turned down slightly. We hugged and I said, "Edna, I didn't know you were going to be here."

"Well, I wrote you day before yesterday that we was a'comin'," she said. "Come on over where we're camped and I'll feed you. I've been cookin' for two days."

Sure enough, by the side of their old station wagon, Edna and Cody had laid out a supper to make your mouth water: a ham, baked beans, potato salad, cakes and pies, a tub full of banana pudding, and a great big jar of iced tea. If the surroundings had been a little more elegant you might have called it a tailgate party.

The food set on Edna Mae's old-fashioned dishes was always welcome to the musicians who had difficulty getting to the concession stands between sets. What with handing out autographs and participating in the "shake-and-howdy" part of the weekend, attending backstage rehearsals and the stomach-twisting anxiety of the performance itself, it was just plain hard to get anything to eat. So the hospitality provided by Edna Mae and Cody was important in a way few people understood.

Nowadays bluegrass festivals are big business, and folks like Edna and Cody Wolfe could hardly afford the price of admission, much less the expense of feeding musicians. Besides, most festivals offer food as part of the musicians' contract "rider"—the part of a contract that covers extras like red M&Ms and bottled water. In those early years, though, it was fans like the Wolfes who sustained players, and their support laid down a fine foundation for bluegrass festivals and bluegrass bands and musicians.

On a warm spring day, when the earth smells new, when the dogwood and redbud trees are in bloom, and the white fluffy clouds dance across the spring sky, I start to think about parking lot pickers and open-air stages, and about people like Edna and Cody who'd go just about anywhere to hear the music they loved, who fed their own souls while they dished out baked beans and potato salad to the rest of us.

Bluegrass festivals began in the mid-1960s, when Carlton Haney produced the first one in Fincastle, Virginia, as a tribute to Bill Monroe. The ticket prices were about $25 for the weekend in those days. Now they can run over $200 for three to five days. Still, they're a great value. Where else can you hear a dozen or more bands, sit in on a bunch of jam sessions, and stand behind an entertainer in a Nudie suit waiting in line for a Port-O-Let?

Here, the season kicks off in May, on Mother's Day weekend, with the forty-four-year-old Appalachian Festival at Coney Island. Our festival was started—believe it or not—as a project of the Junior League of Cincinnati, an organization of affluent women committed to doing good works. Approximately thirty-four percent of Greater Cincinnatians are of Appalachian descent. Back then, Cincinnati was just beginning to acknowledge its mountain roots. In 1970, Junior Leaguers set out to make the city aware of this slice of its cultural pie via a stunning music and crafts festival. There were incredible crafts—art quilts you'd sooner hang on the wall than put on the bed, beautiful pieces of pottery glistening with colorful glazes, and the kind of handmade baskets destined to be displayed on the polished wood of a Hyde Park dining table.

The musical groups were spectacular, too. Roy Acuff was the headliner at the first festival, but I remember the Osborne Brothers best from those early days. Bobby Osborne had a high tenor voice that would shatter glass, and he and his brother Sonny had a hit in the late 1960s with their recording of "Rocky Top." By the time the Appalachian Festival got underway here, "Rocky Top" was a theme song of colleges all over Tennessee, and no self-respecting band at a country wedding could get through an evening without playing it at least once. Audiences drove bluegrass bands to distraction with their requests for the hit. Bands took to putting up signs saying, "We don't play 'Rocky Top,'" and the Red Clay Ramblers actually wrote a number called "Play Rocky Top" just to address the hysteria over the piece.

The song had a refrain—*Rocky Top, Tennes-see—ee-ee—ee*—that proved to be irresistible, and the Osborne Brothers (originally from Hyden, Kentucky, then residents of Dayton, Ohio) became one of the first crossover groups in bluegrass. Their appearance at the Appalachian Festival here drew visitors from far and wide, visitors who bought tickets and stared at quilts draped artfully on hay bales, standing alongside college professors, Junior Leaguers, and first-and-second generation Appalachians who were part of the mainstream for the first time.

Over its four decades, the Appalachian Festival has moved around from Cincinnati Gardens to the Convention Center to its present home at Coney Island. It's still held the second weekend in May, and at under $10 a day, it's the best bargain around.

Just south of us, the Lexington Festival of the Bluegrass is held on the second weekend of June, at the Kentucky Horse Park. The stage is large and shady and set atop a slight rise, with a plywood floor out front for folks who just can't keep from dancing. From the stage, where I have played myself many times, you can see hundreds of festival-goers and lines of merchandise booths—a stretch of real estate where you can buy records and CDs, get a new leather banjo strap or a floppy suede hat.

Promoter Bob Cornett and his wife, Jean, started the Lexington Festival of the Bluegrass in 1974, and it had all the makings of a great festival even then, with terrific performers, food, and down-home merchandise. But this festival's real claim to fame is its outstanding reputation for "parking lot picking"—the informal jam sessions that make bluegrass festivals different from any other musical event.

One year when I played at the festival, I was on stage following a freckle-faced duo—a boy on banjo and a girl on mandolin. They were joined by a guitar player, and all three were singing harmony on Bill Monroe's "It's Mighty Dark to Travel." The girl had on a tee shirt that said "Mandolin players do it better" (it's obvious that she was not particularly concerned with her wardrobe) and the trio was excellent—in tune and in time on the hot summer afternoon.

At 6 p.m. the stage emptied and there was an hour break for dinner. Then, after 7, each band came back for their second set—the all-important evening performance, when you're expected to pull out all the stops and leave the stage to a standing ovation. But it doesn't end there, because on the festival grounds, the jam sessions go on without interruption. So, after playing their second set and slapping on some bug repellent, the freckle-faced girl and her group ran into a bass player they knew, added that instrument to their combo, and took their place among the parking lot pickers.

It was hot and it was late, but they just swung into high gear. As a crowd formed around them, they blasted out Earl Scruggs's version of "Train 45" at breakneck speed. "Sounds just like J.D. Crowe," some man said.

If the players heard him, they didn't take notice. It certainly didn't turn their heads. They just kept playing for the pure joy of the music. But it was a compliment of the highest order. As far as bluegrass is concerned, J.D. Crowe owns Lexington. For that matter, the reach of his virtuosity extends far beyond.

Crowe grew up playing the banjo in Lexington and a kind of Abe Lincoln mythology surrounded his ability. As a boy, he is said to have practiced until the school bus arrived in the morning, then picked up right where he left off when he got home. His father, who knew he was a prodigy, took him to Earl Scruggs for lessons. Scruggs didn't know how to teach what he played, though, so he suggested that the father bring the boy around whenever he and Lester Flatt were in town; that way little J.D. could watch what Earl was doing with his right hand close-up. It might be said that Crowe learned to play the banjo by osmosis. Whether that's true or not, he was in demand professionally by the time he was fifteen, and the album he and his band, the New South, released in 1975 is still one of the most influential bluegrass albums since Flatt and Scruggs took the music world by storm with "Foggy Mountain Breakdown."

J.D. Crowe has never left Kentucky, never moved to Nashville or California as many other star pickers have done. The state has, consequently, lavished him with awards, recognition, even a PhD. Dr. Crowe is in an enviable position: he has a band he can play with when he wants, and, at seventy-five, he can take a few well deserved weekend breaks. However, you will almost always see him at the Lexington Festival of the Bluegrass. This year he will appear on Saturday with the Masters of Bluegrass on the evening show, and that alone will be worth the price of admission.

The following week, June 8 through 15, is reserved for the Bean Blossom Bluegrass Festival in Bean Blossom, Indiana. Bill Monroe had been impressed enough with that first festival at Fincastle, Virginia, back in 1965, that he wasted no time starting his own in 1966, in what is now known as the Bill Monroe Country Music Park.

When I first went to Bean Blossom it was still in its "primitive" phase: there were long lines at the food concession stand (that's *stand* singular—

there was only one for all those people!) and the Port-O-Lets backed up. Ed Pinkston, a local instrument maker, used to say you had to practice hillbilly yoga to attend Bean Blossom. When I asked him what hillbilly yoga was, he answered, "Eat a fried egg every mornin.' That'll keep you out of the Port-O-Lets."

I was there one year when the weatherman warned of a "thermal inversion"—heat the intensity of which I'd never felt before, with not a lick of breeze blowing. That weekend the level of protest about the sanitary facilities reached a new high: It was a lot like the French Revolution. Attendees wanted to drag the Monroe family off to the Bastille.

On the other hand, one of my favorite nights at Bean Blossom was a Saturday night, standing in back of the stage, listening to a group of the best fiddlers in bluegrass tearing up a tune called "Gold Rush." That night there was a campfire, and the fiddlers stood behind a log, which they used to rest one foot on at a time when their solo was over. Fiddlers have to keep their bow arms "oiled up" and limber, and playing onstage with a band for an hour, maybe two, a day just isn't enough practice. Consequently, at a festival like Bean Blossom, where a lot of bands converge with the same repertoire and musical background, you can count on finding plenty of jam sessions at night.

That Saturday night I heard Bill Monroe's fiddle player, Kenny Baker, his Stetson hat tilted just so over one eye, pulling his bow over the strings of the violin like buttery toffee. I heard Byron Berline, and Tex Logan. I heard the West Virginia fiddlers Joe Meadows and the gifted young Buddy Griffin, who later came to play with my own band. I saw Ricky Skaggs that night, too—he was young and still playing the fiddle, and I heard the blood-curdling high lonesome sound of his tenor singing.

Festivals really started seeing success in the 1980s, and bigger, more complex events followed. MerleFest in North Carolina (named in honor of Doc Watson's son, Merle) and the Telluride Festival in Colorado are now the size of small cities; transportation is required between the stages. Both festivals, and others like them, boast hundreds of bands, many not even bluegrass, and the price of a couple of tickets can be truly astronomical.

BLUEGRASS

About ten years ago I was in California at two enormous bluegrass festivals: Grass Valley Father's Day Bluegrass Festival in northern California and the Hardly Strictly Bluegrass festival in San Francisco's Golden Gate Park. I was amazed at the thousands in attendance at each. At Grass Valley, the RVs were huge and rich-looking and lined the park from one end to the other. And that was a week before the festival even started. The price of admittance was so high that the board of trustees had to establish scholarships for talented musicians who couldn't afford it. After all, the festival would not have earned the credibility it enjoyed with no talented amateur musicians watching and playing along.

On the other hand, the Hardly Strictly Bluegrass festival in Golden Gate Park was free, paid for by the late billionaire Warren Hellman. Mr. Hellman, a venture capitalist who played the banjo, started the festival in order to highlight the city's interest and history with the music he loved.

When I was there, I remember the morning fog made the park look like something out of a Tolkien novel: ancient crooked tree trunks, thick foliage, the distinctive look and aroma of eucalyptus. I saw an old Chinese couple doing their morning tai chi, unaffected by the commotion around them. The various stages' sound systems were first-rate, and so were the performers. I was bowled over to see Dolly Parton on one of the women's music stages, though as my old friend, Becky, later said, "She was so far away you could barely see one little sequin."

Still, it was amazing. In my day, I used to sing on hastily constructed stages in the rain for seventy-five audience members sitting in their lawn chairs with trash bags and newspapers over their heads. Now I was in a strange land where the worst weather that could be thrown at me was fog, and that usually burned off by afternoon. Plus, Mr. Hellman flew the musicians out at his own expense and housed them at nice hotels. *O brave new world*, I thought, *that has such creatures in't.*

Bill Monroe used to say that he didn't write all those songs, he just grabbed the notes out of the air before anybody else did. At Golden Gate Park, I realized that bluegrass was magic after all.

CURLY RAY CLINE

We got to the bluegrass festival in Wise, Virginia, early on a Friday morning, and, by afternoon, we had our record table set up. The sun overhead was hot and bright, and there was no shade at all, so we set up a canopy over our little merch mart. When Curly Ray Cline, the fiddler for Ralph Stanley's band, saw our tarp, he asked whether he could put his record table underneath it, too.

I considered that to be a stroke of good luck. Curly was known as the best record salesman ever, and I was eager to watch him in action. Festival money was okay but scarce, so musicians started marketing their record albums (everything was still vinyl in those days). The more industrious musicians started selling 8-track tapes, tee shirts, and key chains, with their picture on one side and their life story on the other.

Curly had all this merchandise—his key chains are worth big money nowadays—plus some of the band's gospel records, with pictures of Ralph Stanley and the boys with their hats off, their faces reverently turned up to the heavens.

It didn't take him long to spread out his wares just so on his folding table, and you could almost hear him sighing, rubbing his hands together in anticipation of cold, hard cash. Although he'd brought along a lawn chair, I never saw him sit in it once during the entire weekend.

Curly was a round man, with a thick, kinky bush of hair that looked like a Brillo pad. He was as merry as a cricket, as my grandfather used to say, and a grin split his moon-shaped face in half. His greedy little eyes narrowed when he looked at our sparse operation.

"Ain't ye got ye any tee shirts?" he asked me, bobbing his head. He was animated offstage, just as he was onstage. His grin never changed: his eyes were constantly moving over the people milling around. Two men in their late forties, with the kind of mountain faces you could spot a mile off, came up to my table. They were wearing railroad bill caps and stiff overalls. They told me they were farmers from Mitchell County, North Carolina, and I could tell they were bashful. They complimented me on my singing.

"You sound a right smart like Patsy Cline," one of them said, while smiling shyly.

Before I could respond, Curly grabbed one of them by the arm.

"Now boys," he said, "them britches. New, ain't they?"

The farmers warmed to Curly quickly, proud that he had noticed their new pants.

"You got to make a good livin' to afford britches like that nowadays." He went on. The three of them discussed inflation and overalls cordially for a few minutes, and when I looked again they were both leaving with two of Curly's albums. One minute I was basking in their compliments, and the next minute Curly had their money.

I sat for a while watching people walk back and forth between the grandstand and the camping area. We were close to Pendleton Gap, Virginia, surrounded by mountains and a rocky landscape. The parking fields in the old fairgrounds were already full of pickup trucks and recreational vehicles, and more were arriving, churning up clouds of red dust as they parked then rolled out coolers and buckets of Kentucky Fried Chicken. The country folk were dressed up for the festival in double-knit leisure suits or short-sleeved white shirts and ties; the city people wore Nike jogging shoes, bleached jeans, and aviator sunglasses.

I was thinking about this unusual mix of music fans when Curly's friend, Mason Little, arrived. Mason was about 5'10" and thin as a rail. He managed Ralph Stanley's bluegrass festival at McClure, Virginia, and he carried himself with an air of gravity, as if he were aware of the authority of his position.

"I heard you been carryin' a couple of dogs around," he said to Curly. Curly answered that yes, he had been carrying a couple of good coon dogs in a special cage on top of the band camper.

"Them dogs traveled three weeks in that cage," Curly said. "Their feet was a little blistered but they were healin' up and rarin' to go the last time I saw 'em. Somebody picked 'em up from me last weekend at the Lexington festival."

Since Curly and I played a lot of the same festivals, I had already seen the dogs. He kept them tied up outside the camper, and I had sneaked food to them on several occasions. Mason stood there thinking for a minute, his arms wrapped around himself, then recalled a dog of his that would tree a coon, fight him, and never make a whimper.

"That durn dog had splits on his ears long as yer finger," he said, measuring off a length with his hand.

One of the members of the Stanley band drifted by our set up to sit a spell and visit.

"You boys still talkin' 'bout dogs?" he asked.

Curly and Mason looked a little sheepish. The visitor was Charlie Sizemore, an attractive young man, and as the afternoon wore on, Curly and Mason noticed that two young girls had been dropping by the record table rather often. They talked to Curly, but they were watching for Charlie, and Junior Blankenship, another of Stanley's young players, and they were not very adept at hiding their interest.

***

When Mason came back from eating supper that evening, he saw the girls hanging around again. He shook his head as they walked away.

"Nowadays a girl don't have no more idea than a rabbit how to get a boy to pay attention to 'em," he said, almost to himself.

Curly agreed, nodding his head. He stabbed the record table with his index finger.

"What we oughta do, Mason," he said, "is tell them girls where they're a'goin' wrong."

Mason considered this for a bit before speaking again. "I raised seven daughters and had nary a bit of trouble with any of 'em, thank the Lord."

By now it was full night, and dark, after a period of deep purple sky. It was time to close up, and Curly said, "Well, when we git here tomorrow, I think you better be the one to talk to 'em."

Then Curly got busy counting out fat wads of dollar bills and handfuls of change. He was almost licking his lips in delight.

"How'd you do?" he asked me, narrowing his eyes and grinning like a fox.

"Well, I know when I'm outclassed," I said.

"Better luck tomorrow," he said, his dark bushy eyebrows arching smugly.

By the time I got back to the record stand the next morning, Curly was already there, down on one knee, playing the fiddle for a small red-haired toddler who was sucking his finger and smiling sweetly. Naturally, his parents bought several of Curly's albums, and he slipped the money in his wallet as smoothly as if it were oiled.

"It ain't so much what you do onstage as what you do off," he said, and I promised to do better.

That afternoon, Ricky Skaggs and his wife, Brenda, dropped by to visit with Curly. They showed him pictures of their new baby, Amanda Jewel, and everybody oohed and aahed over her. Ricky had just put out his first solo album, *Sweet Temptation*, and he was in good spirits. His voice was high pitched and tenor, and he was wickedly funny in those days.

When he saw me with my record table set up next to Curly's, he just shook his head.

"This thing right here," he said, grabbing Curly's *Chicken Reel* album, "cost me a lot of record sales when I was playing with Ralph Stanley. People would come by to see the album Keith Whitley and I had made, and Curly would run right over with that album sayin,' 'Why don't you folks take a look at *this* record? It's got both them boys on it,' and there went my record sale."

I nodded my head in sympathy.

"Well, one day I struck back," Ricky said. "See these chickens on the cover? Well, I sat down at the record table while Curly was taking a break, and I cut the eyes out of the chickens with my pocket knife on about seventeen albums."

Curly looked pained, but just then three men approached the table, looking casually at his display. Curly sized them up, then sprung.

"Got a record player, do you?" he asked one of them shrewdly.

"Naw," the man said.

"How about a tape player?"

The man shook his head again. "Naw."

Curly sold them key chains. Mason tapped Curly's shoulder while he was counting his money.

"Here comes them girls again," Mason said slowly. "I guess now's a good chance."

He straightened, hitched up his pants, and approached them.

"Girls," he said, "You're doin' this all wrong."

They looked at him and blushed.

"Now if you want boys to notice you, just be wherever they are, but don't look to the right nor to the left. Just act like they ain't there and go on about your business."

It wasn't what they wanted to hear; nevertheless, they promised Mason they'd do better.

"Aw," Mason groaned, as if the weight of it were on his shoulders.

I left with my band to do the last show. It felt good: lights just right, mics with just the right edge, and the band rested and enthusiastic.

When I returned to the table it was crowded and I was busy for a while. Still, I watched Curly out of the side of my vision. He shook hands, kissed babies, talked about dogs. I was amazed at the number of people he knew. Talking to that many people would have drained me dry, but Curly showed no signs of flagging, his head just kept bobbing. He could talk to more than one person at a time while congenially collecting and making change from a great wad of cash he held tightly in his fist. His curly hair and ruddy cheeks made him look like a combination of Santa Claus and Nikita Khrushchev.

"Now tell the truth," he said to me when things slowed down. "Didn't you do just a little better on your record sales a'settin' by me?"

"I only lost about a third," I said dryly. Curly tried to look sympathetic.

"Just remember: to sell somethin' you've got to have somethin' to sell, and you gotta set up some place where there's traffic."

He looked over his shoulder to see if anyone was listening, then moved his head a little closer to mine.

"You know what they say about me?" he asked.

I didn't.

"They say, 'Just walk around beside Curly Cline for a while and money'll just fall into your pockets.'"

"That's the truth," Mason Little piped in. He had just sauntered up out of the shadows wearing an expression even more serious than usual. His bill cap was cocked to one side, and he scratched behind his ear.

"I know it for a fact," he said.

I got in the van and waved at them, knowing I'd see them again in a couple of weeks, surprised they had revealed so much to me. I had forgotten about country folks' canny ways with money. My own grandfather had been a respected man in Tennessee because he was a shrewd horse trader. "He kept a cool head," people said as if he'd occupied a seat on the New York Stock Exchange.

Then the teenaged girls came back around for one final consultation with Mason and Curly.

"It worked," I heard one of them say, giggling. "We walked right on by them and pretty soon they came a hollerin' at us."

I settled back into my perch in the van and watched the night stars, so clear out there away from city lights, and I was sure I saw it when Curly winked at Mason, looking a lot like the fox he and his dogs hunted. The moon made hollows in his face, and I could see his eyes glitter.

WALKING THE HILLS

"A green Christmas makes for a fat graveyard," my Aunt Dot used to say a long time ago, waving her crooked index finger at anyone who'd listen. It was her explanation for why people sickened and died even in mild winters. According to her logic, if December wasn't cold enough to freeze the virus germs, a lot of people would die.

I have a new mantra, though: When I get the blues, I reach for my shoes. My favorite walking buddy is Ma Crow, and she and I are intrepid. A walk through snow and slush makes us feel amazingly virtuous. This afternoon, as a reward, we saw a cardinal—a fat male, scarlet red against the dun color of the day. He perched on a tree limb dotted with snow and preened his feathers, puffing himself up as if he were a member of the Cincinnati City Council.

When we started our walks up Sycamore Hill, we were doing some steep climbing and my ragged breath cut through the silence, the only sound I could hear. An old Appalachian woman named Esther used to say, "Aw, I walked up Sycamore Hill ever'day from the Bank Café carryin' two or three kids and three sacks of groceries."

When Ma and I got to the top of the hill, we turned right onto Walker Street, along the woodsy trail where I've often seen deer wallows. It leads to a small city park. We passed the swings and slides and then walked down the long flight of steps, concrete blocks with wrought iron handrails. It was built, like so many beautiful things, by the WPA.

Ma is in better shape than I am; her little legs seemed to fly. Her long salt-and-pepper hair sprang into ringlets in places, and her cheeks were rosy pink.

Her sister died last spring, and she suffered from it but could do nothing about it. It was her younger sister, too, the one she was supposed to take care of, the one who was supposed to outlive her. Ma flew to Knoxville, Tennessee, last fall to hike around the Smoky Mountains, which makes me think of a story about Sara Carter of the singing Carter Family when she still lived in Maces Springs, Virginia. In Mark Zwonitzer and Charles Hirshberg's book, *Will You Miss Me When I'm Gone?: The Carter Family and Their Legacy in American Music*, Carter says she asked for someone to help her "walk the mountain" one last time before she died. I've heard her granddaughter, Rita, tell the story.

Carter was a tall woman, a traipsin' woman. She had a beautiful alto voice, but she could not stay married to A.P.—possibly no one could have—and it interfered with her performing in the group. Instead, she moved to California and wrote her most famous—and only—song, "Lonesome Pine Blues," which Ma loves to sing.

I knew Sara Carter when she was an old woman, and I once spent time with her and her cousin Maybelle when both of them were back in Virginia for a visit at the Carter's Store Saturday night show at the same time. The Katie Laur Band was appearing, and both women were in the audience. It was like an unexpected glimpse of royalty, because I could feel their power as surely as if they wore crowns or tiaras. Yet they were unimposing women. Sara was taller and raw-boned, and Maybelle was tiny and trim.

It seemed ridiculous for me to sing one of the songs they recorded, the height of foolishness to be singing a Carter Family song with my own band, but Sara always insisted I sing "You Are My Flower." It was one of her songs, and she thought I sang it beautifully.

One winter, on the way back to Cincinnati in our old green van, we got stuck in about nine feet of snow, but everybody in the valley turned up to help us out. That's how it must have been when Sara, A.P., Maybelle, and Uncle Ezra (Maybelle's husband) took off to New Jersey to record for RCA Victor in 1928. Considerable preparations were necessary to get their old Model T out of a snowbank or a mudhole and back up on the two-lane highway.

One of the men got us stuck, but the rest of them got us going again and everybody was laughing and cheering as we slipped and slid our way up the hill to the asphalt.

I knew a wonderful old-time fiddler in West Virginia named John Morris who used to come over to the Carter fold to play music. He was red-haired and freckled with china blue eyes and a high color. He and his father, who was also a musician, were drinking coffee at Janette's house on the top of the mountain on a Sunday morning when the phone rang. It was Janette's cousin, June Carter (Maybelle's daughter), and her husband, Johnny Cash.

"Oh, lord," she said, absolutely stricken. Morris said her knuckles went white on the back of the chair.

Both of them jumped up immediately and said, "Janette, what in the world?" "What's wrong?"

Janette replied, "There's a millionaire a'comin' to my house for breakfast."

Morris and his father had to clean up the kitchen while she gathered her wits, but when she did she served up some perfect biscuits (just short enough to be light), scrambled eggs, country ham and bacon, and two kinds of gravy. Plus, of course, a jar or two of damson plum preserves.

That winter, Ma and I walked a lot, fueled by our new-found virtuousness. Walking was our salvation—and music, of course. Ma's small, short fingers stretched with such precision over the neck of her Martin guitar, as if they'd grow into a C chord like a vine putting out tiny tendrils. "The hard thing for me was to learn to use a pick," she said. She was used to having her instrumental abilities negated, but in fact she's an excellent player, the love child of a girl singer and a guitar player in a country band.

Ma's face is a child's face: two mischievous brown eyes framed by slightly pointed brows, and by long and curly salt-and-pepper-colored hair. She has little use for fashion and dresses conservatively in denim skirts and dresses. She has a couple pair of "frou-frou" shoes as she calls anything with height to it, as if she were strutting across the stage in furred pumps trimmed with caribou feathers.

Men generally find her attractive and probably scary, and for those reasons, and more of her own, Ma Crow is looking for space. "I'm a domestic refugee," she told me once, and her eyebrows pointed, her eyes beginning to tear over. One of the best things to do is to get together with Ma and cry. We do that a lot. "It's not like we're depressed or anything," she said with her wry laugh.

That winter we walked a lot, and we sat in my bedroom, or—when the weather wan't so cold—on a picnic table down by the river. We'd take a guitar and work on melodies and lyrics. When something came, we were as excited as children finding shells on the beach.

We wrote a song called "Rubies on Scepters of Gold," which we liked a lot, and it made me want to write something really visceral like a Larry Brown novel in a song: drinking, car wrecks, cheating, and killing.

Ma says we've done most of the research.

BLUEGRASS ROYALTY

The linden trees along Ludlow Avenue in Clifton's Gaslight District are a particularly lush green on this late summer evening. A slender young man with tattoos and piercings carries a skateboard, pushing his way through the sidewalk strollers, periodically putting the skateboard down and riding it for a few feet. He skates past a couple holding hands, past a man walking his ancient lab toward the kiosk on the corner, which is covered in colored notes. Business cards are attached willy-nilly, along with hand-outs promoting healing crystals and Indian restaurants with optimistic advertisements for roommates (since we're just a jump from the University of Cincinnati).

There is no marquee outside the Ludlow Garage advertising tonight's band. No line has formed; all the seats that have been sold are bought and paid for, so there is no need for a ticket window. The sound system has been set up. "Check, check," the soundman says into the mic. "We need less reverb; we're right on the edge of feeding back ... " It is a tedious routine, testing each instrument and each microphone one at a time, but these musicians are accustomed to the highest production values at any venue. It is vital to their performance.

When I come in, the warm-up band is doing its sound check. They're impossibly young and whippet-thin and wear their hair in pompadours straight out of the 1950s. The band has a somewhat mysterious name, My Brother's Keeper, but it is clear they know their way around the acoustic stringed instruments they play. I listen for a minute and set off to find the "green room" where the Earls of Leicester are probably waiting until time for their performance.

Everything is quiet there when I arrive. But there is an anticipation building in the quietness. An important musical event is to take place here tonight, a musical tribute to Lester Flatt and Earl Scruggs and the Foggy Mountain Boys offered by the Earls of Leicester, a band assembled by Nashville legend Jerry Douglas. He put it together to interpret the bluegrass music of the early 1950s and '60s, specifically the groundbreaking music of Flatt and Scruggs.

One of the most important bands to come out of Nashville in a while, the Earls of Leicester were wildly popular right out of the gate, sweeping the International Bluegrass Music Awards the first year the band was together. They've been called a "tribute" band, a term Douglas doesn't like.

"I started the band to play good music, not to be a gimmick," he says. He didn't want authentic bluegrass to be forgotten. "I wasn't hearing it anywhere," he says seriously. After stints with blues bands, jazz bands, and innovative ensembles of every kind, Douglas was in the mood for hard-core bluegrass, so he opened up his Rolodex and dialed a few numbers, and the band the Earls of Leicester was born. He brings an intensity and reverence for Flatt and Scruggs's bluegrass, and under his leadership "everything old is new again," he says.

The Earls of Leicester is an all-star band. Shawn Camp, the rhythm guitar player and vocalist, is a young lion—a prolific songwriter who writes with and for a "who's who" of Nashville and has won his own Grammy Award. His songs have been recorded by Ricky Skaggs, Garth Brooks, George Strait, and Blake Shelton, and more lately he's had a project in the works with Loretta Lynn. Camp, who looks like he's in his late forties, has an unlined face framed by thick curls. He is an extraordinary singer and guitar player who captures the late Lester Flatt, then transcends him to become an utterly natural *outgrowth* of Flatt.

Charlie Cushman, the banjo player who was hired to "play" the late, great Earl Scruggs, makes even expert banjo players weep. His finger picks fly over the strings on "Pike County Breakdown" so that it's almost impossible to tell his playing from Scruggs's.

Flatt and Scruggs and the Foggy Mountain Boys always carried a fiddler with them on their dates. They played with Chubby Wise, who is credited with writing "Orange Blossom Special;" the flamboyant Benny Martin; and finally Paul Warren, who was more of an old-time fiddler than a bluegrass player. As luck would have it, Jerry was able to get Johnny Warren, Paul's son, for the Earls of Leicester. "I am really an old-time fiddler, like my father was, not a bluegrass fiddler," Paul insists when I speak with him, just as his father described his own playing so many years earlier. (Old-time fiddling differs from bluegrass fiddling in the repertoire and in the style of the playing.) To make the package sweeter, Johnny Warren plays his father's fiddle in the Earls. He is a slender, fit middle-aged man whose day job is tightening up players' golf games on the PGA circuit.

Douglas brought along bassist Barry Bales from Alison Krauss's band, Union Station. Though Bales is a virtuoso, he takes only one solo during the concert, because in the Flatt and Scruggs band the bass player stayed in the background. With no drummer and no electrified instruments in either group, the steady 1-2 1-2 bass beat sustains and drives the music.

Jerry Douglas himself grew up in Warren, Ohio, listening to Flatt and Scruggs, especially Josh Graves, the dobro player. Douglas's father had a bluegrass band, and Jerry got his first guitar at the age of five. In an interview with a Nashville newspaper, he remembers the first time he saw the famous band, detailing "the warmth of the audience, the smell of the popcorn, the outfits they were wearing," and he was hooked on Graves and his dobro.

A dobro looks very much like a guitar with a hubcap in the middle. It's played flat, the back of the instrument parallel to the floor. I was in the audience at the International Bluegrass Music Association Awards Show when Douglas inducted Graves into the Bluegrass Hall of Fame. When the announcer mashed a button and Lester Flatt's lovely crooning voice came over the sound system doing his customary introduction of "Uncle Josh," as he was called, welcoming him up to the "old Mercury microphone" to play a solo, I wasn't the only one who wiped away tears.

Wayne Clyburn was an early fan of Douglas. "We were at Ralph Stanley's bluegrass festival down in Virginia, and that night we saw a large circle of people standing by a campfire listening to something. Turns out they were listening to a new player, Jerry Douglas. He was about seventeen or eighteen years old, and he was all over the dobro. Later, I saw him talking to Charlie Waller and Doyle Lawson, and the next thing I knew he was working with their band, The Country Gentlemen."

After Douglas completed a summer with The Country Gentlemen, one of the iconic bands in bluegrass, he got a call to go with another, J.D. Crowe and the New South, a major career opportunity. Through his exposure with Crowe and bandmates Tony Rice and Ricky Skaggs, Douglas became one of the most in-demand session players in the business, and when Crowe's band broke up he landed a highly coveted place in Alison Krauss's Union Station band.

If you Google Jerry Douglas, you'll see at least three screens of discography of between 2,000 and 3,000 recordings, and a listing of fourteen Grammys, CMA instrumentalist of the year, and honors like the National Heritage Award. He and all the players in the Earls of Leicester work other gigs, do recordings, and even tour with other bands. But each musician carves out a piece of time to devote to touring with the Earls. Each is the best in his field, and the variety of work keeps them from being bored.

According to Wayne Clyburn, "Douglas did the same thing with a dobro that Scruggs did with a banjo ... he redefined it." He says that the dobro came from the Hawaiian guitar and was meant to be played slowly, the perfect filler in country music, with its "businessman's bounce" tempos. "Douglas turned the instrument inside out. He learned intricate fiddle tunes, barring the quick grace notes with his left hand, using fingerpicks on his right."

Tonight, Jerry Douglas joins the rest of the band in the green room about a half-hour before it was time to play, wearing a Flatt and Scruggs get-up: a jacket and western-style hat cocked carefully over one eye, the whole thing topped off with an embroidered bow tie. All of the Earls wear this same attire, and from a distance they bear an eerie resemblance to the band they're honoring.

The Earls tune and retune their instruments, laughing and telling stories about Lester Flatt and Earl Scruggs and the Foggy Mountain Boys. Douglas and his bandmates remember that Scruggs was his band's treasurer and carried the night's earnings—mostly nickels, dimes, and quarters—in a cotton pillowslip. Those were the lean years of playing schoolhouses and drive-in theater concession stands, when admission was a quarter. There wasn't much paper money to deal with. Once they got famous, Scruggs carried the night's receipts in a tackle box.

The first few years, Flatt and Scruggs traveled in a single car with five or six band members and instruments plus an upright bass tied on top. Those conditions were short-lived, so before long they had a bus, and road conditions grew a little more comfortable. Still, how did they manage to stay together as long as they did without killing each other, I wondered. The Earls, on the other hand, fly to their gigs, renting a van when they hit the ground and driving sensibly, within a comfortable distance, from one gig to the next.

When I look at my watch it's ten minutes until show time, so I leave the green room to take my seat in the audience to enjoy the performance. The lights come up, the band steps out to play, and the energy is palpable. The concert starts off with high expectations and hot licks from all the players. Wayne Clyburn, Bill LaWarre, and Harry Sparks are seated near the front of the Ludlow Garage room anticipating an evening of good music. The audience is mostly male and presumably well-heeled, since tickets for the event start at $30 and climb all the way to $65 for front row seats.

The music is immediately as rich and satisfying as Sunday dinner, and the audience settles in their seats, propping their elbows on the arm rests. Shawn Camp sings "All I Want Is You" to the delight of Lester Flatt fans, and Johnny Warren kicks off a fast version of "Black Eyed Suzie."

During intermission the fans stand up and mingle, some of them drinking beer. These aren't just fans, they are "aficionados." They know the difference between Flatt and Scruggs recordings of the 1950s and early '60s and Flatt and Scruggs recordings from 1946 and 1948 with mandolin player Bill Monroe. They can also discuss why the difference is important.

Clyburn, a true aficionado, is here because when he was in college he blew off a Flatt and Scruggs concert thinking, "I can see them anytime." Flatt and Scruggs broke up the following week. He has never gotten over his moment of bad judgment, and, he announces a little sadly, "This is as close as I'll get to ever seeing Flatt and Scruggs."

Sparks, an architect who has been active in the bluegrass and old-time music scene for most of his life and is a respected instrument broker and luthier, says, "Put it this way: People are always asking me, 'What does such-and-such a banjo sound like?' Well, I can compare it to another banjo or describe whether it's a thin sound or not, but when push comes to shove, you have to go listen. The Earls of Leicester are playing the roots music of bluegrass, and Jerry Douglas is doing everything he can to memorialize Josh Graves. It's like looking back and allowing us to see inside the history of the music."

LaWarre, a virtuoso mandolin player himself, has much the same opinion. Listening to the Earls, he says, is like being backstage at the Opry, hearing stories, musicians cutting up and joking with each other while they're warming up. It's informal, just plain fun. "I heard the original Flatt and Scruggs twice," he says. "Once at Holmes High School in Covington and once when they played on top of a concession stand at the drive-in. I had just discovered bluegrass, so I was thrilled." He pauses and laughs a little. "As for the Earls of Leicester, I think Jeff White does a great job as Curly [Seckler] on mandolin and tenor singing."

One thing he misses, LeWarre says, is "the choreography of Flatt and Scruggs, the original band. They had only one microphone for the whole five-piece band, and getting into and out of that mic was something like a dance. You kept expecting them to run into each other stepping in and out, but they never did. It was wonderful."

As the band comes to the peak of their performance, Charlie Cushman changes his banjo for a guitar and begins to play a song wearing his finger picks on his right hand. It is what bluegrassers call "a sacred number," and four of the band members gather around the microphone to sing a quartet on the chorus. For a few minutes I am enraptured by the music, by how full it sounds. The singing is rich in harmony, and Charlie's guitar playing is as delicate as calligraphy. He dances up and down the neck of the old Martin guitar adding notes where the music is thin, propping the whole thing up with his rhythmic right-handed three-finger roll.

At the other end of the stage, Jerry Douglas starts an up-tempo tune on the dobro, whipping the audience into a frenzy of appreciation. After an encore, we stand and applaud some more; then Clyburn, LaWarre, Sparks, and I walk out into the summer night, satisfied. As we go our separate ways, we wave at the Earls of Leicester standing at their "Merch Mart," what we used to call the record table, signing CDs and chatting with fans.

It's been a good night, with a sense of intimacy some might call a "moment." Clyburn, LaWarre, Sparks and I have been friends for over forty years, and that relationship has served us all well. Our easy camaraderie carries us into the street. It is early yet, but the traffic has picked up, and there are more pedestrians, more dog walkers. The old dilapidated Clifton apartment houses appear to be propped up for the time being—they've looked "on the edge" for years, but they are still standing. We say good-night, the four of us still standing, knowing we will talk about this evening's music for a long time to come.

FOX ON THE RUN

John Morris was a fiddler who had hair the color of a carrot. He had freckles and blue, blue eyes, and he was from Clay County, West Virginia. He liked to act like he was a rube, though in fact he was better traveled and educated than most folks.

"Why don't you ever come see me?" I'd say, sitting outside his house in a lawn chair in the sun. A couple dogs lolled in the heat. He lived on land that was used to grow things, in the shadows of great mountains. He didn't have a lot of trees around his house.

"Aw," he'd say, "Kate, I'm just too hickey." He talked in a high, clear voice, like someone who's never smoked a cigarette. He had kept the same vocal range all his life—a little falsetto, a little mountain tenor.

For a couple of weeks, we played together in Denver, Colorado, at a contentious United Mine Workers meeting. We'd do our shows each day, wrangle consecutive days off, and the whole band would drive through the Rocky Mountains in a car called a "Rent-A-Lemon." Although there was snow on the ground, it never felt cold. The air was like champagne—the best kind of cold, the kind that makes you feel exhilarated for no reason at all.

We scrambled over the rocks hiking around the mountains and in the evening stopped to see a bluegrass band with Dorsey Harvey Jr. (originally from Dayton) playing mandolin. He was wonderful. His rhythm was right on the knife-edge of swing.

Back in Denver, John and I ate lunch most days in a restaurant that served fifty varieties of homemade pies. Sometimes we were joined by a folk singer named Utah Phillips. He was popular back then, a songwriter of some renown. He'd written "Rock Salt and Nails" and given it to Alice Gerrard and Hazel Dickens. Hazel told me so herself.

"Old Utah," as John called him, told us about how Denver used to be a railroad depot, how the 'boes stayed there right by the tracks, how it was one of the most notorious stops for the bums back in the days of dust bowls and depression. I told him about seeing the homeless sleeping in the glass windows of the May Department Store downtown, and he nodded as if that explained things.

"They're still here," he said. He wore the outfit of a logger, which is to say overalls hemmed short. While he was between stories, John pointed at his bowl of stew. "If you're through with that," John said matter-of-factly, "could I have it?" John was not into sentimentality. "Ol' Utah's a good guy. He's just full of crap."

It's the little things that stay with you. Hiking in Colorado or looking over a rock in Elizabethton, Tennessee, and seeing such rare beauty that it takes your breath away: a view of pink and white dogwood, watercolor splashes next to redbud trees, almost Oriental, the tender green of trees in spring.

※

Over-the-Rhine is like that for me: an unlikely source of buried treasures. I turn a corner, cross the street, see a hidden recess of green foliage up some alley, and I'm hooked again.

This morning I walked past the Walnut Street Baptist Church, its sign still written in German with the date 1861 on the front. It's an old red-painted brick structure with neat white trim, a little ragged around the edges. It needs someone to give it a facelift, just for the sake of making it beautiful again.

I see the group of buildings at the north end of Main Street that Vern Rader wants to re-build into viable loftspace, stores, cafes and galleries. I see true visions everywhere.

In Denver in 1978, John Morris got up early every morning and carved a set of tools for me out of any old wood he could find. He was doing it because whittling kept his hands busy. He started out with a pocketknife he colored with shoe-polish and adorned with my initials. The next day he did a pick axe with great long prongs on it like a longhorn cow, and he carved a "magic screwdriver" that I'd never lose and would just whirl up like a superhero's weapon into my hand whenever I needed it. John sat alone in his room, drinking coffee and carving the tiny wooden implements in that beautiful Denver light.

HARRY SPARKS, GUITAR MASTER

The only time I ever busted up a guitar was at a party in Rabbit Hash in the backyard of E.W. Scripps chairman Bill Burleigh. I was doing a job there with a bluegrass band, and I had the guitar around my neck as we strolled and played to various clusters of guests at the party. Unfortunately, I was walking in deep shadows at the back of the house, and I tripped in a big hole. I was surprised when I hit the ground—you always are—but I was even more surprised when I realized I'd broken the neck of my Martin D-28 guitar. I couldn't move, but I could feel the guitar's jagged edges where the neck used to be.

About twenty-five people came running, and I was briefly flattered that so many were concerned about my welfare. I started to say, "I'm all right," but nobody was interested. "How's the guitar?" they demanded.

I didn't even have to look at the limp neck of the instrument. Instead I told the banjo player, "Put it in the case and take it to Harry Sparks."

Harry doesn't build instruments, but he is known in the bluegrass universe for the almost surgical repairs and fret work he has done on the necks of guitars, mandolins, and banjos over the years, instruments belonging to everyone from Cincinnati friends to Nashville legends. Bela Fleck has flown in with his banjo, mandolinist Sam Bush thanks him on every single CD he releases, and Nashville superstar Vince Gill has called him a friend for more than thirty years. In fact, back in the '60s Harry was asked to dress a fret on a young folk singer's guitar. The man was playing with the Mitchell

BLUEGRASS

Harry Sparks, the Rabbit Hash rambler—When a guitar, banjo, or mandolin got damaged, the musician's first and usually best advice was "Take it to Sparky."

Trio and later, when he politely sent Harry tickets to all his concerts, Harry learned his stage name: John Denver. The future pop star got to experience what bluegrass players in our town have known for years: If you want to buy a guitar, sell a banjo, or heal a mandolin, Harry Sparks—"Sparky" to his friends—is the man to see.

Harry has a feeling for structure. He is an architect by trade, an instrument repairman by passion, and there's something about bluegrass and old-time music that appeals to his Kentucky roots, something about the very framework of the music. Harry himself is built to last. His lanky, six-foot-plus height is straight and strong-looking, even at the age of seventy-three. His hair is a mixture of gray and gold, and his eyes are thick-lashed behind his plain wire-rimmed glasses. He is affable, soft-spoken and soothing when he's telling a musician what's wrong with his "ax," and equally encouraging when he's assuring you that everything is going to be all right. When he told me my guitar was beyond him—that it would have to be returned to Martin & Company for work—the ground gave out beneath me.

"I know this doesn't look good," he crooned in his best bedside manner, "but they do repairs like this all the time. It'll be in the hands of the experts."

Mandolinist Brad Meinerding, who Harry mentored in instrument repair, has a telling story about what a player goes through when an instrument is broken, and what a really talented repairman can do to heal it.

"My guess is one of Bill Monroe's lady friends got upset with Bill and smashed up a couple of his mandolins," Brad says. "I mean, like, into hundreds of pieces." Bill gathered up all the pieces and took them to Gibson, the company that made them. There, a gifted repairman named Charlie Derrington catalogued each scrap and began reconstruction.

"It must have taken six months to a year," Brad says. "But in the end Gibson was able to return Bill's favorite Lloyd Loar mandolin to its former glory." As for Harry's work, Brad says, "I didn't know Charlie—he was before my time—but I think Harry's in the mold of Charlie, in that he's the most talented guy I've ever met, and he is generous with his knowledge and time."

The issue of reworking (or "dressing") frets—the small metal strips embedded in the neck of a stringed instrument—may seem like a small thing. But Harry's great friend, banjo player Wayne Clyburn, gives a reasonably cogent explanation of what Harry does and why it's so useful.

"A uniform curvature on each fret makes the string vibrate more easily and makes it easier to play," he explains. And getting those little pieces to be uniform is a tedious process. "What he does is take a flat metal file and move it back and forth across the fret, and as he does that the shavings drop off on the neck," Clyburn says. Harry's genius is that he can tell by those shavings how consistent the frets are in their height. "That's why people fly in all the way from California to get Harry to do their frets. It's painstaking and very methodical, but it can make a tremendous difference to your instrument in the way it plays and the way it sounds."

BLUEGRASS

Harry's instrument work and his music dovetail nicely with his love of black-powder muzzle-loading, a study of precision in itself. In fact, the first time I met him, back in the shaggier 1970s, was at the Muzzle Loaders' Convention in Friendship, Indiana. I had tagged along with a friend, and I had no idea what to expect. The muzzle-loading aficionados had set up camp around Friendship, and the scene was similar to what a tailgate party at a Rolling Stones concert might look like—if Stones fans dressed in buckskin and wore powder horns around their necks. Stew pots of burgoo bubbled on campfires, and men and women in Revolutionary War costumes wandered from tent to tent, discussing who had the most authentic Colonial set-up and listening to the old-time musicians jam.

I was fairly new to bluegrass back then, muzzle-loading was a bafflement to me, and I had no idea why the two belonged together. But I do remember it was fun, and recently, when I sat down with Harry at Arnold's, we found ourselves reminiscing about those events and how they became the nexus of his two loves.

"At Friendship, you'd shoot all day and play music all night," Harry said, a little wistfully. "I liked to camp fifty yards from the firing range," he added with a twinkle, "and wait for the 8 a.m. announcement to come: 'Ready on the right; ready on the left. Commence firing.' That's when the fun began. All the unsuspecting campers positively levitated."

It seems to me that black-powder muzzle-loading fits in with Harry's passion for structure, design, and precision. All you have to do is ask him to describe the process, and you can hear it: "You mix buck and black powder and you cover it with a card that's quite rigid," he explains. "Then you put the shot into a second wad and cover it with a thinner card. In the old days, these cards would have been made out of leather," he adds, a stickler for historic detail. "You've got to top it with that second card so the shot doesn't fall out of the barrel before you are ready to shoot."

Harry's muzzle-loading hobby is not simply an idle pastime: In 2008 he took top honors in an international competition in Australia. He's as well known in that genre as he is in bluegrass. Harry makes a quizzical expression to indicate that this conflation of music and target-shooting was not planned. "The muzzle-loaders and the music, both old-timey and bluegrass, were part of the same culture," he says, taking a sip of water. "They went together naturally. And working on instruments came out of that same culture, of course. One thing led to another, and it was all organic. The best things always are."

Harry first heard bluegrass in Murray, Kentucky, in the 1950s when Flatt & Scruggs played the local drive-in theater. He said it hit him like a hammer, and he spent years trying to find that sound again. When, as a college student, he dropped into a local bar in Cincinnati and heard Jim McCall, Earl Taylor, and Vernon "Boatwhistle" McIntyre playing, he was thunderstruck. "There," he said. "That was it—and I knew that was the music for me."

His first beat-up guitar had a "bow-and-arrow" action (a term which signifies how high off the neck of the guitar the strings are.) "I developed strong hand muscles from pressing down on those strings," he says, laughing. "Later I bought a Goya"—a folk guitar. "Of course, when I discovered bluegrass, about the time of what bluegrass players define as the 'folk scare,' I had to have a Martin guitar." By the late 1960s, he had opened the Famous Old Time Music Store near Pleasant Ridge in partnership with a guy named Mack Smith. Mack was happy giving lessons and keeping store while Harry worked his day job as an architect. There was nothing fancy about the Old Time Music Store. A few dusty glass cabinets held instrument strings and capos for sale, and the tall drafting board in the back always had an instrument or two that Harry was working on, their necks clamped while the glue set.

It was a place where Harry could work easily, and the store quickly became the hangout for musicians to jam on Saturday afternoons, take lessons during the week, or just sit around and talk about banjos, guitars, and bluegrass.

BLUEGRASS

Nowadays he owns a Martin D-45—an instrument that is widely revered in Cincinnati music circles. It is a pre–World War II Martin with a bass sound that rattles the rafters. It has dazzling abalone pearl inlay all around the neck and the body, and if that guitar doesn't deafen you with its volume, it will blind you with its brilliance. Its pedigree comes from the quality of materials that went into it: real Brazilian rosewood—now a protected species—for the back of the instrument, and black ebony, the hardest wood, prized for guitar fretboards.

He has played for years around Cincinnati, starting back in the 1960s with a group he formed to play at a small folk festival in Kentucky. Getting together for the gig was a bit slapdash; Harry and his group hadn't bothered to choose a name, and they weren't entirely sure where they were when they finally got to the festival. So when the announcer asked him the name of the band, Harry said, "Well, what's the name of this little town around here?"

"Why, this is Rabbit Hash," the man said.

"Then we're the Rabbit Hash Ramblers," Harry announced.

Back in the 1960s, he took a band to Friendship, Indiana, and called it the Famous Old Time Music Company. "We weren't famous," he says now, "but the music was, and we had the store."

His most recent project as an architect was designing a new Gruhn Guitar store in Nashville for his long-time friend and business associate, George Gruhn. When the shop was opened in June, Nashville pickers gave a lavish concert at the Ryman Auditorium. Harry was there, and so was documentarian Ken Burns. Burns announced at the Ryman that he was launching a new documentary and its subject would be country music.

It is appropriate that he made that announcement at the Ryman, the Mother Church of country and bluegrass music. With its oval interior, its perfect acoustics—it was originally built to be a tabernacle for a fundamentalist Christian sect—it is an awesome experience just to enter the doors and see the bare stage where Hank Williams took so many encores singing "Lovesick Blues" that Nashville could no longer ignore him, and where Lester Flatt and Earl Scruggs played the first time with Bill Monroe, and Earl's three-fingered banjo playing tore the place up.

In the middle of the concert Vince Gill went to the microphone and paid tribute to his old friend, Harry Sparks. The two men had been friends since Vince was a blue-jeaned youngster, playing bluegrass in Louisville. Harry, who had been tipped off that he was likely to be asked to sing, was ready. He walked through the backstage area carrying his beautiful D-45 and made his way to the stage.

Harry is not a man who is easily dazzled, but he says he was blinded by the footlights shining up from the floor and amazed at the roar of audience approval. He began with the haunting "Satan's Jewel Crown"—a song that he had learned from Emmylou Harris before he heard the original recording by the Louvin Brothers—then sang "Hot Corn, Cold Corn" with Vince on mandolin. Like so many other performers before him, he was caught off guard by the waves of applause. But he relaxed a little by the second song and was able to feel the soul of what he was singing, the beautiful intervals of the melody. He was more controlled this time around, and he looked out occasionally at the audience in the venerable old auditorium.

Vince joined him on the harmony lines, and Harry thought they sounded pretty good. He smiled a little, to himself. When the last line was sung the audience applauded again. Then, one by one, some enthusiastic listeners began to stand up. A groundswell of approval swept the Ryman, and when Harry looked out again, they were all standing, clapping enthusiastically, embracing him with their affection and their appreciation.

Harry said later it was one of the best things that had ever happened to him, better than fretting his first guitar and getting it right, better than seeing his first building rise in front of him, better than winning that muzzle-loading championship in Australia.

Music is like that: you're in the moment, and it carries you like a wave in the ocean and drops you gently, almost unexpectedly, upon the beach again.

BLUEGRASS

VOICES FROM THE MOUNTAINS

On a hot Sunday afternoon in May, Hazel Dickens sat in a dining room in an upper-middle-class Cincinnati suburb, drinking iced tea, relaxing after three days of performing at the annual Appalachian Festival. She was a lean, dark-eyed woman, about forty, dressed in jeans and a colorful gypsy blouse, with a blue bandana tied girlishly around her straight brown hair. She had the look of an Appalachian in her face, the chiseled, hollowed-out look of the mountains.

She wrote songs and sang them in a voice that was pure emotion and older than time, about coal miners and low-down men and Jesus Christ. As half of the popular duo, Hazel and Alice, she carved a niche for herself in a predominantly male music arena. She was a solo performer now, recording for Rounder Records, singing in concerts around the country, and involving herself in special projects concerning the Appalachian culture. She did most of the singing for the highly acclaimed documentary, Harlan County, USA.

Her voice was low-pitched, softened by traces of a southern accent.

"When I was little," she said, choosing her words carefully, "creative things weren't encouraged, to say the least. You didn't read, or draw pictures or sing anything but church songs. When I got married, I think it was my husband who gave me some paints, and I sat there with the paints and didn't have any idea what to do with them. I was like a child in first grade, and that's how my pictures looked. But I kept at it, and I got better, and I liked doing it."

Hazel laughed, a little self-consciously. "Once," she said, continuing, "I made a picture of a musician hunched over a guitar. When I did that picture, the same thing happened to me that happens to me when I write songs. Something from outside me seems to take over, and I do something better than I thought I had the ability to do.

"People call me a creative person, an artist, a songwriter, and I don't know what to think about that. In the bars where I started singing people thought all women were just dumb broads and easy marks. They hardly seemed to think I was human, much less an artist. But then," she said, thoughtfully, "they never thought much of themselves either."

In the lull of the summer afternoon birds were singing outside the window, and soft, diffused sunlight slanted through the glass and fell on Hazel's face. She got up and made herself another glass of iced tea and placed it in front of her on the table, just so, on a wicker coaster.

She started to talk again. "I need a lot of time alone," she said. "I need to think, just let my mind wander. I don't drive, and I'm paranoid about flying so I ride the bus a lot. I see old women and children, and all kinds of men. Sometimes I can sit and make up things about them in my head, and it helps the time pass. At home, I feel guilty about taking time to do that. But," she added, "I'm getting better at it."

"I stayed with my friend Phylis Boyen in Knoxville for two weeks, and we did lots of things to pamper ourselves," she said. "We were too lazy to cook, so we sat and remembered like two old women.

"Phylis is from a family of singers, and she said in the old days lots of families in her community sang. People would live in separate valleys, hollers is what they were, and at night, they'd go out on their front porch and rehearse what they were learning for church. Sometimes you could hear the families from one valley to the next, singing, then mocking one another and competing with each other ... all those voices from the mountains in the late evening.

"Phylis and I were amazed how much came back to us when we thought about it, about the old Primitive Baptist Church services, how the minister would put his hand over his right ear—kind of cup the ear—not to hear better, but it was a gesture of some kind, perhaps anguish or despair—and when things got emotional his voice would rise in a sing-song rhythm while he preached.

"My daddy was a preacher in the Primitive Baptist Church. He'd lead a song by singing out the first couple lines in a monotone, sort of like a chant. Then the audience, joining in, drawing it out so that it was real long and slow. 'Amazing-grace-how sweet-the-sound,' they'd sing, lingering over each word. We called it lining out a song. People always ask me to do that on Amazing Grace at concerts, but it just wouldn't be correct. Women don't preach, and they don't lead singing, so it would be wrong for me to do it."

Hazel looks down at her hands and shakes her head. "I can't assert myself," she said. "When I was young, the women served the men at table and stood over them, fanning the flies away from the food with long tree branches. The women ate what was left. Some men were thoughtful or maybe not too hungry and left food; others never did. The women ate the scraps.

"My Daddy," Hazel said, "was the sociable one, always the one who smiled." Hazel smiled a tight dishonest smile when she said this, imitating him, revealing all her mountain-bred disdain for charm.

"My mother never talked much," she added, "but when she did she could pulverize you with a few well-chosen words."

"From them both and from my culture I received a legacy of fear. I'm afraid to fly, afraid to drive, afraid to do things by myself. But once I make the commitment I nerve up and do it and try not to tear myself apart over it. Sometimes, when I look back I am amazed that I ever had the nerve to do what I've done, and I'm sure I'd never have done anything without a lot of support and coaxing from my friends.

"My partner, Alice Gerrard and I were among the first singers to perform at the Galax Festival in Virginia. Clarence Ash had sung there in the old style—unaccompanied—but someone said to me, 'I don't think you'd better try that. Sure, he was good, but I don't think you could pull it off.'"

Hazel made a sour face and tossed her head with spirit. She took one last drink of iced tea and began to sing a little, tired from the long, unaccustomed talking. "Well, that made up my mind for me," she said finally. "I sung 'Little Bessie' unaccompanied, to my mother's old tune. I was scared and shaking, and some drunk in the first row was mouthing off. Finally a man stood up and said, 'Aw, sit down and shut up. This girl can sing!' And of course it went over great. Sometimes, underneath, I'm made of steel."

4
ON THE ROAD

JEFF TERFLINGER, KATIE, LARRY NAGER, AND JEFF ROBERTS PLAYING AT THE STONE VALLEY BLUEGRASS FESTIVAL.

ON THE ROAD AGAIN

In 1975, I started a bluegrass band. Nobody had ever told me I couldn't do that, and I had had a couple years' experience in a local band. I figured what the heck. And from the very beginning, the band took off, a little faster than I was prepared for. I had a shoestring budget, no sound system, no van and no stage show to speak of, but I had great musicians and the innocence that only the young can have about what life holds for people with impossible dreams.

My old friend, Becky Hudnall put up the money for the "starter" Peavey sound system, then Buddy Griffin, our fiddle player, and I went up north and bought a dark green Ford extra-long Econoline van, from a band called the Hutchison Brothers. It had no power steering, no air conditioning, no power brakes, and no radio, but the price was right, and I signed on the dotted line and let Buddy drive it home. Parking it turned out to be like wrestling an alligator, so nobody much wanted to borrow it. Summers in the van were an inferno; winters were frigid.

I remember a school we played called Alice Lloyd College in Pippa Passes, Kentucky. All mountain girls were welcome there, even the ones with babies. We had done a couple of one-nighters in eastern Kentucky on our way to Cumberland. At one stoplight in Hazard, Kentucky, where the road was so steep it was almost vertical, the van began to smoke. It billowed dramatically from under the hood of the vehicle, and my heart stopped somewhere in my throat. Buddy, who happened to be driving at the time, pulled the van over on the steep hill in Hazard.

He released the hood, went to work and within several minutes the problem was solved. Back in the winter we had put cardboard in front of the radiator one night when the temperature was 28 below zero, and we were driving back from Cleveland, huddled under blankets. Now, the first warm day of spring, the van was overheating as it climbed the hills of Hazard.

When Buddy emerged from the engine block with the cardboard pieces, he held them up. "Ta da." he said, and we cheered wildly and got back on the road a little more lighthearted, our fear and then our euphoria lifted our spirits and got us to Pippa Passes without any arguments or further car trouble.

I was riding in the back, microphone stands rolling around as the extra-long green van took the curves of the highway. As we rolled down the highway, we played Flatt & Scruggs on the cassette tape player at top volume. Earl Scruggs was bearing down on the banjo playing "Foggy Mountain Breakdown" with Lester Flatt keeping time on the guitar, and it seemed to me it was a perfect day.

Lying flat on the mattress, like Huck Finn on his raft, I watched the clear Kentucky skies. Everything was green, and the newly leafed-out trees were punctuated by white dogwoods and flowering crabapples. As we got closer to Cumberland, the trees were so thick it looked like virgin territory. In fact, when we first saw the tiny town of Pippa Passes we almost missed it. There it was, though: old, laid out like every other small town in that part of Kentucky with a stone courthouse and a few wooden storefronts. The college looked out over everything from its position on the highest hill in town. We parked and walked up the steep hill carrying our heavy instruments.

Someone was waiting for us at the door. They gave the guys box lunches but asked me if I would be good enough to eat with the women in their dormitory. They were hoping I might inspire them I suppose, though I was doubtful about what I might inspire them to do. One of the girls showed up at my elbow out of nowhere and took my guitar and led me to the dormitory.

Inside, I found about twenty-five young women, some with babies, doing laundry and reading movie magazines, watching soap operas on television with their hair rolled up in orange juice cans, like girls in dorms everywhere. I tried to stir up a conversation about music by asking about Madonna, and they shrugged their shoulders, but I named a popular country singer and got a better response.

"You one of the band?" they asked finally, cautiously curious.

"Yes." I said. "I am."

"What do you play?" someone else asked.

"I play guitar and sing," I said.

"Wow!" a woman said. "How'd you learn to do that?"

"I just always did it, ever since I was a kid."

They looked at me doubtfully and went back to playing with their babies and complaining about their boyfriends.

I managed to fix my hair and put on a little make-up and change clothes in this small space (I've done miracles in worse places, frankly), and grabbed my guitar and headed for the auditorium.

The campus was beautiful, as that part of the country can be. One of the best things about traveling in a van was we got to see the country in all its shapes and sizes and seasons, its colors, its smells. I don't think I ever got over seeing a place in Elizabethton, Tennessee. The guys in the band were playing basketball on an outdoor court which was attached to a high school where we were going to do a show for Eastman Kodak. I wandered over and looked down a steep drop-off at the edge of the mountain into a fairy-tale prehistoric-looking chasm of endless pale green leaves dotted here and there with redbuds and dogwood trees, newly flowered in pink and white. I don't think, to this day, that I have ever seen anything more lovely.

Back at the stage at Alice Lloyd College, the guys had set up the old Peavey sound system like a cheap string of Christmas lights strung straight across the stage. We didn't have strobe tuners back in those days, but then we weren't playing rock and roll. We tuned our guitars and fiddles and banjos to the standard "A" with a pitch pipe. That done, we sat the instruments in their stands and got ready to start the show. I'll never know where audiences come from, but about fifteen minutes before show time, I looked out from behind the curtain and the little auditorium was full, the people warm and welcoming. We finished the show with Buddy's version of the "Orange

Blossom Special" which involved the Gillette theme song, twirling the bow on his nose and other entertaining side-tracks, and got a standing ovation and a couple of encores.

When we were packing up, the girls who had been in the dormitory came backstage and insisted on carrying my guitar and my purse back to the van. It was a sweet gesture I'll never forget. I remember lying on the mattress in the back of the van, crying softly. (I usually did cry after a performance. It was a quick way to unwind.) I thought that life was impossible and wonderful all at the same time.

"Put on Earl Scruggs, Buddy," I said. "And turn it up." The mic stands rolled around me on their round flat bases, and I sat up and looked out the rear window and waved good-by to the girls. They stood there until I couldn't see them anymore through my tears.

Because we were a bluegrass band, the Econoline was often headed south, back to the places where that music came from. For us in the late 1970s, a popular destination was the Carter Family Fold in southwest Virginia. The original Carter Family—A.P., Sara and Maybelle, had started their own careers from this Valley in the 1920s; now, A.P.'s daughter, Janette, had "kept the family business a'goin'" as she said, just like she'd promised her father many years ago. They were the first family of Country Music, in fact, having recorded for Ralph Peer in Bristol, Virginia, in 1927 on the same day as Jimmie Rodgers, also known as the Singing Brakeman. Modern audiences may remember Maybelle Carter's guitar version of "The Wildwood Flower."

The Carter Family Fold was located in a place called Poor Valley, because there was no coal there. Consequently, the land was untouched and serene and everywhere there were beautiful rolling hills of green grass and corn fields. Janette's little house sat at the top of a high, high hill (which she walked up and down every day with little difficulty). We'd drive up the rutted gravel road, get out of the van, and smell the open country. Janette always kept some little feist dog which barked vigorously then bit Buddy. Janette would laugh her slow, warm laugh and say, "Well, come on in. You've had a long trip, and I've cooked you a little supper. It's not much ... "

The little dinner would include biscuits and ham and gravy, fresh tomatoes, fried pies, whatever she had on hand—homemade jams and jellies. Going there was as rich and as comforting as Sunday dinner. Janette's father, A.P., had lived in the same house for years before moving down to the little grocery store he owned. The place was like most country places, useless furniture side by side with antiques, prized musical instruments. The boys would always get to play A.P.'s old guitar. Once I slept in a bed made for Sara's or A.P.'s parents. The headboard, which was intricately carved, went clear to the ceiling, and I sunk into a feather mattress fortressed by feather pillows and piles of old family quilts. I learned years later that Janette's cousin June Carter and Johnny Cash had bought the old bed, and I was glad it stayed in the family.

That weekend, during our Saturday night performance at the auditorium, a huge snowstorm had come, and we had to stay in Poor Valley. There was no getting the big green van on the road until someone could come and pull it out with a tractor. I could have stayed a week in the feather bed, but when I woke up the next morning, Buddy was playing the fiddle and Jeff the guitar, and I could smell coffee and red-eye gravy. One of the men in the valley pulled us out with a tractor, much as they had pulled A.P., Sara and Maybelle out of a ditch when they had to go to Camden, New Jersey, to record.

We went to Janette's about once a month and to her festivals in the summer to see genuine old-time musicians, but we also went north. We'd stop in Cleveland and play, then head for Princeton, New Jersey, and work the Princeton University Folk Club. Or we'd stop in Bucks County, Pennsylvania, where a fan could usually find us a gig when we were coming through. We played a wedding up there, we played the Elizabethtown Music Hall in New Jersey. When we stayed with our fan, Dodie Murphy, I'd take a nap in the afternoon in her pre-Revolutionary house, and a woman would slip in and give me a full massage, as a tribute. On the road, people could be kind and understanding.

We played the sports facility in New Jersey when it opened and met a very young Robin and Linda Williams and the fiddler Jay Unger. Robin and

Linda went on to be regulars on Prairie Home Companion, and Jay wrote "Ashokan Farewell" many years before it was used as the theme in Ken Burns' Civil War documentary.

Of course we went to Manhattan every trip we took to the East Coast, and played a respectable Irish pub called O'Lunney's which featured bluegrass on Sunday nights. That's where we were in May of 1977, staying in a very nice condo in midtown, when we heard the news on television that the Beverly Hills Supper Club had burned. We all stood there watching the screen, listening for the names of the dead, wishing we were at home.

*

Winters were hard in the van, though we brought quilts and covers with us, but summers could be unbearable. Air conditioning? We didn't have it. I can remember starting out for a festival near Knoxville, Tennessee. The temperature that day was hovering around one hundred degrees. The highway was so hot, the sun so unrelenting, that our tires started exploding, one by one. "Pop," we'd hear and we'd have to pull off to the side and change the tire. We got back on the road, cross and sweaty, when we heard another "pop," and we knew we'd lost another tire.

Buddy checked the last two tires and declared that they were sound before we got back on the road again. We hadn't expected the radiator to overheat. "Pull her over and shut 'er off," Buddy said, and the boys hoofed to a nearby farmhouse for water while I stayed to guard the instruments. Every fifty miles or so that day, we had to pull over and put water in the radiator. We got to the festival, bedraggled, hot and half-sick, already exhausted, and put on one of the best shows I think we ever did. We were young and healthy, and the heat relaxed our muscles so we could play better, looser.

A band is like a marriage in the way that time can reshape rough days into gentle memories like the time Buddy's fiddle bow came apart in Cleveland in a nightclub. All the hair simply came loose from the bow and hung as limply as Chinese noodles. That night Buddy restrung it with white thread and sat up all night coating it with rosin. It didn't sound as good as usual, but it was decent.

Then there were the nights that we were out-and-out magic. Buddy was a native of West Virginia, so we were popular there, and when we came to town all kinds of musicians would converge. Musical legend John Hartford's tour crossed ours frequently in West Virginia—Charleston was a river town after all—and John would stop whatever he was doing and come and play with us. He and Buddy would play soaring harmonies on the fiddles, play "Ole Joe Clark" so fast you couldn't keep up, and we'd have so much fun that the nights flew by like mile markers on the highway. I wish I could have some of those nights back.

*

We got to be so popular with the miners that the UMW flew us to Denver in 1977 to play at their convention. We played with Frankie Yankovic's polka band, Hazel Dickens, Utah Phillips, the Morris Brothers, the Red Clay Ramblers, and the delightful Lilly May Ledford of the original Coon Creek Girls. While the factions who had supported Yablonski (who had been murdered only a short time before the convention) and the supporters of Arnold Miller, the president at that time, carried on in the streets of Denver, we did our two shows a day and found something called "Rent-A-Lemon" so that we could explore the Rocky Mountains when we had time off. As cold as it was, it didn't feel cold, and the air was as bracing as a plunge into a cold body of water.

The Road took a toll on the band, though. One of the young men in the band wanted to move to Minnesota (he was later driven out by enormous black flies). Buddy wanted to return to West Virginia, and I just wanted a good night's sleep and some time to myself. The center wasn't holding anymore. The view along I-64 from Lexington to Ashland no longer captivated me the way it used to in almost any season.

Of course one doesn't just quit like that. We had "honeymoon" times where we'd say, "Let's throw some things in a gym bag and drive to Canada." I forced myself to fly a few places to give solo concerts, and I flew to New York and sang with the Harlem Blues and Jazz Band at the New York State

Jazz Festival. In other words, I tried as hard as I could not to be over it; but it didn't work.

It wasn't just us. Many of the bands we had passed on the road were hanging up their suitcases, and we missed the fellowship of our fellow travelers. Looking back, it was one of life's great adventures. We made lasting friendships; respectful associations with colleagues; and we saw a good part of the United States we wouldn't have seen if we'd gone as tourists. We learned to read maps (in the days before the GPS), to take care of ourselves and each other in difficult situations, to cooperate when we felt like fighting, and we came out of the experience more mature, responsible adults than when we started. Of course a lot of that had to do with age, but I prefer to think there was some magic in those nights in the van, listening to Flatt and Scruggs tapes on the cassette player, all of us in the dark, listening to Earl Scruggs play the banjo. The beat he played was the same as our heartbeats, and we synchronized our heartbeats to him.

BURNIN' UP THE ROAD

I was getting ready to fly to the Soviet Union to perform in 1990, and I was worried about taking my prized 1951 Martin D-28 with me. American airline companies toss valuable instruments around like pickup sticks, so I decided to use a Coffin case—the kind of sturdy molded plastic guitar carrier that professional musicians swear by. It was too late to buy one, so I made arrangements to borrow Cal Collins's. The jazz man lived in Lawrenceburg, Indiana, and frequently traveled to Europe and Australia to perform.

"You're welcome to it, honey," Cal told me good-naturedly, "but you can't hardly lift it."

The good thing about a Coffin case is that it is virtually indestructible. If the plane crashes, the guitar will be safe; if you're lost at sea, it will float. Cal's offer looked like the answer to my dilemma, but I met opposition immediately.

"You can't drive that ancient jalopy of yours to Indiana," a musician friend protested.

"I don't know why not," I said, defending the road-worthiness of my 1977 Ford. I don't remember the model, only that I called it the Green Hornet. "It's just been tuned up, and it's running like a top."

"Just the same," he said, "I wouldn't draw an easy breath if I thought you were broken down somewhere on I-275 with nobody to help you."

And so I set off for Indiana on a fine, clear morning in April to pick up Cal's Coffin case in a borrowed Chevrolet Impala.

I was driving along nicely, down I-75 and on to I-275, when I saw a small plume of smoke coming from under the hood. Surely it was nothing, I thought, but I pulled to the side of the road anyway. I turned off the ignition, but the smoke kept getting worse. So I positioned myself reluctantly in front of the Impala's grill and released the hood. The smoke billowed out in much bigger plumes.

I ran as far away from the car as fast as I could and looked around for help. A passing car slowed and the driver shouted that he'd stop at the next gas station and send a fire truck. It couldn't come soon enough. The front of the car was already burning, the black smoke climbing in the air. Suddenly, in front of my horrified eyes, the entire automobile exploded into flames. I heard four small pops as each tire exploded—then one more as the spare in the trunk bit the dust. In no time at all, the chassis looked like the bones of a picked-over Thanksgiving turkey.

That's about when the firemen arrived. "Whoa!" one said, surveying the scene. "You won't be driving that one home."

The Highway Patrol cordoned off the area. With a sinking heart, I realized my purse and wallet had been on the front seat of the car: I was on west I-275 with no money and no idea what to do. One of the television stations arrived with a news crew ("Car burns on I-275; film at 11"), then a patrolman dropped me off at the airport and suggested I have a friend come and pick me up.

I did that, but I still had to tell the car's owner that he was no longer in possession of a Chevy Impala.

"I know we'll laugh about this some day," he said, absorbing the blow on one knee, "just not yet."

If I were going to give up driving, that would have been the day to do it. My night vision was beginning to go, I was tense behind the wheel, I'd had every mechanical problem in the book, and I'd collected enough parking tickets to wallpaper a room. Only a few months before, I had trashed a golf course by accidentally running across the greens on a rainy, wintery day. Helicopters were involved in the chase that ensued. As far as car karma went, mine was dangerously close to empty.

My problems started when I was a teenager in Detroit. My father attempted to give me driving lessons when I was fifteen, and the minute I took the wheel I drove right into a good-sized tree on Ellsworth Avenue, where we lived.

"God a'mighty," my father barked. "Where did that come from?"

Shortly after my disastrous first driving attempt, our family relocated from the Motor City to Huntsville, Alabama, where—after spending about three hundred hours practicing parallel parking—I got my license. I promptly had another accident the very same day, backing into a large pole at a strip mall on the way home from the drug store. My confidence in my driving skills was dwindling.

Still, my relationship with auto ownership continued into adulthood, when it took working out a budget for me to see that there was no way I could continue to operate a car on the income of a musician. I needed to live car-free. And for that, I needed a plan.

I had lived in Clifton, in the gaslight district, in the 1970s. It had been an easy place to maneuver without transportation. Back then, Keller's Market was still open, so a good butcher and relatively fresh produce were within strolling distance. I could eat a hot turkey sandwich at the Busy Bee and ice cream at Graeter's. Bus service was good in Clifton; from there, I could get downtown easily. And there was the convenience of Hyde Park: When I used to house-sit for friends there, I'd walk to The

Echo for a good, inexpensive lunch and pick up prescriptions at the old drugstore on the square. But house-sitting gigs never landed me in Hyde Park on any kind of permanent basis, and the rents in Clifton had grown out of my reach. So when I gave up my car for good in 1995, I decided to move to Over-the-Rhine.

At the time OTR had a few corner convenience stores and a lot of artists and musicians. Bus transportation was plentiful, but the schedule took some effort to master. One of the buses that ran right by my apartment on Main Street was the No. 46—a route that made a beeline for University Hospital. Unfortunately, I didn't always require hospitalization. The No. 53 was handy because it went to Clifton, but it proved to be unreliable. To get to more destinations, I had to walk to Twelfth and Vine, to the bus stop right across the street from Ensemble Theatre.

Today, Vine Street bus stops have been renewed, along with the neighborhood. In the Gateway District you can sit and wait for your ride—even get out your laptop and take advantage of WiFi. Back when I lived there, if there was a bench, it was bound to be damaged; if there was a shelter, it was warped or leaking. You'd find yourself standing for thirty minutes in the cold or the rain or sweltering in the sun, waiting for the next bus.

I patiently explained all this to the Metro people during my seasonal telephone calls. I'd helpfully query, "Did you realize that the bench at the stop on Twelfth and Vine is gone?" Or missing one leg. Or whatever misfortune had befallen the public convenience.

"Yes," the polite response came back. "We're aware of that. We're cleaning up all the OTR bus stops this spring."

When spring came with no improvement, I was back on the phone. "Remember that bus stop at Twelfth and Vine I complained about last winter?"

"Yeah," the voice would say. "We're working on it. And we got more buses on that route so you won't have to wait as long. You probably don't need the bench." I felt like Bob Newhart doing a telephone comedy routine.

Jim Tarbell—who tried going without a car himself for two years—has pointed out to me that the planned streetcar will connect OTR to downtown. So people who work on Fourth Street will be able to lunch at Findlay Market and still be back in the office for their afternoon meeting. But in terms of making the city a go-carless neighborhood, "it's just a drop in the bucket," he says. "So much more is needed."

I had a rich life in Over-the-Rhine, even without a car. I lived above Kaldi's Coffee House. If I got lonely or restless, all I had to do was walk downstairs and I would more than likely meet someone I knew and find a spirited conversation. Maybe it was the espresso talking, but I learned the art of conversation there, and I learned a lot about art, too. In fact, I spent so much time in Kaldi's that I eventually got a job there singing with a band and booking performers. For me, a neighborhood couldn't get more "walkable" than that.

*

When you live without a car, people always wonder how you get your food. Most of my meals came from the neighborhood. There was no fresh food at the corner bodegas, but nearby Court Street boasted an open-air produce market several days a week, as well as the Avril-Bleh & Sons butcher shop. I used to walk to the Court Street market and Avril's every Wednesday afternoon—a tradition that made me enough of a regular that the butchers stopped work and got out the rubber chicken and the trombone on my birthday. I still had my dog, Sister, in those days, but nothing could entice her into Avril's. All the staff tried coaxing her with bits of steak, but she would not budge. "It just don't look right," somebody said, "a dog not wanting to go into a butcher shop."

Tony Sparta's market with its glossy tomatoes and expensive specialty foods was another Court Street favorite. Tony stocked Italian meats and cheeses, and on Wednesday afternoons a man came to the shop and made mozzarella balls, and you could eat the whey, a delicious by-product of the cheesemaking. In those years I was meeting weekly with a trio of musicians—not to practice, just to play for the love of it. I'd pick up produce and polenta at Tony's and we'd have a light dinner of vegetables and Verdi or whatever we happened to be working on at the time. It always felt like a feast.

Living in Over-the-Rhine meant that downtown's great resources were handy. My friend Kate Schmidt and I regularly swam in the big old-fashioned pool in the basement of the YWCA, floating on our backs and enjoying the boomy silence. One day the fire alarm went off and a voice came over the PA directing everyone to evacuate the building. Kate and I looked at each other in horror. We would rather have burned to death than to go out on the sidewalk in our bathing suits. Luckily, it was a false alarm.

The main branch of the public library was across the street from the Y, so I was never short of reading material. And if I couldn't find something there, I could always call the Mercantile Library on Walnut Street. If they had a novel I wanted, they'd mail it to me with a stamped self-addressed envelope to return it in. Sweet!

Life on Main Street really got interesting when Diva's opened. It was an edgy salon, a bit ahead of its time, with spiky hair, lots of "product," and one stylist with pink locks. You had to bring your own magazines, but it was right next door to my apartment building so I wasn't about to quibble; I was finally able to get a haircut! A young stylist named Amy Lake took on the maintenance of my hair—a challenge she met until Diva's closed. I tracked her down at a salon in Hyde Park—too far away for me to cab on a regular basis, though I took the bus once or twice. Amy booked me as her last appointment and drove me home herself. I went through her divorce with her, babysat for her youngest daughter, and watched her children grow up. She was a ferocious mother and she had a sweetness, a kindness, in her nature. I wouldn't have known about any of that without those car rides, where both of us let our hair down, so to speak.

By happy coincidence, Amy has settled in a salon called Bang Bang on West McMillan, a $5 cab ride away from where I live now. Amy gives me "good hair days," and I find I can handle just about anything life throws at me because of her expertise.

Amy is one of the few people left from my old network. Several years ago I moved to Klotter Avenue, and I've had to retool and rebuild. No buses lumber up and down the nearest cross street, so I tend to get more isolated than in my days in Over-the-Rhine, and I find myself more often prevailing on others. My neighbor, Lee Hay, takes me to the vet if my dog is feeling poorly. If I run out of kibble, Pet Wants at Findlay Market delivers. I read way too much, so Cedric Rose, of the Mercantile Library, will either drop a book in the mail for me or deliver two or three on his bicycle on nice days (I live on his way home from work). For years, WNKU lined up volunteers to ferry me to the radio station for my shift each Sunday; now my old friend Leona Durham drives me there, and my radio partner of twenty-three years, Wayne Clyburn, drives me home. Wayne and I call that sacrosanct time of driving and unwinding our "production meeting;" we make decisions about our show, what music we might want to explore, that sort of thing. One grand transportation bargain is Findlay Market: from Klotter Street, it's just a short cab ride to one of the great food centers of the city.

Still, I could not get along without a car if I didn't have friends behind the wheel. I find it difficult to ask for a ride, but I have to do it now and then. I am independent and "necky" about it, but I also find getting into a car and riding twenty minutes with a friend can cheer me up as much as a chocolate milk shake.

I suppose we're all of us resistant to car-pooling. It's a low-grade fear of intimacy, I think. What will we say? How should we act? I have had a fellow musician say to me, "I can't handle having a passenger tonight. Work has been a bear all day, and I was looking forward to a few minutes of downtime when I'm in the car." That is candid and understandable. I like to think I can make it as easy to opt out as to opt in. Mainly, when I open the passenger door of a car and get in, I try to come prepared with good conversation and a few stories, if that seems to be called for, and good listening skills if the driver wants to do the talking. I have come to believe that riding alone is something lonely people do.

Perhaps the growing of a relationship is the long journey, the big adventure. Hopefully, your car won't blow up. I think we'll both enjoy the encounter and come away from it feeling like we've had the best kind of adventure, the kind that leaves us feeling warmer, more connected, and a little bit better prepared to face the world.

QUEEN CITY COWBOY

January of 1994 was a bleak one in Cincinnati. I was stuck in an isolated apartment in Mt. Auburn, frozen like an insect in an amber bead. Sometimes, though, the very thing you need can come along just when you need it most. As my old friend Tom Cahall used to say, "Sometimes things can turn around on Double Jeopardy."

So when the phone rang, my heart lifted. It was my pal, bluegrass mandolin player Bill LaWarre, who in those days owned the ad agency Northlich Stolley LaWarre. "How are you?" he asked without identifying himself (powerful men seldom do). Then, after the pleasantries: "How would you like to fly to Montana next weekend?"

Bill and I had been playing in bluegrass bands together for years. He was a top-notch musician and a good tenor singer, but he had a day job that was hardly conducive to touring, so this request was totally unexpected. What had changed? He had recently acquired a second home—a log cabin close to Yellowstone National Park—and he was putting a band together to play on a radio show called *Main Street* on Montana Public Radio. He had already lined up a banjo player there—a guy named Joe Rockefeller. I had met Joe and the guitar player Tom Fish at Bill's house once when they were passing through town. They were the kind of musicians you can walk on stage with anywhere and feel confident they'll make you look good. I had no reservations about having them as part of the show.

"Well, are you working that weekend?" Bill said.

A night to remember. Bill LaWarre with Katie and a host of musicians after a Tall Stacks event. That's John Hartford down front.

"No," I said, and began pulling a suitcase out of the closet.

"Good. We're leaving at 6 a.m. sharp from Lunken Airport."

"Six in the *morning*?" I shrieked.

"Six a.m." Bill said. "And we've only got one refueling stop, so don't drink a lot of coffee."

"What about my REM sleep?" I said. But it was useless; Bill had hung up and gone on to his next project.

A week later, when he and his date, Claudia Massey, actually showed up at 6 a.m., I was dozing on my suitcase, packed and ready for the western journey. Bill and Claudia were in fine moods, talking about Roy Rogers (Bill's childhood hero) and their shared passion for collecting vintage mangles—old-fashioned ironing machines.

At first glance, Claudia didn't seem to be a cowboy-and-antique-tchotchke kind of woman. She was dressed in a cashmere turtleneck sweater and a jacket with the cuffs rolled up, and she had an elegant stillness about her. She carried a round wicker basket packed with snacks and sandwiches on whole wheat bread with lettuce and sprouts. I didn't know her very well then, but somehow I sensed there wouldn't be any doughnuts in that basket. I was right. I helped myself to a sugarless pudding cup and observed the two of them on the drive to Lunken. Bill gave her such tender looks that I thought, *Aha. This is serious.*

I remember nothing of the flight except waking with my half-eaten pudding cup just long enough for the bathroom stop. The next time I opened my eyes, we were nearing Montana. When the plane began to descend, I saw Yellowstone looking like a snow globe, white flakes falling silently, wilderness everywhere, nothing moving. We landed rough on a gravel strip in a valley surrounded by mountains—stone outcroppings with glacier-scraped surfaces, everything else buried in snow.

Bill's property manager met us at the little airport and drove us to the two-story "western chalet" Bill was renovating. Heat was the first priority, so he set about bringing in wood for a fireplace so big it seemed like it could swallow up several adults. I had seen Bill make fires before, and he was always meticulous, but this time he outdid himself. Within ten minutes, we had a glorious blaze, flames leaping and logs snapping in the dry mountain air.

The place was homey, with Indian blankets and landscape paintings adorning the walls, roomy leather couches, a small Remington sculpture, and a floor-to-ceiling art quilt done by Rabbit Hash artist Jane Burch Cochran. A second-floor gallery ran around the upstairs where I was to be quartered in the guest suite. Its renovation was not complete, but there were baskets of shampoo bottles and pretty soaps, an old china cup, and soft, thick towels stacked like a picture in a magazine.

I fell asleep again for a few hours, and when I woke everyone was gone. I figured I had missed dinner, but I felt so much better that I didn't mind. I rummaged through the pantry, which was filled with P&G products—a very comforting sight—and found something to snack on.

When Bill and Claudia returned, holding hands and blushing, I was in good spirits, well rested, and ready for what we—well, I—had come for: music. I tuned up my guitar, and Bill got out the fiddle he was just learning to play. We rehearsed for hours, working out tunes like "Soldier's Joy" and "Whiskey Before Breakfast."

We went to sleep quite late, confused by the time change, and when we finally woke and headed into town we were three friends, more at ease with each other, armed with instruments, spirits high, anxious to perform.

*

It was Claudia who saw the eagles first: two enormous predators, swooping and gliding in the bright blue Montana sky. Their wings were spread out for what seemed like miles, and their beaks and claws were poised to nab any small animal and rip and tear it apart to pieces. They were both magnificent and frightening.

Bill slowed the beat-up old pickup truck and slipped and slid in the snow onto the shoulder of the switch-back mountain road.

"Are those the eagles we've been seeing around the cabin?" Claudia asked, and Bill said he thought they were.

"That looks like their nest," he said, pointing to an aerie high on a rocky outcropping. We sat and watched their acrobatic loops. The sky was cloudless and cold, the snow piled high. We were close to Livingston, Montana, north of Yellowstone, not far from the valley where the movie *A River Runs Through It* was filmed.

"They're golden eagles," Claudia said in her soft voice.

"You think?" I said, a little thrilled. I had only been in Montana for twelve hours and I'd already seen something exotic. I shielded my eyes from the sun and gazed at the red mountains in the distance. The rocky ledges and cliffs looked like something from one of Bill's old Roy Rogers movies, and the big, blue sky was all around us.

We drove on, past small ranch houses, a strip mall with a large supermarket, and a double-wide house trailer with a large tire lying on its side near the edge of the property. I figured in summer the tire would be planted with petunias, and a mongrel dog would be lying in the sun.

Livingston itself looked a little like Dodge City waiting for Wyatt Earp and Doc Holliday to show up. We grabbed coffee and a sandwich at a local saloon in a dining room full of ranchers wearing fleece-lined coats and eating steak and eggs. Then we hurried to the radio station.

Playing always starts with tuning up—no small thing, especially with a mandolin. Nowadays young musicians have fancy accessories, including electronic tuners, but Bill and I had come up in the old school. Tuning was a job we had to do on our own. And where I had six strings to tune, Bill had the nearly impossible job of tuning eight strings, paired, and each pair of strings had to match each other perfectly. He paced as he went through this ritual, gazing intently at his small, ornate instrument, playing fast riffs and fills to warm up.

When Bill was playing full throttle, I was always amazed at his big hands speeding across the slender neck of the mandolin. *How did he get the right fingers on the right frets on that skinny fingerboard?* I wondered. Yet he did. Banjo player Jeff Roberts once attributed the virtuosity of some musicians to the fact that they had fallen in love with a particular instrument, and that had happened to Bill. He'd had the good fortune of finding a rare Gibson F-5 mandolin when he was young. Besotted, he bought it and it became his love. Sometimes, even when he wasn't playing, he'd pick up the F-5 to admire its clean lines.

Before long we were joined by Joe Rockefeller, his five-string banjo hanging around his neck, his picks bristling on the ends of his fingers, running scales up and down while Tom Fish, dark and scholarly-looking, accompanied him on the guitar. We introduced ourselves and discussed repertoire, and before we knew it, it was time to play.

It was a live radio show with a real stage and an audience dressed in jeans and flannel shirts. The air crackled with energy and the excited expectation of entertainment-starved folks in winter. There were mothers with babies in carriers strapped to the front of their bodies, and standing across the back of the room, a row of ranchers wearing exquisite Stetson hats. They reminded me of Garrison Keillor's "Norwegian bachelor farmers"—men who might bolt at the first sign of social interaction.

We played for nearly an hour—all the classic tunes—then I began "I'll Fly Away" to end the show, and by the second verse the audience was singing along, too. We all got a standing ovation, and we felt lighter as we put our instruments back in their cases. Everyone was smiling, a few people were humming as they rose to leave. One couple was holding hands as they filed out with the crowd. We'd achieved what every performer hopes for—we'd made contact with our audience, and we were all a little better for having done that.

Back at the ranch that evening, I was wide awake and Bill and Claudia were sleepy. We made a fire in the huge hearth of the great room, and Bill and I played tunes on the mandolin and guitar into the night while Claudia dozed on the couch. When Bill went outside to replenish the firewood, I followed. With no city lights to dim their brilliance, I could see the great round moon and billions of stars in the cold night sky. Somewhere people were moving and driving cars and playing jukeboxes, but not here. Here there was a stillness, a quiet beyond anything I had experienced.

The next morning, I woke to the smell of bacon frying, coffee perking, biscuits baking, and the promise of adventure. After breakfast we set off, Bill fixed on driving across Yellowstone, all the way to Wyoming and back, intent on showing me this place he loved so much.

As we made our way through the park, the weather turned blustery until, it seemed to me, we were in the middle of a blizzard. In the blowing snow, the park bristled with life. The wild animals had headed down to the valley where food was easy to find, Bill explained.

"Look," he said, and pointed to some elk walking slowly, wearing their tall antlers and looking like Las Vegas showgirls.

When we came upon bison along the sides of the road, I was speechless. They stood like a small herd of black behemoths, their shaggy hair blowing in the stiff wind, and when they grazed, their heads swept from side to side as rhythmic as metronomes. Once the patch of grass they were browsing on was bare, they didn't lose a beat—just side-stepped slightly until they found more under the snow.

Bill stopped the truck so that I could get a better look at them. If the golden eagles had been mystical, the bison felt primal—like creatures from the beginning of time.

"It's an inspirational place," Bill said as we took it all in. "I heard Tom Brokaw say in a speech once that he had never made an important decision in his life without first going to Yellowstone."

What I knew about Yellowstone is what I'd heard from others: that it was magical; that the geysers were spectacular; that this important, remote spot has drawn life here for millions of years—amoebic creatures multiplying in the thermal pots, then dinosaurs, then Paleo-Indians, then trappers and hunters who lived off the thick herds of animals. But I didn't really appreciate the hold Yellowstone had on my friend until I visited it with him.

Here's an odd thing about friendship—you start out being pals because you have something in common—liking softball or enjoying the same movies or, say, playing the heck out of "Orange Blossom Special" for a room full of winter-weary Montana ranchers. But your bonds don't really deepen until you get a good look at the other things that your friend holds dear—especially when they are so far from your own experience that they seem otherworldly.

Long after our trip, after Bill and Claudia had married, they were honored by the Yellowstone Park Foundation for their work on the organization's board of directors. In the intervening years, Bill served as the foundation's president and Claudia had helped raise money for projects at the park. I attended the ceremony proudly. After all, I felt I had been present at the creation.

We ate out that last night in Montana, but I don't remember much about it. The sounds of music were re-playing in my head, accompanied by the blowing snow, then the deep silence of Yellowstone. When I closed my eyes

I saw the eagles' nest and the buffalo grazing, and the stars strewn across the heavens like diamonds.

Then, having thought it all through one more time, I slid into sleep as peacefully as a child.

RABBIT HASH

Rabbit Hash sneaks up on you. One minute you're rolling along the gentle sweep of Route 18 in Burlington, Kentucky, beside rich fields and deep green foliage; the next minute, you round a curve and slow down for a sign that reads: "Rabbit Hash, Population 1." There are a half-dozen buildings scattered on either side of the road, along with Rabbit Hash's dominant landmark—the large, white-washed General Store with the Coca-Cola logo on the top of the roof.

Not exactly Shangri-La, but there's something artful about the way the tobacco barns hug this bend in the Ohio River, something particularly lovely about how the dappled sun glints through the leaves of the trees and dances on the water.

I am visiting Rabbit Hash for the first time in many years, and I see it through a haze of fairy dust. Its residents are old friends who peopled my life in the 1970s and '80s, before Rabbit Hash was recognized on the National Register of Historic Places, back when it was owned lock, stock, and barrel by native son Lowell "Louie" Scott, who built wood-burning stoves and slept on a roll-away bed in the back room of the General Store.

Rabbit Hash might be little more than a memory if it weren't for Louie, who had the presence of mind to start buying it up when the population dropped to nearly zero. And if it weren't for the political turn it took a decade and a half ago, it might not even be on the map. Those of us who knew and loved the town always felt that it was natural that Rabbit Hash should rise like cream to the top of the churn. But it took a special election to get the ball rolling.

In 1998, civic leaders called a press conference and declared the town was going to run a dog—several dogs, in fact—for mayor, and that voters were invited to stuff the ballot box with their dough. Each vote cost a dollar, and anyone who owned a dog could buy as many votes for that dog as they could afford. Furthermore, anyone could run, even humans—though it was easy to see early on that the race would go to the dogs: affluent canine owners from all over were spending like it was going out of style.

The race brought all the elements of politics into play: greed, vote-buying, influence-peddling, and newspaper photo ops. Television news got behind the event, too, and Wayne Clyburn and I were asked to do a remote radio broadcast on WNKU from Rabbit Hash.

On the day of the election the temperature was nearly 100 degrees with humidity to match, but it didn't slow the speechifying. Dog owners wandered from group to group, snapping their suspenders, passing out pamphlets, and brazenly soliciting votes in exchange for zoning restrictions, highway construction, and other promises equally impossible to fulfill.

The race between a black German shepherd named Goofy and a black lab named Herb was especially heated. While Herb was well groomed and made a fine presentation, Goofy showed a tendency toward laziness and looked eager to resume his usual position, sprawled under the front porch of the General Store. One voter was overheard saying, "That's one sorry hound." Another: "I wouldn't elect Goofy for dogcatcher."

Goofy kept right on scratching himself in embarrassing places, and in defiance of his critics won the race, costing his owner and his supporters a substantial pile of cash. Since the proceeds went to the Rabbit Hash Historical Society—the whole affair got national attention—even the losers weren't too sore. And this tiny Kentucky town began its ascendency to glory.

Or, at the very least, a sleepy notoriety.

Now, years later, I am here again for a friend's art show, looking out the car window as we drive slowly into town, eager to see how the place has fared in its role as an icon of Americana. Will it be chic and upmarket, overrun with tourists and traffic? Will everyone be eating arugula? Or will it still be the kind of place where the mayor is free to lift his leg on any tree?

In 2002, Louie Scott sold the town's land and buildings to the historical society (it was a deal made possible by the out-of-nowhere bequest of a retired P&G secretary, but that's a whole other story). Now the General Store is under the management of Terrie Markesbery, a young woman who moved here with her husband a little over ten years ago. They keep the place stocked with chewing tobacco, Orange Crush, and microwave breakfast sandwiches.

I am pleased to see that the General Store itself, the beating heart of Rabbit Hash, seems to be the same—freshly whitewashed, the broad front porch running the length of the structure, with rickety steps on each end. But the Rabbit Hash Visitor Center is new since my last visit. Well, not exactly new: one of the old log cabins has been "re-purposed" for this purpose. This is where you'll find the historical society as well as the Department of Tourism, which offers a stack of flyers anchored by a stone paperweight.

The current mayor's office is a shelter located behind the barn. Mayor Goofy was widely celebrated when he died, and his successor, the late Mayor Junior, was very nearly worshipped by constituents. Now the citizens of Rabbit Hash are fond of saying, "Boy, the new mayor is a bitch!" Lucy Lou, a border collie, is the first female dog to hold the office. Several signs indicate the proper way to interact with Her Honor. "Do not feed the Mayor!" they implore. "Foods that are not on her regular diet plan disrupt her system and her figure."

A woman who introduces herself as Lucy Lou's secretary offers to wake her from her nap so that I can meet her, but I decide to leave her to her rest. Instead, I visit the General Store, look at Terry's selection of Indian jewelry, and buy a box of ginger chews. I sit down on the bench outside to savor my treat and people-watch.

Rabbit Hash used to boast that there were no children in the town. Now, I see a young couple in Nike Airs pushing a fancy stroller. The benches are filling up, mostly with men in shorts, a few wearing tee shirts with "Rabbit

Hash" emblazoned on the front, the lettering stretching across their girth. I don't know if they're tourists or locals, but in Kentucky, they call it a "dunlop" stomach when a guy's belly has "done-lopped" over his belt. So these men have captured the spirit of the place.

The name Rabbit Hash would be famous even if the mayor was human: it's that memorable. The website of the historical society explains its origins, and I'll repeat it here for anyone who has missed out. In 1847 a terrible flood raged through the community between Thanksgiving and Christmas. As you can imagine, it put quite a damper on celebrations; it also drove the rabbits to higher ground. Residents worried about the future of their holiday dinners, the historical society's entry claims, causing one man to joke that at least there should be plenty of rabbit hash. It became the town's nickname, and in 1879, when the town had to change its actual name from Carlton (because of confusion with Carrollton and Carroll County), Rabbit Hash was the obvious choice. Maybe there's something in the water, or maybe it's the name, but somehow Rabbit Hash seems to breed characters the way boggy ground breeds mosquitoes.

Case in point: Doc Baker, the resident obstetrician. Back in the 1970s, Doc Baker used to ride a mule to clinics in the backcountry to treat expectant mothers. Legend has it that he arrived at one facility to find a heavily pregnant women smoking. Baker fired off a pistol in the air. His mule reared up on its hind legs and Doc Baker fired again. Once he had everyone's attention, he shouted something to the effect that pregnant women had no business smoking cigarettes and said he'd be back when they could "stop sucking nicotine."

Rabbit Hash was also the home of Crazy Clifford. He was, I was told, a former scientist whose outlook on life was altered by a terrible motorcycle wreck. Clifford lived in the woods near town—nobody knew quite where or how—and he appeared on full-moon nights to drink beer and get into mischief. I encountered him once, many years ago, when I was playing music there. Clifford, on a tree stump in cut-off shorts, was dancing like a wild man. His skin was so tan, and his hair so black, that I seemed to be watching a cut-out silhouette writhing in the night to his own inner rhythm. He never even noticed me.

I don't remember where I met Fiddlin' Joy Sibcy, but a lot of our time as friends was spent at Rabbit Hash, listening to bluegrass bands or drinking "sassyfras" tea with Mike Fletcher—Shantyboat Mike—on his floating Rabbit Hash home. Fiddlin' Joy, as everyone called her, was tall and slender with thick strawberry blonde hair that fell down to the middle of her back. She wore garments she got from second-hand stores, long skirts divided in the middle like riding clothes.

Once, when she was reading want ads and looking for a job, she circled one ad for a carpenter. When I saw her a few days later, she was jubilant. "You must have gotten the job," I said.

"No!" she said, bubbling over with excitement. "But I found the outfit!"

She held out a paper bag that contained actual carpenter's pants—the kind with a loop for a hammer and pockets for nails. "I got it at the Goodwill for .99 cents," she declared proudly.

Given Fiddlin' Joy's penchant for accessories, it should not come as a surprise to learn that she could not actually play the fiddle. She simply carried it under her arm as a violinist might do, the bow hanging from the crook of her finger. If someone came along and requested a tune she would say, "I've just been in a jam session and my arm's worn out. I'm sorry." If they wanted to know where she'd be playing next, she'd point to a distant campfire and say, "I might be over there a little later on tonight."

Fiddlin' Joy might have been my friend, but her best friend was Jewel Rose, a wealthy girl whose father owned a coal mine in West Virginia. Jewel Rose and Joy kept an antique show wagon locked up in Rabbit Hash, and they liked to pretend they were ladies in an old western saloon. I guess that's how Jewel Rose met Crazy Clifford. I'm not sure, but I do know they were madly in love for a time.

Rabbit Hash has always been a peaceful place. Of course, that was before bikers discovered the spot during Mayor Goofy's term. Now nearly every day motorcycle riders roar in to enjoy the serenity and ruin it at the same time. But by and large they are good guests: As Don Clare says, "They don't leave nothin' behind but their money."

Don Clare is president of the historical society, and as such, tends to be the administrator of Rabbit Hash, dealing with its present issues as well as its past. "This is a wooden-town community," he tells me. "All these wooden buildings right on the river are a real concern when it comes to flooding." And so the floods that gave Rabbit Hash its name still threaten its rickety existence.

But nothing much seems to damage its image. Rabbit Hash celebrates its own history more than any town I know. Visit on Old Timers' Day in late summer and you'd be amazed at how many people consider this place their own. They come in droves, folks you haven't seen in forever, wearing frontier costumes and eating barbeque and drinking Coca-Colas. Maybe they lay claim here because it seems like a good place to be from.

One Sunday a few years ago, when my radio show on WNKU was still broadcast in the afternoon, I got a call at the studio from Jane Burch Cochran, the nationally-exhibited quilt artist who lives just outside town. Miss Jane, as she is called, had an urgent request. "Katie, I have lost my pocketbook," she said in her ladylike voice. "Could you ask on the radio if I left it somewhere?"

Sure enough, as soon as I asked, the phone rang and it was somebody at the General Store calling to say they had her purse and to come on back and get it.

As my visit proves, it's still that kind of place. In the office building/barn/art gallery, the last painting has been examined and discussed by browsers (unfortunately, there weren't any buyers), and I help Miss Jane tidy up. It is sticky hot, and since it is Rabbit Hash there's no air conditioning.

"I'm glad you came," Jane says. "It will give people something to talk about tomorrow." She had promised her art colleagues that if they came to the show there would be a couple of celebrities, one of whom was her chiropractor. I was the other one.

I laughed. "Which one of us had top billing?" I asked, grinning. "Me or the chiropractor?"

Jane gathers used plastic cups and forks into a trash bag. She's flying to Montana the next day, to a small cabin she and her husband own there. In Montana, she says, "I don't do anything except read and think about projects. I'm always working on something in my head." She gives me a sharp look. "Do you think artists ever get to retire?"

I laugh and take a drink from my water bottle, pick up my purse, and start toward the stairs.

"Have a good time," I yell to Jane, but she is already lost in thought, and she doesn't hear me. She is probably daydreaming about her next quilting project.

Spending the day in Rabbit Hash is as close to retirement as I am likely to come, I think. But for now, it's close enough.

PLAYING THROUGH

I have always thought my decline began in earnest about twelve years ago when I had a gig with a bluegrass band at a country club in Northern Kentucky. I drove over in a wet winter twilight with zero visibility, one of those dreary days that crop up so often in Cincinnati just after Christmas. The job we were playing was for friends of the banjo player, Jeff Roberts, and the pleasures of his company sometimes could override the chaos that ensued. Unfortunately, by the snake-oil tone of voice he used when he first called me, I could tell immediately that this was not going to be the case.

"We'll be in and out of there in no time," Jeff said, talking really fast like when he's eaten a lot of Little Debbie snack cakes. "The magician and the nun who does the animal balloons are working most of the last hour anyway."

"The nun who does animal balloons?"

"Sister Agatha. I hear she's great," Jeff said smoothly. Then: "Gotta go. See you Sunday."

On Sunday I left the house right on time, threw my guitar in the back seat of the car and turned on the radio. By the time I hit I-275 South, the warmth of the car and the sound of the radio felt like a cocoon. *I could drive all the way to Nashville*, I thought, but I took the right exit and saw a building that had to be a country club.

"Nothing to it," I said to myself. Following instructions, I pulled into a narrow black-top lane in back of the main building. The blacktop lane began to narrow, and I couldn't see ten feet ahead of me, and that is when I found myself driving right onto the golf course.

I didn't know what else to do, so I kept on going; it felt surprisingly good, so I didn't stop. No one was playing, of course—it was winter. The grounds were saturated from the rain, and I had the place all to myself. I inched forward, enjoying the feeling of my tires sinking into the ground, gouging up hunks of costly green turf, and I liked the little sucking sound it made every time the wheels pulled clear again. I began to hum a merry-go-round song in my head, and for a few minutes I was a little girl again, playing mud pies. But when I had to gun my car to get up a small hill, I found myself stuck in a trap somewhere on the fourth hole.

Crime doesn't pay. I saw the klieg lights before I heard the walkie-talkies. Suddenly, a uniformed man was running towards me yelling, "Stop!" which was silly since my car was clearly wedged between two trees. When he got to the car window and got a good look at me, he seemed a little red in the face, and he pressed the "talk" button on his radio and said, "Aw, Darryl, it's just a woman."

Maybe it was the way he said it—"it's just a woman"—that brought me back to my senses, but suddenly I felt ridiculous sitting there in my old Ford all dressed up for a party wearing a snazzy pink sequined baseball cap.

"Lady, do you know you're in the middle of a golf course?" the guard said gently, giving me a look that suggested I might need my bifocals changed very soon.

"Yes, I know I'm on a golf course," I said in my best haughty voice. "I thought I was on the right road, but it seems I wasn't."

Then, he led me through the trees, off the course and onto the main highway, much the way you'd shoo a housefly out an open window. I was late for the gig, of course. Sister Agatha had already twisted ten or eleven balloons into dachshunds by the time I walked into the room, and she gave me a pinched superior look while I was taking my guitar out of the case. I had to explain the whole thing to Jeff, without looking obvious, and he snickered, then just started laughing outright, and I noticed he was having trouble tuning the banjo.

"You drove through a golf course?" he asked again.

"I did," I responded. "And I can prove it."

"I can't believe you drove through a golf course," he said, again, just before he kicked off "Shuckin' the Corn."

We walked outside to the car when the gig was over, and he examined the back fender where the rolls of turf had wound around it about twelve times.

"Do you think you could help me knock some of this dirt off?" I asked. "It's making a rubbing sound."

"I think we're going to need some tools here," he said. "Didn't you see the sign?"

"What sign," I asked.

"The one that said 'Don't drive on the golf course.'"

I gave him a hard look. He was laughing. I was to hear that laugh years later when a car I was driving caught fire and burned up. The tires made little popping sounds as they blew. But that's another story.

Jeff always says just because a joke is old doesn't mean it shouldn't be told anymore. "Why, sometimes," he says, "You're just beginning to get the hang of telling it on the fourth go-round."

I'm writing this story again, just for Jeff. It is a true story, and it made him laugh, and frankly, I've never heard the end of it anyway.

A PRAIRIE HOME COMPANION (1980)

Garrison Keillor was standing on his front porch in Minneapolis the first time I saw him. It was very early and still dark when we pulled into his driveway. He was very tall, and he had a large dark cat wrapped around the back of his neck. Now *A Prairie Home Companion*, which has had many incarnations, is a movie directed by Robert Altman, and my old friend Garrison has become a movie star. I went to see the movie recently, and it brought back many good memories of the three times my bluegrass band played on the radio show created by Garrison out of a writer's yearning for another time.

Back in the late seventies, Garrison Keillor located the Katie Laur Band through our record albums, and he called our bass player, Larry Nager, about luring us to Minnesota. He heard something in us he liked, he said. We had never heard of him, and I was less than enthusiastic about driving that far. For all we knew about Minnesota, they had snow and ice ten months a year and still hadn't made peace with the Indians.

Nevertheless, our first performance was on May 17, 1980, the second *A Prairie Home Companion* to be nationally broadcast. (Who'd have thought it would go on and produce 477 live shows during its first ten years?) The oriental rugs were there, as was the backstage curtain fold where we gathered to play fifteen or twenty minutes at intermission. This small performance went onto the radio, but not to the live audience, and allowed stations to identify themselves and whatever else it is they do to satisfy FCC regulations. I think it was Swedish Independence Day, and Garrison had found a traveling Swedish band. They sang in Swedish, except for one song, "Fox on the Run," and this song they obligingly performed in a kind of phonetic English.

In those days, Garrison still had a radio show, the original *A Prairie Home Companion*, named after a local cemetery. We got to Garrison's house, had an hour's nap, and had to get up, drink coffee and go to his early morning radio show to promote our appearances. Being interviewed by him meant staying on your toes. He was a brilliant man, a virtual encyclopedia of music.

In those days Garrison shared a house with the producer of *A Prairie Home Companion*, Margaret Moos. It was a great house in a pleasantly old-fashioned part of Minneapolis. It reminded me of the square in Clifton in Cincinnati. At Garrison's house, he had a lot of books on natural wood shelves all over his living room. Jeff Roberts recalls vividly that Garrison had no shower curtain. It was one of those things that outraged Jeff occasionally. How could anyone have a hit radio show and no shower curtain? Garrison not only had no shower curtain, but Jeff felt sure he was not even thinking about acquiring one. "What would cause a man not to have a shower curtain," Jeff would say, fixing his listener with an almost hypnotic gaze.

Garrison always got us a weekend gig at a local Extempore Coffee House to defray expenses. It had mismatched chairs and wobbly tables, and I think we played for the door and sold some records. (Fiddler Buddy Griffin always grimaced when I said we were playing anything "for the door." He'd say scornfully, "I've got a whole basement full of doors.") Nevertheless, it was a new audience, and they ate us up like cream. (It's always good to be from Kentucky when you're out west; they think you're authentic.)

The Saturday night of the broadcast, the tension was palpable. Garrison paced a lot, then rode to the theater with us in our old Ford van. The roof sagged. When Garrison leaned his poplin-suited arms on the window, a sluice of water from the previous night's rain ran down his arm. We arrived at the theater with plenty of time for him to get the stains fixed. The World Theater was a wonderful place to play. It was old and needed some sprucing up, but the production was stunning. The sound system was the best I had ever heard. We had never heard Garrison's "Tales of Lake Woebegone," but I stood backstage listening to him and thought of ways I could get the program to Cincinnati.

We did about six songs. I'm sorry I can't remember what they were. We returned to the coffee house for another set with the Swedish Independence Day Band. We sang "Fox on the Run" together. Then the music started flowing, and we could all feel that flow, that being in the moment which is what keeps you going through sixteen-hour road trips and no sleep. In no time, we were laughing and having a wonderful time with the audience. They liked us; they really did.

5
OVER-THE-RHINE

MR. SPOONS IN FRONT OF THE REAL AUNT MAUDIE'S MURALS.

SATURDAY NIGHT AND SUNDAY MORNING

I walked into Aunt Maudie's at 1207 Main Street on a summer's night in the late 1960s. I was young, and there was a sweet breeze and the promise of a new season in the air. Sometimes, when your whole life is about to change, you don't really notice anything out of the ordinary, and that was the case with me. I was with a few other people, people whom I didn't know well, and we had heard about a place downtown where you could listen to a bluegrass band and drink beer out of Mason jars. It was the first of my "Cincinnati Experiences," as I came to call them. Experiences when, just like that, I walked out of my everyday life and into the future.

We paid a $1 cover charge at the door and entered a long room that widened as we went. Every step took us farther into the underworld, it seemed to me. My eyes had to grow accustomed to the darkness. In this part of downtown—called Over-the-Rhine—old buildings were often arranged with the least possible footage on the sidewalk. You had to walk in to get a feeling for the largeness of these spaces. Years later I heard that it was done for tax purposes: you paid property taxes on how much room your property took up on the sidewalk, so the crafty Cincinnati German builders went for depth rather than for splashy frontage. I don't know if this is true or not; I certainly wasn't thinking about it on that particular Saturday night.

I don't know if I was thinking about anything, but when I got a blast of a cracking five-string banjo coming from the stage inside the building, it was as if I had been splashed with a blast of ice water. The banjo player was playing something I recognized as "Salty Dog Blues," and at the chorus, three voices blended in a baritone, lead, and high tenor trio so true and so authentic I was dumbstruck.

Let me be your Salty Dog,
Or I won't be your man at all,
Honey, let me be your Salty Dog …

They accented certain syllables with runs on the guitar. The music was so rhythmic it was mesmerizing, and a chubby guy with a flattop haircut was playing upright or "double" bass, just a hair ahead of the rest of the musicians, giving the music a kind of hard rhythm. "Folk music in overdrive" is how one critic described bluegrass, and I still believe that's about as accurate as you're going to get.

When I finally looked around, I saw that the room was reasonably bare except for a long bar and some four-top tables with mismatched chairs scattered here and there. A pool table sat a little bit off to the side and some Appalachian women gathered around it talking to each other about men.

"Harold's got to where he don't even take me to the doctor no more," one of them complained. Her eyes were small and black in her head, like a bird's. "He's just laid up drunk all the time." The other woman shook her head at Harold's husbandly shortcomings, and they went on with their familiar litany—none of it good. They might have been plump, but they crammed themselves into spandex, and oddly enough, many of the women had their hair rolled up in those pink foam curlers you used to see before blow-dryers became part of our culture.

Bill LaWarre, an advertising executive whom I met at Maudie's, was as amazed as I was by the foam curlers. "It was Saturday night," he'd say, shaking his head. "Were they going some place after Maudie's that required they set their hair?"

If I had to guess, I'd say they were getting ready for church. I was to learn pretty quickly that the residents of Over-the-Rhine were as conflicted about religion as they were about many of life's basic values. They drank, they smoked, they hung around in bars, but a lot of them were in a little storefront church pew the next morning.

This kind of juxtaposition would become familiar to me as I delved deeper and deeper into the music. I was fascinated when the band on stage followed a drinking, cheating song, like "Dim Lights, Thick Smoke and Loud, Loud Music" with a lively gospel number, "Prayer Bells of Heaven," or a song like "Mother's Not Dead; She's Only A'Sleepin'" (in close, eerie four-part harmony). Over-the-Rhine had you coming and going: Saturday night and Sunday morning.

Joe Jones, or Mr. Spoons, as everybody in Over-the-Rhine called him, was a Child of the Divide. He lived in various parts of the neighborhood with his mother, his brother, and his sister. His father had left them when Joe was ten years old, and he stepped up to the plate to help his mother put food on the table. He had already discovered he had a knack for spoons-playing and rhythm: he had reached for his first set of spoons before he was five years old.

In his adolescence he became a drinker and a sinner, passing out, as he once told me, on the tracks of the bridge to Newport. His Mother never gave up on him. It was she who spotted the genius in what he did. It was she who sewed his "Nudie" suits. He became a fine entertainer and the main breadwinner of the family—he told me once he had sent his brother to U.C. with the money he made from playing spoons. His brother was the first one in his family to graduate from college.

Several men in Cincinnati have called themselves "Mr. Spoons," but if you ever saw Joe Jones in action you saw poetry in motion. When he danced into Aunt Maudie's, quiet whispers passed up and down the room. "Mr. Spoons just came in," the college kids would say. "Reckon Joe's gonna play us a tune," an Appalachian man smoking in the corner added.

"Spoons, Spoons," you'd hear the calls all over the bar. When he started playing, the room exploded. He'd start with just a spoon or two, keeping time on the back of his hand, maybe walk the spoons all the way up the back of his head, then switch to playing on a customer's head. Or he made it look like he was playing against the customer's head, by hitting the spoons against his fingernails. If he had a good audience, he'd add a few more spoons to each hand, and the band would kick it up a notch or two. The faster the song got, the faster he danced, and the looser he got. He would play the spoons in great, shining arcs, sweat beginning to run down his forehead, the dance steps more vigorous, looser.

His mother bought polyester jackets and decorated them for him. One of them had fringe everywhere, and his name embroidered in large letters. One of them had spoons sewed on the back as if they were walking somewhere. He carried a flat board on which he displayed plastic corsages for sale, nothing you'd really think about buying normally, but when the playing was over, he started to sell the corsages. He sold them for $1, and I read in photographer Cal Kowal's book on Spoons that, on his best night, he had sold sixty-nine corsages before he left Aunt Maudie's. If you live in Cincinnati and own any of the original corsages, you might want to start planning a trek to Antiques Road Show—you could very well have something valuable.

Mr. Spoons was quite professional with his instruments. He carried his spoons (which he said he stole from the Salvation Army) in his back hip pocket. The handles were wrapped in white adhesive tape to make them easier to grip. He started out with one spoon, and on a good night he might end up playing with sixteen spoons in each hand by the end of the set. He was an average-sized man, with that down home biscuits-and-gravy look about him, a little pasty, his black curls held in place with a lot of Vitalis. His eyes were a startling blue, and for all his awkwardness, when he danced he looked like Fred Astaire. I had never seen anybody as good as Mr. Spoons; he brought the house down with every performance.

My friend, Becky Hudnall, who lives in California now, still has her first Spoons' corsage. A guy everybody called Fast Eddie bought it and presented it to her.

"Thank you," she said, a little surprised.

"It ain't for you," Eddie said. "It's for him."

Years later, when I first saw Johnny Rosebud in a jazz bar in East Walnut Hills, I thought of Mr. Spoons. Johnny had been around the blues bars for years, selling long-stemmed roses to whoever wanted them. If he could talk the band into letting him sing "Kansas City Blues," he knew he'd sell more roses. He wasn't in the same league as Mr. Spoons, but if it was a slow night and the band was bored, they'd let him sit in. He put everything he had into "Kansas City Blues," too, which got the band out of their bad mood. It was a win/win situation. Like Mr. Spoons, Johnny Rosebud was a little eccentric. He was a square peg in a round hole, but he was in his own way, an artist. So was Caldonia.

I didn't run into her until the early eighties. She was a small, Black woman, her hair cut short like a boy's, her body muscular and athletic. She claimed to have been discovered tap dancing on a street corner in Louisville by the band leader, Louis Jordan, and she claimed he had written his hit song, "Caldonia, Caldonia, What makes your big head so hard?" for her, but I have no way of knowing whether it was true or not.

I did see her dance a lot. She'd come into Arnold's carrying her tap shoes in a box tied with twine. If the band was sounding hot and swinging, she'd get her shoes on as fast as she could. If things were a little slow, she took her time.

She wasn't just a one-trick pony: she could dance, and she could sell a song, though her voice was raspy. When she needed tips, she'd go from table to table and make one buttock jump up and down while the other stayed still. This impossible-looking step never once failed to put money in the hat the waitresses passed for her. "Let's give Caldonia a standing rovation," she'd say, and they did.

Nowadays when I read stories about the rebirth of the arts in Over-the-Rhine I wonder where art has flourished more consistently than in

Over-the-Rhine. Court Street has so much painterly atmosphere you can almost smell the turpentine. Even the first European immigrants, the day laborers, gathered at the old photography studios around Court and Main streets. They thought having their picture taken was the height of glamour, and sent the pictures back home to their families in the Old Country.

In a coffee table book called *Prairie Fires and Paper Moons: The American Photographic Postcard; 1900–1920*, I've seen pictures of men sitting on the quarter moon prop who looked exactly like Larry, Moe and Curly. In this book about the early days of photography (by Hal Morgan and Andreas Brown, with a foreword by Wilmington's John Baskin), the proprietors of the photography studios would line up the immigrants who wanted their pictures taken. The customers were not used to America, didn't know the language, but they wanted those pictures to prove perhaps they'd been somewhere as exotic as Cincinnati, Ohio.

The photographer would rush down the line charging "in advance," taking their money. Then he'd go out the back door to buy film and flash powder, run back, put on his photographic clothes and start shooting customers on the quarter moon or the cardboard gondola. By the end of the night, everybody was drunk, and everybody was happy.

Over-the-Rhine had artists hanging around because rent was cheap, and it was as close to Europe as you could get in Cincinnati. In his wonderful book on Mr. Spoons, Cal Kowal has captured not only Mr. Spoons, but the Over-the-Rhine culture as well. By photographing the caricatures of the regulars who came to Aunt Maudie's, he preserved an important bit of the history of this particular part of Cincinnati (the colorful part, I think). If you were familiar with the patrons, you could tell who the caricatures were.

When Ray Mills, the owner of Maudie's died, Fifth Third Bank took ownership of the building and because the walls were dirty, painted over these wonderful pictures. No matter how much we screamed, what was done, in this case, could not be undone. It remained, in the minds of the "eccentric artists" as hideous a crime as covering the Sistine Chapel with Burma Shave signs. Because of Cal Kowal, we have a small piece of those paintings remaining.

By the time I moved on from Aunt Maudie's (the first time) it had turned into a comedy club. After Mr. Spoons won first place on *The Gong Show*, I heard he had met a stockbroker in Manhattan, married her, and was living in a penthouse, playing spoons on a street corner outside the United Nations Building, which is where Woody Allen discovered him. Mr. Spoons started showing up in the going-out guide of *The New York Times*, tap-dancing through restaurants in pricey parts of town. ("You seen one toilet," he said to me once, "You seen the next one.")

In Woody Allen's movie, *Sweet and Lowdown*, Spoons actually played the spoons in a talent contest in a Grange Hall somewhere in the Midwest. His co-star was Sean Penn, and I often pictured the two of them in dressing gowns and ascots playing Scrabble during their breaks.

Eventually it all collapsed: the marriage, the movie career, the ascots, and Spoons was left playing on his street corner by the United Nations Building. He got a couple of choice gigs out of that: playing in Japan, where he was revered much like Lafcadio Hearn, the *Cincinnati Enquirer* newspaper columnist who was treated somewhat shabbily in Cincinnati and moved to New Orleans, and was buried in the final resting place of the Japanese Royal Family.

Pigmeat Jarrett was surely the oldest of the Cincinnati street artists. According to one biography I read of him, he died on September 5, 1995 (9/5/95) at the age of ninety-five. Like many performers his real birth date was unknown, but with the nine's and five's in the date of his death, it makes a colorful story.

Pigmeat slipped onto my radar screen with great stealth. I first saw him playing cocktail hours for tips at Coco's on Greenup Street in Covington. After that, he was likely to slide onto the piano bench at Arnold's on Eighth Street in Cincinnati. He came and went so quietly, he reminded me of a wisp of fog on the Ohio River. You'd look around and there he was, so thin you could slide him under the door, a fedora hat pulled down around his head like Hoagy Carmichael. His eyes were ancient-looking, rheumy, slightly yellowed, and his hands were thick-knuckled with arthritis. "His brand of blues was a combination of boogie and story-telling," according to Tom Beck, who played bass with him for two years.

Pigmeat had worked at most of the Black clubs around town: the Cotton Club, the Bucket of Blood, and more than likely the Swing Bar on Vine Street. The Swing Bar was a successful bar catering to a white, Appalachian clientele, and in the forties, fifties and early sixties, they had a "hillbilly" band as the main headliner and a Black jazz trio to play breaks. A man who was a regular at that bar, Jonny Wolfe, told me once the Black trio sat at their own table when they weren't playing.

Pigmeat had also worked as a cook on the old Delta Queen steamboat in his younger days. He considered it an ideal job. He would say, "Well, you see peoples on the land. They jest lookin' at you on the boat, wonderin' where you're goin'." It was often difficult to understand Pigmeat's patois, but I did understand him one night during Tall Stacks when we talked about the steamboats. "Ever' boy needs to get hisself out on the river and see where she goes. It make a man understand things."

Right around the corner from the studio where Ruth Lyons did her daily show (women who made up the studio audience were required to wear white gloves), all kinds of hillbilly, blues, and swing music were being recorded at the Herzog Studio on Race Street, Cincinnati's first commercial recording studio (it was where Hank Williams recorded "Lovesick Blues," and Flatt and Scruggs recorded "Foggy Mountain Breakdown").

While others see Cincinnati as a dull place, populated by men in suits who write insurance policies or sell soap, others, who've been around, know it as the magnet it is for strange artists and the characters who passed through here on their way to someplace else. Cincinnatians leave you alone; if you have something that needs doing, this is a good place to do it. There is a richness to the riverbanks, and what washes up here leaves a little of itself behind when the tide goes out again.

OVER-THE-RHINE

A GOOD NEIGHBOR

Kaldi's Coffee Shop has sold its liquor license, and even the bums are feeling the pinch. When the lights started going out by 9 p.m., guys like Ricardo, our friendly Street Vibes vendor, got left in the dark. The perky little stained-glass coffee cups are still dancing on the transom above the door, but lattes have replaced martinis for the time being, and Kaldi's is on the wagon.

At first, an existential gloom pervaded this block of Main Street after dark. If Kaldi's could start closing early, what's next? Of course, you can still get your morning coffee (and you can get it starting at 7:30). People are still coming in for lunch and the youngsters who come by in the afternoons after school continue to toss their coats and book bags in a communal pile by the piano. One boy who sits at a booth by himself has on a leather jacket, and his hair stands up on top of his head like a Roman helmet.

The guys who hang out in front of Jordan's Market are complaining. "It's hard to make any money when ain't nobody on the street," somebody said. "We've got to get people back down here some way." I laughed, thinking that if I closed my eyes I could be at a city council meeting, but it isn't funny. It is always the poor who are the hardest hit. To them, fewer drinkers translates to fewer merry-makers to toss a $5 bill into an outstretched hand. I remembered a favorite Street Vibes vendor, Grady, I think, who would look remorseful and say, "I ain't makin' my jack."

James, another man you'll see on the loose down here, has always scuffled but he's always worked. When I first moved down here in the late nineties, he used to load and unload for a man who operated a storage center next to the Circle A grocery on the corner of Thirteenth and Main. Then he worked for awhile at the Cuban Restaurant (don't even get me started on the adventures at the Cuban Restaurant; just the potted palm outside the door with the balloons hanging from the limbs says it all). Anyway, James worked there until the first time they closed. One night I was short with him after a bad, bad day, and he said, "Don't go being so snippy with me, Miss Lady. I'm a GOOD neighbor."

To my eternal humiliation, a few nights later, I had to ask him to help me break into my own apartment. I had come home from my shift at WNKU without my keys. Normally I could cut through Kaldi's into the hallway of my apartment, and I was home. But Kaldi's was closed. I had forgotten my keys, the code on the front door wasn't working, and I didn't have a cell phone or money. James showed me how to get the fire escape stairs down to street level. I climbed up, opened my window, and slid through like a practiced cat burglar. I had to pull the fire escape stairs up behind me, and with James offering encouragement, I made it. The next time I saw him I gave him some money for his help.

"Don't be offerin' me money for doin' what any good neighbor would do," he said, as he snatched the cash. You have to be realistic down here.

Our neighbors to the north have flourished. Thirteenth Street is full of trendy lofts and galleries lit up and crowded with art buyers on Final Fridays. Thin, slinky young women in bias-cut dresses and high, high heels congregate here for art openings. Even the Peaslee Neighborhood Center looks a little more upscale with its herb garden and spiked lavender plants and its outside mural garden. It blends comfortably with the design shops and rehabbed warehouses across the street. In one of those warehouses a few summers ago, a consortium of artists rented one of these spaces for an art show called "Volk." It was temporary, but for a few months the venture presented some thoughtful, entertaining art. You could wander down there for a show, drink the Kool-Aid, and see everybody you knew.

Our end of Main Street, the "entertainment district" is not doing as well. Davis Furniture, a little south of Twelfth Street, has closed, as well as the Jump Café, and the upscale art gallery next to it. Last fall we lost Diva's, too, our edgy, punky, hair-styling salon. Now, the high school students who don't go to Kaldi's sit in ragged rows behind where Diva's used to be and talk in the fervent way of teenagers before they head home for supper, band practice, and all that jazz. The mean concrete streets and sidewalks are dingy and littered. Neon's, whose previous owners kept it so immaculately tended and manicured, is looking seedier although it's still in business.

Jordan's Market, next door to Kaldi's, doesn't even pretend to sell groceries anymore—just lottery tickets, beer and wine, cigarettes, and candy and snacks for the kids who go there after school. MD 20/20 and Wild Irish Rose promise relief from the cares of existence, and people on the corner clamor for change from the well-heeled patrons parking Beemers and Humvees in poor neighborhoods. For the yuppies from the suburbs, the Main Street Entertainment District is a walk on the wild side.

Over-the-Rhine serves many populations, and Kaldi's plays a large part in weaving together the threads of those occupations, furnishing a yeasty atmosphere for the artists, architects, builders, lawyers, educators, and social workers who come here. Kaldi's continues to be full in the daytime hours with business meetings, hurried lunches for suited customers carrying laptops and reading newspapers, couples or friends meeting for an early dinner on their way back home. However, nights are another matter. It has always been difficult to get crowds downtown on a weeknight, even at Arnold's, where I used to play before I came to live above Kaldi's, and in the bleak midwinter, nighttime bar-hopping is minimal. Getting up at 6:30 or 7:00 a.m. looks so much worse when it's still dark. Busy lives stretch scarce resources, and the expense of a bottle of white wine and a jazz trio is sometimes more than the budget allows.

One group who meets regularly at Kaldi's on Wednesday night is a group of congregants from the Hyde Park United Methodist Church. They come seeking a vision or a way to serve this neighborhood. They have felt their way along, learning more about us as we learned about them. I like them, because they don't necessarily have an agenda, and still they come every week and remind us to be good neighbors. I'm amazed that other communities quarrel! I thought we were alone down here; we're not. People in Hyde Park are having a hard time coming to terms with social services being "Back in your own backyard," as the song says. Watch out Indian Hill. Meals on

Wheels is coming soon to a church near you. Here in Over-the-Rhine, we have a lot of soup kitchens: sixteen of them to be exact. Across the street from my apartment, homeless men and a few women line up for showers.

Meanwhile, different representatives from Impact Over-the-Rhine show up on these Wednesday evenings. We come together to fit the pieces, to polish the edges. We are determined to be real. It helps if the left hand knows what the right is doing.

I feel as long as the Methodists are with us when they can be, we will be all right. Kaldi's is at least selling coffee and black bean chili. Last night after Bockfest the place was full again, just like it used to be, except that people were nicer and listened to the music.

Since no one was drinking, more families came in with children who wanted to see us play, sitting in a semi-circle, all of those guitars and one bass. Ma Crow and I gave up a few hours into the singing, but Andy, Brad, and Scott kept on playing, drinking coffee. I always hope people find a way to feed their better selves.

BREAKING THE MOLD

Brenda Tarbell calls herself the Grandma Moses of pottery. It's a catchy image, this comparison to the legendary folk artist, but it's misleading. True, in her sixties, Brenda has finally come into her own as an artist. But she is slender and agile, enviably able to crouch on her knees for hours, lost in her work. And there's nothing primitive about that work, either. Case in point: her elegant installation recently unveiled at the Duke Energy Convention Center.

The piece, a sixty-foot-long riot of ceramic flowers, is titled *Buds, Blossoms, Branches, Boughs to the Queen*. I'd heard others talk about it, using words like "ethereal" and "perfectly crafted." When I finally went with her to see it, it lived up to its billing.

Brenda made the pale flowers from a creamy white stoneware clay; her son David, a metalworker, fabricated branches from steel tubes and she shaped delicate copper wire into stamens. Three interns from ArtWorks Cincinnati—the organization that commissioned *Buds, Blossoms, Branches, Boughs*—assisted on the project, as well. Its placement in a hall on the south side of the Convention Center is just right: sunlight hits the work, and it seems to expand.

Brenda made the piece to explore the strong connection between Cincinnatians and nature. "I picture people from the deep South looking at the magnolia blossoms, and feeling closer to home," she says of the first grouping of flowers. She chose serviceberry for the second cluster, because, "in the mountains, it was the first blooming tree in the spring. If you lost a loved one over the hard winter months, the budding of the serviceberry was the first indication that the ground was thawing, and services could be held for the deceased.

"It's pronounced *sarvisberry* in the mountains," she added. "We have serviceberries growing in Friendship Park right downtown on the river."

Her representation of the dogwood is stunning. The whiteness of the boughs looks Asian; the lip of the blossom, tissue thin. Indeed, in this region it's hard to imagine spring without the dogwood scattered across our hills, its branches like delicate flushes of color in a Japanese print. Even in a city resplendent with parks and gardens, the beauty of the dogwood stands out. In Brenda's work, it marks her slow ascent from pottery to ceramic artistry.

The 1960s and '70s were creative times in Cincinnati; you could feel it in the air. The network of young artists and musicians was at its peak. Potter Mike Frasca established the Spring Street Pottery in the Pendleton Art Center in Over-the-Rhine; Greg Seigel's digs were south of town, but he'd drive into Cincinnati when he got enough pieces together and sell them out of the backseat of his car. Painter Tom Bacher created giant canvases of skyscrapers, streets, and fancy cars, rendered in fluorescent paint that glowed in the dark. Jane Cochran was just beginning the fabric art pieces that found their way into international quilt exhibits. Those of us who made up the audience for these luminaries wore dangling earrings purchased from quirky little shops in Mt. Adams. We went around, as arts patron Lib Stone once said, "looking like the Mamas and the Papas."

That was the scene when Brenda arrived in 1973 with a BFA from Ohio State University. Her first studio was Clifton Earthworks, where Cincinnati Art Academy faculty member Bob Hasselle ran a gallery. But her hands quickly found more work to do. Helping her husband, Jim Tarbell, with his restaurant, Arnold's Bar and Grill, sidetracked her. So did raising their three children. But she continued to work on her craft, with discipline, out of the limelight. Her great friend and pottery partner, Pam Korte, says she wishes young artists knew the value of simply showing up to make art the way Brenda Tarbell has. "No one knows how she did it all," Korte says. "She just did it, putting one foot in front of the other, quietly and without assumption."

My early memories of Brenda are vivid: I recall her dressed for one of her husband's first "Odd Balls"—looking like a Gibson Girl in a "gently" used gown which she bought for $5 at a thrift shop. I remember her at Arnold's, helping out in the kitchen, and I recall her at any number of art openings in Over-the-Rhine on Final Fridays. Always lovely, always original. At an opening in Sarah Jane Bellamy's ultra contemporary gallery, she created a pleated skirt from folded plastic bags, and with her hair in a stylish chignon, she looked as if she had walked out of the pages of a fashion magazine.

Recently I was invited to have lunch at a house in Hyde Park where the hosts had filled the walls with contemporary art. Our meal arrived on ceramic plates and cups so fragile, so tiny, they looked like dishes fairies might have dined on. I knew immediately they were Brenda's work. They reminded me of pieces she'd shown at a holiday art and craft show: small mushroom caps made of thin white ceramic material. They were utterly original, nothing like the sturdy, earth pottery pieces of the 1960s and '70s. It was the first time I noticed that Brenda was going in a new direction, leaving craft and stepping up into art.

"I no longer throw on the wheel; I work with paper clay now," she says when I ask about the change. Her medium is clay that's blended with a fiber such as cellulose—delicate-looking, but strong. "I hand-build: I pinch, I prod, I poke my material into shapes," she says. She's had the opportunity to practice her new techniques in good company. She worked one summer after college at the Banff Centre in Alberta, and a Summerfair Foundation grant enabled her to study with Curtis Benzle at La Meridiana International School of Ceramics in Tuscany. Heady stuff. But, she insists, "I still call myself a potter."

Several years ago, when my family gathered in Cincinnati for a holiday weekend, Jim and Brenda invited us to their wonderful old house on Broadway for breakfast. There was food to spare, beautifully prepared and served on handmade plates. Jim was in excellent form, slicing heritage tomatoes to spread on a beautiful platter. He scrambled eggs into a frittata with onions, green peppers, and cheese, and everything was served up next to stacks of bacon and sausage. My sister snagged a piece of cured ham on a beaten biscuit, moaning softly as she bit into her treat.

Though the day had started gray and colorless, inside it was all cheer. When Brenda brought out the coffee, it was in handmade cups—handle-less ones, meant to be cradled in your palm like a warm hug. And just then, a ray of morning sunlight beamed through the window, anointing all of us with holiday spirit.

Around the Tarbell house, what Brenda hasn't made herself she has swapped with other potters of distinction, people like Bob Hasselle and Michael Frasca, and her friends Louise Jenks, Terri Kern, and Pam Korte. Her friendship with Jenks, Kern, and Korte has culminated into the annual show that they do in Jenks's driveway in Hyde Park. They call it "Pots and Lemonade," and it's one of those really friendly, get-there-early-and-chat affairs.

Jenks, whose sturdy, colorful stoneware pieces grace so many Cincinnati tables, is awed by the way Brenda can turn clay into ethereal art. "She is absolutely fearless. She will try anything," Jenks says. "The strengths of her shapes carry the delicacy of her work."

On a recent visit, Brenda wore cotton pants and an old turtleneck dabbed here and there with something, paint or clay, and her longish dark and silver hair was pulled back and fastened with a barrette. When the subject turned to growing old, she held up her hands to show her knuckles beginning to swell. "This is arthritis," she says, laughing. "This is old age." We sat companionably for a while, feeling the aches in our bones, the pleasures of having work to do, and the pain of having to do it. I wanted to ask her how she'd managed it all: the husband, the big house, the children, and the work. But I didn't. It seemed to me a question nobody could answer satisfactorily—not a woman who is an artist, maybe not any woman.

Pam Korte, who teaches at the College of Mount St. Joseph, has some observations about the joy and pain of making art. "There is a lot of talk nowadays about 'Putting in your ten thousand hours.' It's the new trend in talking about art," she says. "I'd say that Brenda has done that and more. The discipline of it, the years when you're just slogging through, showing up at your workspace."

I thought more about it: about the dewy days of youth, followed by the slackening of energy in middle age, when the children are sick or the house is a wreck or money problems are hanging over your head like storm clouds. The years when you're golden, and the years when you're not. They're followed by what I like to call the Sagging Chin Years, when the skills you have mastered finally begin to pay off. Perhaps it is "just showing up" that shapes the artist. But I think it's more complicated than that. I think it has more to do with spirit. It is hard to create beauty with a pinched soul.

"Brenda is one of the most generous artists I've ever known," says Korte. "It's been a privilege to work alongside her while she put in her ten thousand hours." Then she paused. "I can't wait to see what she does next."

OVER-THE-RHINE

STREET OF DREAMS

One cold, winter day back in the late 1990s, the pipes in my Mt. Auburn apartment froze and burst, and I had no choice but to move. It is hard for me to pull up stakes; I'd like to be a large sea turtle and carry my house on my back so I could duck when troubles threaten. In this case, though, I knew exactly what I had to do, and where I wanted to go.

A couple of years before, I had met a landlord named Bill Baum in a small studio apartment on Main Street in Over-the-Rhine, which he was rehabbing all by himself. Bill was a quiet, interesting man with graying hair and a red pickup truck and all kinds of credibility. The room where we met was simple—nothing except a drum stove and a window air conditioner—and I almost rented it. But I let myself be seduced by a place on Walker Street in Mt. Auburn—a bi-level apartment with glass walls in the bedroom, which was just like living in a tree house.

It took the frozen pipes to get me to Over-the-Rhine, and then my apartment luck held. I got a great place in a building called the Belmain, right on the corner of Twelfth and Main. I started moving my stuff into my new apartment that very day, and by nightfall everything I owned was safely stowed, except for a picture I had finagled out of a disc jockey—WNKU's Mr. Rhythm Man, for all you kats and kittens with pep in your step. It was a 3-D painting of a cat coming out of a television set (Mr. Rhythm Man had been heavily influenced by Nam June Paik, I believe). The piece was packed in a cardboard box in the hall downstairs, and when I turned my back somebody snatched it. That was Over-the-Rhine for you.

The neighborhood was all about art, and though I lamented the loss of the cat in the television set, I figured I'd find something else. I moved all my boxes up two flights of stairs like a college student; then I gave up my car, which was an old clunker anyway. I would become a long-distance walker, I

Linford Detweiler and Karin Bergquist: Over-the-Rhine's favorite couple. Photo by Michael Wilson.

decided; maybe even get a bicycle and some of those cool, tight shorts and a V-shaped helmet.

I had moved so much stuff in one day, my adrenaline was running pretty high. Anything seemed possible.

The next morning I slept late and went downstairs to Kaldi's Coffee House, where I had my first latte. The long, L-shaped bar was full of artists with paint on their clothes, and their banter was as heady as a hot loaf of bread from Shadeau Breads down the street: art, music, politics. Jim Wainscott, a painter of beautiful, rich nudes, was there. Knowledgeable about world affairs, he liked to rant a bit about the Republicans. Kate and Greg Schmidt, the brother and sister who created work in welded metal, were there, too. Kate—six feet tall with blonde curls spilling down her back—would be the first woman I ever saw in safety glasses.

Betsy Reeves, one of the smartest girls I ever met, who would later manage ArtWorks during the Big Pig Gig, was a waitress at Kaldi's back then. She had a different take on art, too. She'd wrap a box in tinfoil and rig it with batteries and tiny lights, then she'd create an old-fashioned diorama full of found objects like feathers and tiny stones, and the whole thing would blink on and off, on and off, like Christmas tree lights. Her best friend in those days was a young woman named Linda Hartley, who did stunning pieces of cloth art and photography. They hung out with Kelly Wenstrath, who was the most outrageous of all: on Final Fridays, when all the galleries were open late, her large, carved wooden giraffes and rocking horses were frequently on display in Kaldi's windows.

It had been a long time since I was around young women, and it was good to see what they were up to—the way they'd taken the women's liberation movement so many of my friends and I had worked for in the '60s and '70s, and what had they done with it. For one thing, they still cried over boys. Even though I called them the "pretty girls"—and they were—Betsy pointed out that no amount of liberation would stifle their biological urges. When she said this, she looked at me as if she were speaking to a slightly slow learner. "Nothing's changed," she told me, "except we have more options now. Biology is no longer destiny."

Kelly didn't talk much about such things, didn't even "journal" as the other girls did, but it was she who came up with the Orange Party—a huge gathering of artists in an old church by the river near Sayler Park. Everyone was to come in costume; everyone was to wear orange; anyone who wanted to exhibit had to pass scrutiny; and any bands who wanted to play had to have their own sound system.

"Why do you call it the Orange Party?" I asked.

"Because, among artists, orange is the color of insanity," Kelly said. Her thick shining brown hair framed her beautiful young face and deep brown eyes. *She's a work of art herself*, I thought, *and she doesn't even know it.*

To replace the lost cat art, I ended up buying a picture from the painter Tim Tatman. I still have it. It is large and hangs in my living room, and when people see it for the first time, they call it "interesting." It looks like the Marlboro Man on acid, with great, burned-out eyes. I first saw the work when he exhibited at Base Gallery—a cooperative of painters, sculptors, and new artists. The artists who belonged to Base paid dues, which in turn paid the gallery's rent and the utilities, and they took turns sitting in the gallery on Saturdays and Sundays, welcoming potential buyers.

Final Fridays were one way artists could sell their work in Over-the-Rhine—scheduled on the last Friday of each month to give them a chance to scrape together enough money to pay the landlord. Everyone scrubbed the galleries, washed the windows, even brought in bands. I remember a Final Friday when the wine was flowing freely at Base Gallery and two artists got in a fight over a woman. I was thrilled. *They're going to start cutting ears off any minute*, I thought to myself, but nothing of the kind happened.

Emotions often ran high in the neighborhood where affairs of the heart were concerned. One artist married a woman he called "Girl," a flaming redhead with a temper to match. The intensity of their relationship could not be maintained, though. When she came home from a trip to find an unfamiliar bra behind the sofa, she started throwing her things in cardboard boxes and marching down five flights of stairs with him following behind her, pleading, "Now, honey." But Girl had had it. She took the salt out of the shakers and the linoleum off the floor.

Like the artists, the street people in Over-the-Rhine were as amped up as Damon Runyon characters: *Guys and Dolls* updated. In particular, the Street Vibes vendors and the con men hitting up the suburbanites for money provided a continuing saga. There was an elderly, addled woman who met all comers by pleading, "Can you give me thirteen cents, sir?" One night, a grad student named Mike Templeton had heard it one too many times; he slammed into Kaldi's declaring, "I'm going to write her a check. I'm going to say, 'Excuse me while I go back inside and get my checkbook,' and then I'm going to write her a check for thirteen cents."

Sooner or later, everyone ended up at Kaldi's. At 11 o'clock every night, Tom Bacher would breeze in the door. Tom was the first artist I ever met who worked with phosphorescent paint; he had to charge his paintings with a flashlight, then turn off the lights in the room and listen to everyone gasp as the paintings, in the dark, came alive with twinkling lights. Each evening at Kaldi's he would take his usual table on the café side of the shop, and order a cup of coffee. He would be joined shortly by John Steele, another artist, who had worked a day job, gone home, fed the children, taken a nap and a shower. He showed up at Kaldi's to mark the shift from his day job and his nocturnal vocation—art. Their routine was always the same: a couple of cups of coffee, and he and Tom would disappear to their respective studios, prepared to paint most of the night. The discipline of it amazed me and eventually carried over into my own work.

"Mother Art"—sculptor Pat Renick's nickname—inevitably appeared on Friday nights with her longtime friend, art historian Laura Chapman. Patricia's wide-brimmed straw hats were as well known as she was, and she looked at whomever she was talking to from under the brim, her hazel eyes twinkling like stars.

It was she who was the star, though, and everyone was in awe of her. She was a professor emeritus in sculpture at the University of Cincinnati with a storied past. Back in the 1970s she had acquired a Volkswagen Beetle, took it into her studio, and turned it into a metal dinosaur. Jimmy Carter was president and we had a hostage crisis in the Middle East, which had led to a gasoline shortage: people lined up at service stations to fill their tanks. Pat's enormous sculpture announced "Cars are obsolete" at a time when Detroit was afraid it might be true. She also morphed the remains of a Vietnam-era combat helicopter into a triceratops—a reflection on war. Her work put Pat Renick on the same footing as artist Judy Chicago, whose "Dinner Party" installation, a table set for history's fascinating women, was touring the U.S. at the time.

Over-the-Rhine wasn't just about phosphorescent painting or sculptural social commentary. The musical group Over the Rhine was coming into its own in a studio space across the street from me. A young, dark Mennonite guy named Linford Detweiler had teamed up with a blonde singer of ethereal beauty named Karin Bergquist.

My radio show, *Music from the Hills of Home*, was on WNKU from noon to 3 p.m. on Sunday afternoons and when we first met, Karin told me about how she'd get in her car and drive east toward Georgetown until she lost the WNKU radio signal, then she'd turn around and drive back to Cincinnati. She did this every Sunday, because, as she told me, I played women artists—interesting women artists that she didn't hear on other stations—and she wanted to know what they were doing.

I was equally charmed by Linford Detweiler, equally drawn to his intelligence and to his measured way of doing things. When we talked he paid attention, his head cocked, his shaggy brown hair just brushing his collar as we discussed music. He was kind and softspoken. Most musicians are endlessly fascinated with music. "Who's your favorite band?" "Whose songwriting skills do you admire?" Linford was a remarkable young man who had the good fortune to meet his soulmate. He understood her gifts; and she understood his.

The magic of what the two became when they came together to form Over the Rhine was due in great part to the way that Linford was able to translate Karin's vibe into an ensemble style using different musicians. From the first, they took Cincinnati by storm.

Early on, they captured their music on small, four-track machines in their space on Main. Here was garage-band music-making at its best—as inventive as Les Paul and Mary Ford, who figured out back in the 1950s how to overdub singing and guitar playing on a four-track tape machine and revolutionized recording. Since they wrote all their own music, Over the Rhine had no royalties to pay, and they teamed up with photographer Michael Wilson, also on his way up, who did their wonderfully moody CD covers. Every news release that went out, every picture, every publicity hand-out was done by Wilson. His sepia-toned images of them became as iconic in Cincinnati as Andy Warhol's Campbell's soup cans.

Over the Rhine started out with a small, enthusiastic group of fans who came to every concert, and as tradition and legend grew up around them, people gradually began leaving gifts of roses on stage, as reverently as Europeans do. A couple of years ago I read a poem called "The Hills Before Christmas" at their annual Christmas concert. Behind footlights piled high with roses, I stood at the podium and looked out at the audience in the Taft Theatre. I was amazed. Every seat was full; the Taft was as packed as I had ever seen it.

I was a musician myself, and I know how hard Karin and Linford worked in those early years. What I don't understand is why we all did what we did, unless it was that magic, freewheeling, raucous world that was Over-the-Rhine.

I remember when the New Year arrived in 2001 because I had just written my first sonnet. It was about the moon at its apogee—the apex of its trip around the earth. There were painters and dancers around me who had created works to celebrate it, and I was inspired too. It was a privilege to be part of the community, and the richness in spirit there had never been so strong. The year ahead promised splendid achievement piled on splendid achievement. At least, that's the way it seemed to me.

Then, on April 7—a Saturday—a nineteen-year-old named Timothy Thomas was shot and killed by a police officer in a dead-end alley off Republic Street. Thomas was unarmed—the second unarmed Black man to die in police custody in five months. The first question a lot of people asked was why was he running. But it seemed obvious to me. He was running because it was the middle of the night and that's what you do when you're in the wrong place at the wrong time in Over-the-Rhine.

Anger and frustration hit the Black community in Over-the-Rhine hard. In the oppressive heat and humidity the following week, it passed from person to person in lightning bolts of rage. One afternoon, just as a rainstorm hit, I saw the bottled up energy explode—hot dog carts in front of the court house being overturned, newspaper stands being knocked down. As the mob moved up Main Street, they broke out windows in Kaldi's, in the Over-the-Rhine Foundation office. A few blocks away, at Findlay Market, they did enough damage to bring business to a screeching halt.

I spent as much time out of doors as I could, watching events develop. On Sunday—a week after the killing—I sat down on the back step of the Belmain with one of Main Street's homeless denizens—a guy called The Bluesman. He was puffing on a hand-rolled cigarette, talking fast, more than a little manic, his eyes a washed-out blue, his skin a puffy red color from sleeping in doorways in the sun. The Bluesman had epilepsy—among other problems—and his brother came down to Over-the-Rhine almost every day to bring him his medication. I didn't know it then, but by the time the year was up, the Bluesman would be dead.

After a few minutes, I walked to the front of the building. The entire terrain had changed. The street was blocked with at least ten police cruisers. Helicopters were flying low. A large unruly line of people was walking towards us on Twelfth Street. I'd later learn they were coming from Timothy Thomas's memorial near Washington Park.

The sun was shining, and except for the drone of the helicopters, a deathly quiet permeated the air. For a long time it was a stalemate. The protestors stared at us, and we stared back. For a while it seemed like nothing would happen, then the earth under our feet seemed to move and the police fired a volley of rubber bullets. It all seemed to be happening in a kind of slow motion, as things do when the situation is desperate and too extraordinary to be quickly understood. But in that frozen moment, I understood one thing for certain. *Now*, I thought, *a change has come*. I wanted to scream, to stop it, but no sound would come from my throat.

It would take months for the change to play out; musicians played benefit after benefit to keep Kaldi's open. But eventually the doors closed on so many places.

"Nothing gold can stay," the poet said, and those were golden days. All my young friends have gone on to at least moderate success, so the seeds that were planted back then must have fallen on fertile ground. The last time I was down there—and it is still painful for me to go—I saw the Belmain looking beautifully restored, with Dan Korman's "green" store where Kaldi's used to be. Best of all, the corner of Twelfth and Main has a large, freshly painted bicycle rack.

Maybe it's time to revisit my old dream of urban cycling. Or maybe I should just stick to walking. I've always been good at that.

OUR LADY OF COURT STREET (2010)

"I've always pictured myself playing the guitar," Bobbie Corbean said to me one morning the summer before last when we met on the corner of Court and Vine streets. "And I think you're just the person to teach me."

I choked on my cappuccino and prepared to run from the prospect of correcting yet one more chord progression played by one more struggling novice ("Let's just try a C there instead of a B…"). But I hadn't reckoned on Bobbie's determination. Which is how I happened to find myself on a hot afternoon in June climbing three flights of stairs in the graceful old building where she lived, armed with a package of guitar strings I'd just bought at a pawn shop in Over-the-Rhine.

My friendship with Bobbie wasn't new. We'd known each other since the 1980s when we were always turning up for the same awards or grants. I remember the meetings, the photo shoots, the wonderful camaraderie with other artists and community activists, even though I don't remember who won or what the awards were. But I never really got to know Bobbie until the last few years of her life, which ended last October.

When I moved from Main Street to West Ninth—what I jokingly call "Midtown"—I was delighted to find that Bobbie lived across Vine Street and one block up from me on Court, in the Court Vu apartments. The Court Vu, like the legendary Dakota in Manhattan, was one of those buildings coveted by artists, actors, and musicians who longed to live in the high-ceilinged rooms with Rookwood tiled fireplaces and marble in the baths and hallways. Outside, pin-tucked brick patterns accented the facade, and large shade trees protected the building from hot Cincinnati summers.

The drawback was that the Court Vu had no elevator. Bobbie, who was 81, dismissed the three flights of stairs she climbed every day as "good exercise." To me it felt like climbing Mount Rushmore. When she reached the top, she was as serene and untouched as a yoga master, and I was panting like a second-rate nag at River Downs.

Going in her front door made it all worthwhile, though. It felt like happening upon an ancient souk in Marrakech. The thick, smooth walls of her foyer were hung with zebra skins, and every available space had been filled with art, plants (she had gorgeous orchids), pictures lovingly framed, and interesting pieces she had collected from friends and lovers from all over the world. "Good" art hung beside paintings she'd kept for sentimental reasons, incense burned, and gauze diffused the light that poured through the windows. The effect was exotic. If Sidney Greenstreet had walked into the room wearing a fez and offered us Turkish coffee, I wouldn't have been surprised.

"Now I have to tell you," she apologized when she opened the door to me for the first time, "this is a no-shoes environment. Shoes bring in the outside world."

"Good point," I said and started unlacing. (Jazz pianist Ed Moss later told me he always checked to make sure he didn't have a hole in his socks before visiting Bobbie.)

The strings I'd picked up at the pawn shop for her guitar were the wrong kind: they were for a flat-top guitar like my own; she had a folk guitar instead. I tried to explain it to Bobbie, but she was disappointed. "Well, damn!" she said, as if she had intended to learn to play the guitar that very afternoon. Bobbie did not like being thwarted. She didn't pout long, though, and after awhile we had a glass of wine and promised ourselves to try the guitar lesson another day. While we drank, she talked a little about her long and interesting life. "I was born over in the West End, honey," she told me. "But I had my heart set on Paris."

I could picture her there, like Josephine Baker on the Left Bank, framed by feathers and diaphanous chiffons. But Paris had to wait. Before she could light out for the City of Light, Bobbie had responsibilities to a husband, Walter Corbean, and two daughters. She knew she was creative, and she operated within that skill-set to earn a living for her family. She worked in retail and in the 1950s opened a "charm school"—the kind of place where she could help girls, specifically African American girls, learn manners and modeling skills and develop the self-esteem that would help them navigate social and professional settings. She became the buyer and fashion coordinator for the Lane Bryant store downtown—the first time a Black woman had held that sort of position in Cincinnati.

By the 1970s, Bobbie's children were grown. And although she would forever call Walter Corbean the love of her life, her marriage had ended. She was ready to spread her wings, and the opportunity came through another bold Cincinnatian. Doug Crutchfield, the son of a Baptist pastor who had defied his family by going to New York to study dance, had moved to Copenhagen to perform and teach. When Crutchfield suggested Bobbie visit him there, she did.

Copenhagen was a revelation to her; it set her free. She admired Scandinavian fashion—the subtlety of design, the lightweight fabrics, the clean lines. In Copenhagen, that twinkling city, she honed her sense of style and launched into the kind of life she'd only dreamed of, in a place unlike any she'd ever seen. She began modeling almost immediately (the Danish took to her brown skin and curly hair and lithe figure—traits "that weren't selling in the United States at the time," she told me dryly, but without rancor), and eventually landed a job with a government department created to promote the fashion industry.

"I was the first American director of the Scandinavian Fashion Center," she said. She managed press relations, launched shows, and kicked-off seasons. It was an era when companies such as Dansk and Marimekko were setting the style, and she was in the middle of it. She'd gone from Lane Bryant in Cincinnati to working with the great fashion houses of Europe, and she made herself at home.

※

Once she established herself in Copenhagen, she was finally able to travel, and she did it as she did everything, with great flair. She walked the banks of the Seine in Paris, saw the fashion centers in Milan and Rome, and eventually found her heart in Africa. Her Court Vu apartment was filled with the mementos of those trips: Kenyan weavings and jewelry, an antique ivory broach, a necklace of what looked like tiger's teeth, and copper ankle bracelets to ward off "Old Arthur," as she called her arthritis.

Traveling changed her, or perhaps it accented who she already was. She learned to love the ocean and exotic islands. The sea, that giver of life, was part of her vision of herself, and as she got older and traveled less she still managed to walk the beaches once a year in Cancún. "Taste the salt from the ocean and be healed," she'd say.

One morning, I saw her standing on the corner of Court and Vine, looking as willowy as a girl, dressed in tan pants and a brown tee shirt, a kerchief tied just-so around her neck. She was wearing large, dark glasses, like Greta Garbo. She kept one hand in her pocket, because she didn't carry a purse.

"Have you ever had a shot of wheat grass?" she asked me when I caught up with her.

"No," I said, "but it sounds like something I'd like to try." So Bobbie and I walked up Vine to Total Juice Plus, where Bobbie insisted on paying. "The first shot is on me," she said, laughing like a crafty drug pusher. "You can buy the next."

The green liquid came in small pleated paper containers, like pill holders, with a choice of orange or lemon slices offered like salt and lime after tequila. The juice tasted like the essence of life—or maybe that was just Bobbie. She had a way of making ordinary things seem memorable.

After that first shot of wheat grass (which did make me feel strangely energetic) we saw each other every few days on Court Street, swam at the YWCA on Walnut, or ran into each other at the bus stop on the east side of Vine Street. She was such a buoyant person she lifted the atmosphere just by standing on the corner talking.

Her closest friends were Rob Dorgan and Steve Bolia, a pair of designers she had met when they owned the Left Handed Moon, a quirky gift shop just down Court Street from where she had opened her own place, Ms. B's Marketplace, in 1990. Rob, now a partner in the Over-the-Rhine design firm Studio Vertu, remembers her as an artist. "She loved the process more than the finished product," he says. "Even a dinner party, for her, began days before the event. Shopping for the food was part of the process. She'd go to Findlay Market and pick just the right ingredients. After dinner, when we offered to help with the dishes, she'd insist that we leave them until the next day. 'Tomorrow when I do the dishes I'll re-live everything and visit with all of you again,' she'd say."

On a crisp day last winter, Bobbie and I met outside the Court Vu by chance, and she told me that her doctor had found a mass in her lung. She was scheduled for a biopsy.

"Are you afraid?" I asked, and she dropped her eyes. The good news came back later that week that the tumor was benign.

"Good," I said. "We'll still have time for those guitar lessons."

Meanwhile, I had my own medical situation to attend to: back surgery. I had been diagnosed with a lot of fancy names like "stenosis," "scoliosis," and "degenerative disc disease," but Bobbie simplified things. "Honey," she said, "it all means arthritis, and it's a misery."

Not long after, she started complaining of pain in her chest. She said she thought the anesthesiologist had nicked her lung when the biopsy was performed. But that wasn't it, of course. The tumor turned out to be malignant. "I'm not going to have chemo or radiation," she said. "It might kill those bad cells, but it will also kill the good cells. I need to concentrate on keeping those good cells healthy."

She began packing her fine art and having it photographed and appraised. She wanted to sell it and use the proceeds to establish a foundation for young girls. She donated a classy dress and hat to the Cincinnati Art Museum. Like a guest who had stayed too long at the party, she was getting ready to leave.

It was Ed Moss who reminded me that Bobbie was a great jazz fan. In the 1980s, after she returned from Europe, she ran a contemporary version of the Cotton Club, an old West End nightclub, newly envisioned by Bobbie to inhabit a space by the Convention Center. Ed was the music director. The new Cotton Club was short-lived; what endured was her relationship with Ed, which went back many years to the days when they had worked at Babe Baker's, the city's premier jazz joint before the Blue Wisp. In the 1960s, everybody stopped in Cincinnati and played at Babe's, according to Ed, who led the house trio along with tenor saxophonist Jimmy McGary. Bobbie was Babe's right hand. Ed's impression was that she was a partner in the business and a facilitator. Or, as he put it, "She was the cat that poured the oil on troubled waters, you know?"

In those days, with race issues coming to a boil all across the country, the NAACP was leaning on Babe to put a Black trio in his club. "Biggest Black club anywhere, and they had a white trio," Ed said. "We had to stay in the kitchen during our breaks, because the place was packed every night."

According to Ed, Bobbie persuaded Babe to keep Ed's trio in spite of the fact that they were white. "I would not deny myself the privilege," she famously said, "of knowing someone just because they're different."

Ed still laughs at the memory. "Bobbie never drank anybody's Kool-Aid," he said. "I'm going to miss her. I never had a bad time with her."

Michelle, one of Bobbie's daughters, developed multiple sclerosis, which is what brought Bobbie home from Copenhagen in the early 1980s. She worked at the elegant Gidding-Jenny department store for a while, did fashion shows for Shillito's, even put out a quarterly high-style magazine called *Mode*. In the 1990s, she opened Ms. B's, her charming consignment shop on Court Street. The Court Street area was a lively neighborhood back then, with the Left

Handed Moon, Avril-Bleh & Sons Meat Market, Tony Sparta's Italian grocery store, and open-air market stalls a couple days a week. Bobbie's store was stocked with the kind of "gently used" merchandise—vintage coats, dresses, hats—that only Bobbie could have put together.

The hats she'd collected—some of them with elaborate, starched veils—would have been a boon for the costume department of *Mad Men*. They were small, fitted to Styrofoam head forms, a feather going this way, the tilt of the hat fixed with pins at clever angles. I remember seeing a lovely, buttery cashmere cardigan in that shop, too, alongside Bakelite jewelry you might have expected to see at the flea markets along the Seine in Bobbie's beloved Paris.

There was never a trace of disappointment that life had circled back to Cincinnati, separating her from the excitement of Europe and the rich pleasures of the world's fashion capitals. It was as if there wasn't a place in her vocabulary for a word like regret. Rob Dorgan likes to quote her mantra, that "life is what you make it."

"She'd say, 'If you get stuck in the fact that you are Black or gay or whatever, that's your decision,'" he recalls. "'But, honey, be sure not to blame the world or wait for it to change. It won't.'"

Bobbie eventually hung up her own hat and retired, but she never lost her discipline, her passion, her love of life. She always had some kind of project going on, and she always wrote—diaries, notebooks, and journals overflowing with her stylish script lined the shelves in her apartment. As a child in grade school in the West End, a teacher had told Bobbie she had beautiful penmanship. "Nobody had ever told me anything about me was beautiful," she told me once, matter-of-factly. So, for the rest of her life, she wrote to express herself with the one trait she'd been complimented on.

She never drove a car, but it didn't hold her back. Ed Moss told me she kept right on visiting his club at Schwartz's Point until a couple of months before her death. "Omar brought Bobbie down whenever she could make the scene," Ed said.

"Who was Omar?"

"I don't know," he said, smiling. "He was part of Bobbie's world."

Bobbie died in October and was buried at Spring Grove Cemetery. I didn't know how to feel. I had lost the sound of her voice, lost the memories, the small fantasies that make life bearable. So one day I put on all the make-up I could find in the dusty drawer where I keep it for "special occasions." I used a tiny bit of silken eye cream, dabbing it on gently with my little finger. I followed it with concealer, then just the tiniest bit of powder to set it. I blushed, bronzed, fluffed, and buffed and put on my best outfit and went to Saks Fifth Avenue.

It was the perfect thing to do. The sales personnel at Saks knew Bobbie and were sorry to hear of her death. They put blush on "the apples of my cheeks," as they called them, and slipped tiny gift packages in my shopping bag.

I realized I'd stumbled into Bobbie's milieu. It *felt* like her. At the perfume counter I sprayed myself with a touch of Chanel No. 5, and I seemed to see Bobbie smiling that magic smile of hers, as if a genie had materialized out of the bottle. She pushed me up the escalator to the second floor, where I saw stacks of cashmere sweaters in bright blues and yellows.

"This is more like it, girl," Bobbie whispered in my ear, admiring a turtleneck on our way to the Italian designers. "Look at this," she said, showing me the certificate of authenticity attached to the Armani jacket I was reaching for. She draped me in plum-colored scarves of silk so light they seemed to have no weight at all, then topped it all off with a large-brimmed hat, looking at me mysteriously from under its brim.

"Don't be so serious, girl," she seemed to say, as she used to do back on Court Street. "Forget that arthritis. Strut down the runway like you are somebody. Remember: Get up, dress up, show up!"

What fun she was. For the life of me, I've never figured out why she wanted to take guitar lessons.

6
NOSTALGIA

THE MOON ON MAIN STREET AT RENSLER'S PORTRAIT STUDIO.

HOW HIGH THE MOON

Carteaux and Leslie, a very fine used book store just a few doors from the corner of Vine and Court Street, is presenting an exhibit called *Rensler's Revisited: A Fresh Look at Vintage Works From a Venerable Cincinnati Portrait Studio*. I hadn't noticed when I moved here to Court Street that the elegant book store, with its front door set back from the sidewalk, was the same store I visited in 1980 with author John Baskin, but when the old photographs went up on the last Final Friday, the memories came flooding back to me.

In those years, when John and I went about together, he interviewed the owner of the shop, June Rensler, for a book called *Prairie Fires and Paper Moons*, for David Godine Publishers, and he granted me access to his notes about that long-ago interview.

June Rensler's father opened the shop in 1906. A lot of immigrants, fresh to the city, wanted postcard portraits to mail home and June noted they seldom smiled. "Did they think it made them more intelligent?" she asked herself. John had a different conclusion. He thought it more likely that people didn't smile because the exposure times were long; "hard to hold a smile for half a minute without it turning into a *rictus*," he said.

Photography had only begun to appear in the Civil War, and June Rensler said her father had been influenced by field reports of a younger brother who ran away from home to work with a traveling photographer. And so the Rensler shop coincided with this international epidemic in picture postcards. Her father lived on bananas (five cents a dozen at a little market up the street) and couldn't even afford all the supplies he needed. When customers lined up on the sidewalk, an assistant collected the money from everyone, then ran out and bought film.

For twenty-five years he never had a key to the front door because he was open twenty-four hours a day, ignoring the blue laws, which said he was supposed to be closed on Sundays. (On Sundays, his assistants ran the shop and when they were arrested he came downtown and bailed them out—the fine was cheaper than losing the day's proceeds.) He did this until the laws changed. "I wore them out," he told June, satisfied.

Halloween was a great night for the shop, although it frightened June, this young girl looking at nearby Over-the-Rhine, the costumed adults festively roaming the by-ways and alleys (sort of an extended gallery hop, and probably not a lot different than today, if everyone were disguised as a beggar). Sometimes she locked herself in the car. The same customers came over and over. June remembers one old German from the neighborhood who came in every weekend. "Mama, no flowers tonight!" he said, handing Mr. Rensler the last of his money.

The backdrops were done by itinerant painters who were always a little drunk—pale men who worked at night and, like elves, finished in the early morning hours and were never seen again. According to June, the patrons were infatuated with the moon. They sang to it, counted the days until it was full again, and wanted their pictures taken with it, so June's grandfather made one. It was a great sickle of a moon, with a face on it, and the customers loved it.

If you're too young to remember *Paper Moon*, the movie with Tatum O'Neal, or the song, you might remember the scene in *Sweet and Lowdown*, that Woody Allen movie in which the eccentric jazz guitarist, played by Sean Penn, tried to perform on a paper moon. Mr. Rensler's customers had their pictures taken over and over on it until "the luster wore off of it."

Mr. Rensler taught June the trade, but he would never allow her to have one of the newer box cameras "the little people use." Photography was a respected craft to him and he was treated respectfully. "Like a doctor," he said. "Go back and look at the Rembrandts," he told June. "Study the lighting. Photography is all lighting. It is the play of light on a flat surface that gives the illusion of the third dimension. You *must* have shadows ... "

He thought that in twenty years he had made a half a million prints. He built a new house and told his family it was made of postcards. The business lasted until WWII, and after that time so many things changed.

When John found the shop in 1980, Mr. Rensler's portrait was in the window, one of the few he had allowed of himself. He wore a hat, a topcoat, and held his cigar at a jaunty angle. June was still making postcards, only she used a piece of developing paper and cut it into the correct size. By the time John found her, the moon had worn out.

APOTHECARY

Piatt Park is lit up for Christmas. Its graceful wintery arches are hung with garlands of swag, and the twinkling night lights make it look like a snow globe someone shook up and left to settle. William Henry Harrison, majestically astride his horse on the west end of the park, faces a bronze statue of President Garfield at the other end. Garfield was a politician from Ohio who managed to stay in office for six months before he was assassinated. (People had a shorter fuse back then when it came to presidents.) The park is how I imagine a Parisian quarter might look on a festive, foggy night.

A lot of Cincinnatians say Garfield Place instead of Piatt Park, probably because it's hard to pronounce. My friend, Lib Stone, who is on the park board, says Cincinnatians have always called it "Pie-ette" Park, with a long "I," although the family who gave the land in 1815 pronounced their name, "Pea-ette." In any case, it's Cincinnati's first park, and the land was given to the city for a market almost two hundred years ago.

Benet's Pharmacy is in the Doctor's Building at the east end of Garfield Place. It has been there since 1925, seventeen years short of a century, and the minute you walk inside the door, you know you've made a find. An old-fashioned institutional-green scale sits just to the left of the front door, with a slot where you can put in a penny and get your weight and your fortune. Like the scale, the rest of the pharmacy has been largely untouched by time: the cabinets and fixtures are the same ones pictured on the wall when Jonah Benet and his brother owned the place. The 4711 cologne and the displays of Kent hair brushes and combs have been there since the eighties, at least.

Since its opening, it has been buffeted by the winds of fortune, but the little shop on Garfield Place is still there, looking unlike any drugstore you've ever seen. When the Volstead Act was passed and Prohibition came along, you could buy alcohol at the drugstore, in some form or another. When the downtown doctors moved up to Clifton, Benet's became a "neighborhood pharmacy." Now, with the advent of large chain drugstores selling everything from laxatives to hair spray, Benet's has become more a niche pharmacy. They make many of their own compounds, especially for dermatologists, and they still carry and order the old favorites, like Father John's Cold Syrup, Black Draught, and the infamous 666 Cold Syrup.

Pam Kohrman bought the business from Joe Palermo (who is still a pharmacist there) a few years ago because she feels a commitment to the community and to the spirit of Benet's. "It's truly not like any other store," she says, running a hand through her short, brown curls. She and her employees, are a family of a kind, she says. Mary Lou and Julia run the cash register, the accounts, and the orders, and keep things lively, pick-up and delivery. It can get hectic: phones ringing, people demanding to know why they can't get their oxycontin refilled without "goin' through a mess of doctors." The deliverymen come and go quickly, often stopping to call their customers from the phone behind the counter to tell them, "I'm leaving now … please be ready for delivery."

"I think we provide a service to the community," Pam says, juggling my questions, a phone call, and a customer who is asking for a special order of Camay soap. "We used to just deliver within a five-mile radius, but that is expanding. We try to serve Over-the-Rhine, too," she adds. In Over-the-Rhine, there are no drugstores at all, and many of the older folks in that community have no way to get their medicine.

I asked her if she had any favorite creative ways of circumventing the doctors' orders on prescriptions. She laughed and said, "Our customers are a pretty good bunch, but I do remember one person who came in one time and said 'the pills flew out of my lap, over the bridge, and into the Ohio River.'

"I felt this sense of continuity, you know," she says, talking again about having bought the place. "Joe owned it for so long, and before that Jonas and Harry Benet owned it. There's just a feeling about the place; it's a great store, I think."

My dog, Sister, agrees. Benet's is her absolute favorite destination. She likes to lie under the ceiling fans on the cool black and white-checked linoleum while we wait for a prescription to be filled. We watch people come in and go out, in various forms of sickness and health, in wheelchairs and on canes and crutches, the lame and the halt. In spite of their physical misery, though, they are friendly with the staff, even cheerful while they're in the restful atmosphere of Benet's.

The outside world is often indifferent and cold, and at Christmas the phony tinsel and canned music can exacerbate our feelings of isolation. Telemarketers flood the phone lines with pre-recorded messages, and old-fashioned pharmacies have mostly gone the way of the small savings and loans we used to patronize. But Benet's is still a beacon: as unique and inviting as it ever was, as much a part of the fabric of Cincinnati as the statue of Garfield, outside the door, its brass arms raised in a seasonal benediction to a proud city, struggling through development to find its own authentic way.

BLUE CHRISTMAS

The first time I went Christmas shopping in Cincinnati was in the late 1960s. I had just moved from Alabama, and I was away from my family for the first time. Lonely doesn't even begin to cover the emptiness I felt. I moped around instead of unpacking household goods. My husband had been transferred to General Electric at Evendale, so I had to make a new path for myself, find a new way of life, and I had to do it all at Christmas.

I knew no one, but I remembered my father's admonitions about being in a new place. "Don't criticize anything about the city," he'd say. "Put yourself out for people." So I didn't complain when I got lost on Harrison Avenue ("Always take a sweater when you're going to the west side of town," a new friend's mother advised me), and I tried baking pumpkin pies and leaving them outside the doors of our new neighbors on Thanksgiving. By Sunday evening after the feast, the pies were still there. My neighbors had, like Perry Como, gone "home for the holidays." Making friends, with my thick Southern drawl and country-girl ways, looked like an uphill climb indeed.

Two Saturdays before Christmas I couldn't shake my lethargy. I felt I had to go someplace where I could see people and lights or I would simply fold. I ended up downtown, at Shillito's department store. I parked in a large covered lot across the street from the old telephone company. It was a dreary December day, snow blowing, the cold seeping through to my bones because the coat I had on was too light. It had been made for gentle Alabama winters, not the bitter Midwest. But I warmed up as I made my way to the most popular department store in town. Its front window glittered with Christmas pleasures: a lavishly lit tree, mannequins in formal dress, oversized tin soldiers, sugar plum fairies, toys of all kinds, and plaster models of joyful children unwrapping bicycles and games. My spirits began to rise.

Inside the store, scarves and hats were nearest to the door, so that someone like me, who ventured out poorly prepared, could accessorize herself against the damp and cold. "You could get great gloves at Pogue's," my friend Susan Abernethy Frank, who started her retail fashion career working at Shillito's, once told me. "But at Shillito's they taught you how to wear them." She pretended to put on a pair of kid gloves, smoothed them down, then ran her right index finger between each finger of her left hand to settle the glove precisely. She grinned at me, her eyes sparkling. "In no time at all, the gloves fit like a second skin."

Shillito's was crowded with shoppers that day—so crowded you had to elbow your way to an escalator or one of the Art Deco-style elevators.

Sportswear and formal wear were up two floors, then another floor up it was foundation garments. (Years later, the Katie Laur Bluegrass Band played for a bra and girdle-fitting clinic at the top of this escalator. The young men in the band kept imagining they were going to get a peek of forbidden fruit; no such luck.)

Housewares and furniture were on the top floors where I eventually purchased my first grown-up bed, after years of sleeping on a mattress on the floor. Carpets hung from the ceiling, along with lavish drapes and lacy cotton curtains. Walk a little farther and you were in the linens and then the small appliances, whirring away on the display counters like tiny robots: magical coffee grinders, blenders, pasta makers—anything that could be plugged in. And all the while the loudspeakers played "Let It Snow!" and "White Christmas" to get you in the mood to shop.

I roamed through the store, bottom to top and back again, and Christmas shopping worked its magic on me. By the time the Muzak was looping through the second chorus of "Silver Bells," the throngs of busy shoppers and decorations and lights made me chipper once again.

In those years, Fred Lazarus III was still president of Shillito's. He was part of a dynasty of retailers (his family owned Bloomingdale's in New York), and he had his own ideas about class. He had been stationed in France in World War II and was a connoisseur of food and wine, so Shillito's had an excellent selection of imported wines, cheeses, pâtés, and a very good lunch counter, with a menu selected to offer new and different food choices at reasonable prices.

I'll never forget Fred and his inimitable wife, Irma, coming to a bluegrass festival where I was performing years after I got to know them. I had told Irma to pack a picnic lunch, and she brought a sparkling white wine, pâté, Brie, fruit, and a baguette. Picnics were Irma's favorite activity and she didn't mind that she was seated next to people who were eating baked beans and corn bread, hot dogs and potato chips.

I came to know the Lazarus family in the 1970s, and one night when Fred and I were alone in his study having a brandy, he told me a little bit about the store. Shillito's had been started, he told me, by John Shillito, who worked as a clerk near the public landing in the early part of the nineteenth century. He sold dry goods to the steady stream of steamboat passengers, riverboat gamblers, and people on their way west: the adventurous spirits who floated down the Ohio River to Cincinnati on flatboats, where they outfitted ox-drawn wagons for the next leg of their journey.

While Fred talked, the fireplace crackled, and I heard the occasional barge making its slow, mournful way down the river. In my mind, I could see the raucous scene at the public landing, smell the smells and hear the noise: dock workers coiling and uncoiling the ropes that moored the boats to the harbor; steamboats picking up and discharging passengers, packet boats dropping off mail and other goods. There would have been many merchants like John Shillito, I'm sure. But his business prevailed, growing into the department store that the Lazarus family acquired in 1930.

When Fred came home from World War II, things were about to change in Cincinnati's retail scene; he saw to it. "We wanted to move party dresses," he said dryly. "Irma was involved with the symphony, the opera, the ballet, and I suggested they host some dress-up events. So ... women had to have party dresses for these events, and we'd fill the windows with mannequins wearing wonderful dresses with blown-up pictures of the event invitations. That got the women buying dresses at Shillito's. And, as I said, we helped support the arts organizations."

He took a sip of his brandy—looking satisfied with himself, his eyes hooded like a snake's—as the fog moved over the river, covering everything like a vaporous blanket. It could be downright spooky up there on that hill, especially in the winter.

I never knew much about who owned Pogue's, the department store in the Carew Tower, but I knew it was definitely "for the carriage trade"—the wealthy customers who shopped for jewelry at the exclusive Newstedt-Loring Andrews on the south side of Fourth Street, Bankhardt's Luggage, and of course Closson's, where you could buy heavy silver flatware, exquisite china and crystal, notepaper from England, even soaps from France and—on the second floor—fine art in Phyllis Weston's gallery.

Pogue's lingerie department displayed its merchandise with the same reverence that Closson's bestowed on Baccarat crystal; the silken peignoirs and the spaghetti-strapped charmeuse confections were all kept under glass. I especially remember the bedroom slippers: mules with two-inch heels and marabou puffs on the toes—the kind of shoes you'd see in a Fred Astaire movie, worn by Ginger Rogers with a long silk dressing gown tied at the waist. A lot of men came to Pogue's lingerie department for their wives' Christmas presents. You'd hear them telling the sales clerk, "Well, she's just about your size … maybe a little shorter and broader in the hips."

Downtown was a retail mecca then. People drove up from Louisville and Lexington, stayed at the Netherland, and ate at Maisonette or Pigall's before they started their Christmas shopping. They'd stop at Henry the Hatters for men's ties, and at Henry Harris, a small, exclusive women's dress boutique tucked into the southwest end of Carew Tower arcade, where old-fashioned fragrances like Lilly Daché were packaged in luxurious striped boxes with silver bows. Serious shopping went on at Henry Harris, and at Christmas they kept a well-stocked bar to fortify their clients.

But the jewel in the crown of Cincinnati's retailing community was Gidding-Jenny. You'd walk in the front door, smell the fragrance of Odalisque, the store's "signature" scent, step onto the thick cream carpeting, and you were in holiday shopping heaven. Cosmetics were on the first floor, and not just cosmetics, but luxury creams, fabulous oils, expensive perfumes: Estée Lauder, before it became a household name, and Chanel No. 5. Does anyone besides me remember Polly Bergen's Oil of the Turtle? It was touted as the most luxurious of creams, sure to give wrinkles the slip.

The beating heart of the store, though, was behind cosmetics. It was where your purchases were toted up, your charges made, your packages wrapped. I don't think I ever saw a cash register at Gidding's. Instead, your purchase slip was placed in a pneumatic tube along with your check, your money, or your charge account information. The transaction was sucked up to the office, where charges were OK'd or denied, change was made, and checks approved, then the bill of sale was returned through the same tube, flashing back like something out of science fiction.

At this same counter your purchase was packaged in ridiculously thick royal purple wrapping paper and placed in a royal purple shopping bag with the name of the store in gold. In fact, at Christmas, everything was gold at Gidding's: the wrapping paper, the bags, the bows were an orgy of gilt. Straight back through sportswear, at the other end of the store, was the table with Gidding's legendary eggnog bowl. It was silver, and when you approached, a man dressed in white livery served you your grog with a sprinkle of hand-grated nutmeg on top—not in a paper cup, mind you, but in a tiny plastic disposable glass which you could walk around the store sipping while you shopped. It was spiked, too; it lowered your inhibitions and gave you a feeling of euphoria, as if you were floating on a cloud. To add to the luxurious holiday spirit, the store hired models to stroll around in fur coats and evening gowns.

Gidding's third floor was for designer clothes. You sat down, gave the sales lady your size and told her what you were looking for, and it was brought out and presented with a practiced flourish. It was all in the wrist: *Whoosh!* The skirt of the dress fell in a peacock spread as if it were being shown to the Queen of England. If that frock didn't suit, another saleswoman was right behind, and—*whoosh!*—another dress.

The prices on the third floor were out of my league, but I went there once with a friend. She wasn't really planning to buy anything, but she had asked me to go with her because she was a little intimidated by the store. My companionship gave her sufficient courage; she ended up dropping about $1,000 on a couple of outfits in one afternoon. It was a breathtaking amount of money to me. But she wore the clothes for at least ten years, and every time she put them on, she looked sensational and felt that way, too.

After Christmas the gloves came off, so to speak. That was when Gidding's had the Attic Sale—truly a dog-eat-dog affair. Women went to the fourth floor well-dressed and well-mannered, and came out looking a fright: hair out of place, runs in stockings, and eyes glazed. They'd go in to the Attic

Sale sane, but when they got in there and saw the prices, they were foxes in the henhouse: fur and feathers flying, teeth sharpened, feverishly snatching up bargains and trying on clothes in the middle of the floor willy-nilly. I knew a woman whose own jacket got sold right from under her nose; she'd taken it off to try on another, and by the time she got back to it someone had bought it and carted it off in a Gidding's bag. The store only had attic sales twice a year—maybe because it took six months for customers (and saleswomen) to recover.

McAlpin's was the people's choice. A popular, moderately priced haven, it was crowded at Christmastime with exhausted shoppers vying for seats in the tearoom for lunch. They served Boston brown bread and cream cheese, and bracing cups of hot tea (something rare for me, a Southerner, accustomed to lots of ice and sugar).

Hathaway's, the only familiar place still open downtown, is famous for its egg salad sandwiches on white toast, and it continues to look like a scene in a 1950s Technicolor movie. The waitresses' hair is swirled up like the curl on top of a Dairy Queen cone or like spun sugar, a pencil occasionally stuck behind an ear, ever ready to take your order.

My first Christmas in Cincinnati away from my family was one of the hardest holidays I've ever celebrated. My theory is that lights and lavish displays were invented to take the weight off our memories, and while the brick-and-mortar stores I miss each year made Christmas magic, it takes more than shopping to make Christmas memorable. Nowadays, we can shop on our smartphones (I'm sure they have eggnog somewhere, and there's probably an eggnog app), but where's the fun in that? Yet every day, I'm aware of more little shops popping up everywhere: small local endeavors coming alive in Montgomery, in Oakley, in Hyde Park and Clifton, even in Bellevue, Kentucky, and my prediction is that we may see an active local retail scene once again.

Certainly we will have joyous holidays, for there's still nothing like a sprig of mistletoe or the pungent scent of a fir tree to evoke Christmas nostalgia. Go shopping. Hide your presents. Surprise people. And have the merriest of Christmases.

URBAN LEGENDS: THE DARK SIDE

A couple weeks ago, I was sitting with Tom Wolfe outside his Chicken Pot Pie Restaurant near the corner of Court and Vine, and suddenly Tom pointed his long arm like a basketball center about to dunk one. "That's the dwarf," he said dramatically, his eyebrows pointed for emphasis.

"The dwarf?" I said.

"The dwarf." He replied.

I looked but just then the 78 Metro bus went past, obscuring the people on the corner for a moment. Suddenly, I saw him plain as day. His upper torso was normal; his legs were short, straight kegs. He had straight brown hair held in place with a band tied around his forehead, so that he looked like an Apache.

"I saw him two years ago on some damn West Coast cop show on television," Tom said. "He got fifteen-to-life."

He laughed and took a drink from the plastic glass on the table. We were sitting outside on Vine Street, just like we did last summer in the balmy spring air. The breeze blew like sweet perfume. Since Tom had put a table and chairs out in front of his business, a young couple walking home from the library sat down and joined us.

They wanted to know what was so remarkable about the dwarf. "Well, he's like one of those urban legends," Tom said. "People who hang out at night in bars downtown have seen him. I think I was working at Japp's when I first saw him. He was incredible."

I remembered standing with Greg Schmidt outside of Kaldi's and watching him do backflips into the dumpster then shinny up a couple streetlight poles. Greg, who admires all efficient mechanisms, admired the dwarf tremendously.

"Look how strong he is," he'd said to me that night.

Tom said, "The trouble with the dwarf was he'd backflip into the second story window and curl up inside a box or under a desk and spend the night. It made the business owners crazy."

I've known a lot of street people who might be called urban legends (they were real, though some of their stories might have been exaggerated). Mr. Spoons was one of the best known. He put adhesive tape on soup spoons and played at least eight at a time as well as I've ever heard them played. He used to dance through Aunt Maudie's on Main Street in Over-the-Rhine when I was singing with a bluegrass band back in the seventies. In those days, before he won first prize on *The Gong Show* and went to New York, he sold cheap, plastic corsages and rolled his eyes at pretty ladies.

"Spoons done won *The Gong Show*," Caldonia said to me once, taking her tap shoes out of a shoebox tied with rough twine. "He's hit the big time now." Caldonia had tried out but didn't make it, and she looked as if she were still mad about the whole thing. "He's beat me forever."

I met Caldonia at Arnold's Bar and Grill back in the early '80s. She was a tiny Black woman who started out tap dancing on street corners in Louisville and she was still plying her trade. "Caldonia, Caldonia," she'd sing, "what makes your big head so hard?" It was the refrain from a Louis Jordan song of the swing era. She said he had named the song for her, but it could be that she took her name from the song. She lived in Section 8 housing up on Reading Road, on Social Security, I guess. She died sometime in the eighties, and I remember hearing talk about a pauper's grave.

In the end I think her family buried her. I hope so. She was one of the best tap dancers and all-around entertainers I ever saw, even if there was something a little off-kilter about her. She was fun for a few songs, then she'd get ready to leave, and she'd always ask the audience to "give Caldonia a standing rovation."

I remember Johnny Rosebud, too. He'd come by with fresh flowers, a scruffy growth of beard, and a ripe body odor. He had one song he liked to sing, and if the band would play it, he'd take the microphone and belt out "Kansas City" in a grizzled voice, spitting all over the ball-shaped part of the mic, his arms stretched out like Jackie Gleason.

Tom Wolfe has been something of an urban legend himself, though he's well groomed and is an elegant conversationalist. He was a Marine, then a seminarian, a profession he supplemented for awhile as a bartender. His longest bartending job was at El Coyote, east of town. He told me once that women had been his ruin, and I have seen more than one pretty girl drive by in a Mercedes or a BMW convertible, blow the horn, and yell, "Wolfie!" It always makes him sheepish.

When he started making chicken pot pies he found his niche, and you could see him nights delivering pies in pizza warmers to bars with hungry patrons, to parties, to offices. He was everywhere, laughing, affable, kind-hearted. He once showed me a letter from Ronald Reagan congratulating him on saving a boy from drowning in a swollen creek in the dead of winter. He framed the letter. It was beautifully written, and it congratulated him on his heroism. "I had Reagan on speed dial for months," he said, laughing.

We liked to exchange stories about the different "characters" we've known. He was the first person to tell me about the 9 o'clock rat, a large rodent which ran across Vine Street from the alley to the back of the library every night at the same time. I watched for that rat many a night last summer, and it was true. You could count on him like the mailman. Every night at 9 p.m., the rat dashed across the street. He hasn't shown up yet this spring.

Tom says it's the economy.

7
GREAT BARS

KATIE AT ARNOLDS. MUSICIANS DIDN'T GET RICH PLAYING THERE,
BUT MUSIC SOUNDED BETTER AT ARNOLDS, AND NO OTHER
PLACE IN TOWN HAD ITS LATE NIGHT AMBIANCE.

ARNOLD'S COURTYARD

Music sounds better when it's played outside, and the best place in town to listen *al fresco* is in the courtyard of Arnold's at 210 East Eighth Street. Nobody knows why it sounds so good. An engineer friend of mine says it shouldn't. "They've got a cement floor and brick walls," he said. "All the surfaces are hard, yet it sounds better than anyplace in Cincinnati. It just doesn't make sense."

Like so many things which are great about this city, Arnold's courtyard doesn't make sense, yet there it is: a paragon of acoustics and sensational sound right in the middle of town. The old wooden stage is hot, and the tables are scattered around so that they are all facing the performers. The lines are strung with Christmas lights, and you can hear the low buzz of plates clattering, patrons laughing and talking, and over it all the sound of jazz bands, banjo pickers, fiddles, washboards and jugs, even Jake Speed's harmonica.

Park your car and walk across the street on a starlit night when the notes of "Moonglow" rise from a clarinet like champagne bubbles, hanging on the heavy, humid air. The bridge, "We seemed to float right through the air," spins down the scale, full of yearning intervals, while the piano fills in the empty spots, and the drummer brushes like Bill Bojangles tap dancing on a sand-covered floor. Or listen to a five-string banjo, bearing down on "Shuckin' the Corn," and feel the rhythm flow through you like your heart beat.

So many interesting musicians have played at Arnold's it's hard to single one out, but Bobby Guyer, who played trumpet with Benny Goodman back in the day, was one of everybody's favorites. He wandered in one night looking bewildered, his glasses crooked, wearing polka dots on top and stripes on the bottom (like the test pattern on a television set, trombonist Bill Gemmer later said); then he licked his lips a few times, put his trumpet to his mouth and blew everybody out of the water. Harry James didn't have a thing on Bobby Guyer. He had played in the big Hollywood musicals with all the stars on the MGM lot. He'd even dated Carmen Miranda, "the chick with all the fruit on her head," he told me. ("We grew pot in the dresser drawers," he said once, talking "under water" as someone described Bobby's raspy, whiskey-soaked voice. "The cops didn't know what it was; they busted us for liquor.")

Arnold's was restored by Jim Tarbell in the mid 1970s, and the story goes that he discovered the courtyard by accident. It was full of rubble, and had been sealed off for years behind a concrete wall. After Jim re-opened it and added the carved wooden doors, he brought everyone in to play—local musicians, plus talent that was passing through.

One night in the early eighties, he called everybody he knew on the phone and said, "Get down to Arnold's tonight," and there he presented the world-renowned jazz guitarist Marty Grosz (who collaborated with Woody Allen on the music in some of his films). That night the place was packed, it was hot, and there were no seats left. Marty was in town from New York to play for the Hamilton Jazz Society, and he worked with his old friend, Cincinnatian Frank Powers, on clarinet. The music was so good that it sparkled in the light like diamonds, and no one moved for three hours.

I went to work at Arnold's about a year after it opened. I played with bluegrass bands and began singing with Buck Pfeiffer and the Rhythm Rangers on Tuesday nights, then later with my own classic jazz quartet, "The Dream Band." Certainly a lot of those summer nights in the courtyard were hot, but we'd drink pitchers of water and aim fans strategically, and by the second set, it always seemed cooler, a slight breeze blew up and played sweetly around our faces. By then we had blown the dust out and sweated out the tension, and our muscles were so loose we came out swinging like angels dancing on the head of a pin.

October marked a kind of melancholy. We played "Autumn Leaves" and "Autumn in New York" as the yellow gingko leaves fell from the Tree of Heaven, as we called it, carpeting the concrete floor of the courtyard like a treasure of gold coins. We always noticed when the first leaf fell. It meant that summer was drawing to a close, and that the beautiful music, riding lightly on the air like the gingko leaves, would fall silent for a time.

We stayed at Arnold's through the winter so that we could have the summers in the courtyard; it was our time to dream impossibly romantic dreams. The leaves were like notes of music riding lightly on the air, falling silently, leaving a hint of sadness in their wake. Those were halcyon nights, and though we put on sweaters to combat the October chill, we couldn't stretch the magic. It was gossamer; we could not hold it.

BLUE NIGHTS

I went downtown on a recent Friday night to see the Blue Wisp Jazz Club in its new location. When I slipped in at Seventh and Race, leaving the rattle of city life behind me, the band was playing a fresh, lilting take on Antonio Carlos Jobim's "Desafinado," the sensual rhythm of the bossa nova wrapping the listeners in its tenderness. The sound of Phil DeGreg at the piano mingled with the tinkling of glasses and the low murmur of conversation. Candles flickered on the black four-top tables. The place was packed; the joint was jumping.

The Blue Wisp, like the Blue Note and the Village Vanguard in New York City, simply refuses to die. It is in its fourth incarnation now, a long way from its beginnings in the 1970s in O'Bryonville. The new trappings are a little slicker than that smoky bar on Madison Road I used to love so much as a wide-eyed, aspiring jazz singer. But the essence of the place is the same: it's all about the music—and the characters who love the music.

Marjean Wisby and her husband, Paul, opened the Blue Wisp in 1977, but it took Jimmy McGary and his tenor sax to put it on the jazz map. McGary assembled a band for the Wisbys' bar—Pat Kelly on piano, Marty Wittow and Don Gauck on bass and drums respectively—and things began to look interesting. Unfortunately, musicians and bar owners will fall out occasionally, and

Steve Schmidt—a wonderful guy and a huge talent on piano.

that happened between Jimmy and Paul. Alex Cirin had the gig "for a minute," as musicians say, and in 1979, pianist Steve Schmidt landed the job at the ripe old age of twenty-two, along with bassist Michael Sharfe (who was followed by the redoubtable Lynn Seaton, now on the faculty at the University of North Texas), and John Von Ohlen on drums. The Schmidt-Seaton-Von Ohlen Trio was so good it raised the bar for all musicians and made it easy to get good out-of-town soloists to come in for weekend guest spots.

Indeed, the players who gigged at the Blue Wisp could have been the Who's Who list for *DownBeat Magazine*: sax man Scott Hamilton; guitarist Herb Ellis, fresh from his years with the Oscar Peterson Trio; Thelonious Monk's sideman, Charlie Rouse; and so many others. The brilliant Art Farmer came in from New York with a young Fred Hersch on piano and Bob Bodley on bass. Then there was "Little Johnny C"—Johnny Coles. According to Steve Schmidt, the legendary trumpeter was old-school all the way, traveling like a no-name. "I'd meet him at the Greyhound bus station every time he played," Schmidt reminisced to me recently. "He was a sweet cat."

One of Steve's favorite acts was Sun Ra's band. Sun Ra was a bandleader who sincerely believed he was born on another planet, and, appropriately, wore robes of state and some sort of celestial space gear on his head. During shows, a dancer performed with a lit torch, and at the end of the night the band walked off stage playing "Zip-a-Dee-Doo-Dah." Steve said the band had some crossover following from the Grateful Dead, some old hippies from the '60s among his groupies, who kept asking Sun Ra if he was a vegetarian. "They would stand there sort of reverently," Steve said, laughing. "'No, man,' Sun Ra snapped. 'I had some friends who were vegetarians, and they're dead.'" As Steve recalled, Sun Ra liked to chow down on Kentucky Fried Chicken or Burger King.

In those days I was a bluegrass musician who loved music, and you know what they say: the more you love music, the more music you'll love. And so I fell in love with jazz—with its longing intervals, its intelligent lyrics, the sheer exuberance of it. Hanging out at the Blue Wisp on my free nights and after my own gigs gave me a window into its magic, and into the complex minds of the people who made it.

In O'Bryonville, the Blue Wisp had an office of sorts behind the bar where the musicians could go to get away from the audience and one another. I used to sit back there working *The New York Times'* crossword puzzle with Al Cohn, a tenor saxophonist from New York City, who had recorded with Stan Getz and Zoot Sims. He'd walk onstage searching his memory for the answer to fifty-one across, then launch into the most cogent, musically intelligent tenor sax solo you might expect to hear. Even when words failed him, music never did.

⁂

Paul Wisby died in 1984, and Marjean became the beating heart of the Blue Wisp. She was as much a presence as a wooden carving of a mermaid on a ship's prow. She was middle-aged when I first got to know her, and she looked like the actress Anjelica Huston—straight brown hair and bangs but with a round, pudding face. She had a distinctive voice, too, a cross between a growl and a witch's cackle, and she sat behind the bar smoking and watching the action unfold around her like a modern-day Madame Defarge. When I'd come in at midnight from a bluegrass gig, she'd look at my clothes to see if I'd been working. "You been screechin' somewhere?" she'd say, smiling at herself and blowing a little smoke at me.

Marjean was fond of many of her customers. She had nicknames for all of them (I was Kitty Litter) and had stories about most of them. One of her favorite tales involved Leo Underhill, a WNOP disc jockey. As she told it, one night at the old Madison Road location, Leo was having a drink and listening to a band. He requested "Green Dolphin Street," a jazz standard. For whatever reason, the band said no and counted off another song—which irritated Leo.

Now, Leo was known to drink a bit, and he could be a character. (He once showed up for his early morning shift at WNOP in the back of an ambulance accompanied by two "unregistered" nurses.) This particular evening he sat and thought about the band's refusal, and according to Marjean's version, decided that the problems jazz was facing certainly had to include the fact that this band did not know "Green Dolphin Street."

Within fifteen minutes or so he was heckling them mercilessly about their incompetence. "Do you even know the first chord?" he asked, his big eyes growing larger behind his glasses. "Well, I do."

With that, he got up and made his way to the front of the bandstand, evidently prepared to direct the ensemble through the treacherous shoals of

"Green Dolphin Street." All of a sudden he experienced a wardrobe malfunction. Just like that, with no preamble, no warning, his pants hit the floor. Leo looked around wildly, grabbed his trousers, and fled to the men's room.

For the rest of the night, Marjean tried to coax him out. "Leo," she said, "People need to use the bathroom!"

"Marjean, don't make me go out there," he responded plaintively. "Ever'body's seen my underwear."

I've heard it said that this was how Leo acquired the moniker "Old Undies" from the other disc jockeys at WNOP. It sounded right when Marjean told it, but I don't know if anyone is still standing who could attest to this story.

⁂

In 1989, Marjean and the Blue Wisp were forced by rising rent to leave the O'Bryonville location. Luckily, downtown had a place for the venerable jazz club—an empty space in the basement of the Doctors' Building on Garfield Place. Getting it up and running took time, but on opening day I was as excited as a Reds fan. I can remember going in through the door, hearing the sound of the music, the scuffle of the horns playing off the swing of the rhythm section. Suddenly I couldn't get down the stairs fast enough.

Wednesday nights were when the Blue Wisp Big Band played, and in the basement at Garfield Place they lifted the roof off the building. Everybody who was anybody showed up: Rosemary and Nick Clooney (George Clooney has already spent a couple nights at the new Blue Wisp, I heard); Tony Bennett; various Cincinnati Symphony Orchestra players; actors from traveling companies; even hair god Vidal Sassoon. Music was happening; jazz was alive and well at the Blue Wisp, and if you were a fan you simply had to be there, to stand in front of the stage and listen to it for a few minutes before you even sat down. That's how strong its pull was; that's how hard it hit you.

Steve Schmidt moved on in 1993; Phil DeGreg soon took the job as pianist and head of an ensemble that included Bob Bodley on bass (newly returned from New York) and Art Gore on drums. I'm sure I sang with that trio at least fifty times during the Garfield Place years—and that's not counting the times the featured horn player was too tipsy to toot the last set and Bob or Marjean might call me and say, "You're gonna make it down tonight, aren't you?"

I'd hesitate. "I thought I might stay home and practice my guitar tonight."

"Well," the gentle plea would continue, "the trumpet player isn't holding up too well, and it would be totally cool if we had somebody to help him make it through the last set, you dig?"

Of course I'd hop in my old Ford and head down, in case the trumpet player passed out or something equally dire occurred.

In those days at the Blue Wisp, you could anticipate the arrival of various local musicians around 11 or later. They'd turn up after their own gigs were through, dressed in tuxedos. Cal and Susie Collins came, if Cal was in town; Terry Moore and Bob Poe stopped by after their nightly gig with Shirley Jester at the Terrace Hilton; Ron McCurdy usually stopped by with a bit of Irish brogue and twinkling blue eyes. The pianist Ed Moss made the scene nightly about 1 or 1:30 a.m. in his signature beret, his hair pulled back in a ponytail, a cigar in hand. And when major stars were booked into the club, Dee Felice would be sure to show up, his long face serious behind his hep-cat goatee and aviator glasses, his own tux the sharpest outfit in the joint.

I was usually the exception to all the swell dressers, dropping by in blue jeans after my gigs. (I recall hocking possessions to make the stiff cover charge when Scott Hamilton was in town.) If you didn't know what was going on you'd think a flock of giant, suave penguins had invaded the city under the cover of darkness. But it was the cognoscenti, the true lovers of the art form, the people who practiced jazz day in and day out. Their presence was a clear tribute to the music that emanated from the club.

I can say I heard some of the best music I've ever heard in my life sitting among them in the audience at the Blue Wisp. And as a performer, it was always an honor to be behind the mic. I even got to sing with Cal Collins and Warren Vache at the first Blue Wisp location, after Cal and I had done a special for Channel 48 in 1981.

"Here's one you better know, sugar," Cal said, grinning like Wile E. Coyote. Then without further ado he kicked off "Stars Fell on Alabama." I was completely taken by surprise, so my knees were knocking like ball-peen hammers. But I made it through the first chorus, gave Cal and Warren a chorus each, and came back in on the bridge. It was hard coming back in on the bridge, but as I recall I pulled it off. I was just a chick singer, and I had no idea if it was the right key or not.

In 2000 Marjean's lease expired and she moved the Wisp again, this time to 318 East Eighth. I went along for the ride, but I never really "made the hang," as the musicians would say. My ardor cooled as so many friends and colleagues died. Cal was gone and Kenny Poole, Terry Moore, Dee Felice, and Morgy Craig, too. Then, in 2006, Marjean herself died. After that, I went down to the Wisp a couple of times. But I couldn't make myself stay long, and I couldn't make myself return.

While I was out of circulation, the musicians and fans who loved the Wisp scrambled for a way to keep it alive. Cincinnati attorney Eddie Felson bought the club in 2007 and last winter moved it to its present, more advantageous location at 700 Race Street. After years of scuffling, it seems like it's finally in the right place at the right time, with a little something for everyone. The jazz room is separate. The bar area features plenty of enormous plasma TV screens for sports events, and the club books in blues as well as some occasional New Orleans music for different tastes.

Some things haven't changed. The Blue Wisp Big Band still gathers on Wednesday nights, still led by charismatic drummer John Von Ohlen. And now with hipper digital leadership, the Wisp has its own website. This makes me smile. I remember how hard Marjean used to work to figure out how to program the club's small telephone answering machine. Every week she'd laboriously recite the names of the featured acts for all seven nights. There'd be glitches, mispronunciations, start-overs, some laughter, and more start-overs. Many times I recorded the information about the upcoming acts because everybody else got tongue-tied.

What would Marjean have made of a website? I think she'd have been amused. She'd have taken a puff off her slim cigarette, tossed her hair back slightly and said, "What's a web?" Then she'd have turned to important things, like musicians who'd been on break for way too long.

"Hey, Richie," she'd have yelled at the red-headed bandleader. "It's time to get the animals back in the pit! You dig?"

A COMET OVER NORTHSIDE

It is a lush, green summer evening in Northside. Inside the Comet, a popular bar on the corner of Hamilton Avenue, the crowds are already claiming tables and taking seats. In front, a group of women holding places for friends chatter about homes and families and jobs. The rise and fall of their voices makes a soothing sound, like cicadas, and the light streams through the window behind the stage. The early evening seems somehow comfortable. Old friends, a familiar setting, the anticipation of entertainment.

About 6 or 6:30, the band members drift in one by one, carrying instruments. They are the Comet Bluegrass All Stars, a bluegrass band that has played Sunday evenings at the Comet for about nineteen years, according to their leader, Eddie Cunningham. "We started playing here on Sunday afternoons," he tells me, with a wry chuckle, "but we kept moving it back to accommodate the crowds until now we go from about 7:30 to 10:30."

The Comet All-Stars Band has been accommodating crowds since their inception. The band has served as an incubator for some of the finest string players in bluegrass. Guitar player Tim Strong started with this band, and Brad Meinerding started here on mandolin before his move to the popular band, Over the Rhine. Jeff Roberts has played banjo with Eddie for most of those nineteen years. Missy Werner plays mandolin and sings lead and harmony. Her husband, Artie, plays bass. John Cole, who is relatively new to the local bluegrass scene, plays dobro.

Years ago, I had been sure the band could not sustain the loss of a musician like Tim Strong, but I hadn't reckoned with Harold Kennedy. Harold has taken over the guitar slot, and the band is rock solid. He takes outrageous liberties with the timing, grinning impishly as he makes you wonder whether he will make it back to the melody line on time. He does, of course; he is always in control. Harold Kennedy has brought originality, a totally different sound, to the band. He came from Nashville where he traveled for years as lead guitarist with country bands like Rascal Flatts and Hank Williams III. He married a woman who lives here, decided to quit the road, and Nashville's loss was our gain. Harold is a joyful player to watch. The stage is his playpen: his guitar licks are exquisite, elegant and surprising.

The Comet Bar is popular with many bands (Steve Schmidt holds his annual jazz Christmas concert there); and that could be because it has wonderful acoustics. It is an old wooden bar with stools on the tavern side and tables and chairs on the musical side. It is decorated with black and white pintucked tile like a bar from the '30s or '40s. The bartenders are neatly dressed men with white butchers' aprons wrapped around them. If they had parted their hair in the center and worn handlebar mustaches, the setting could have been the early 1900s.

I order a Diet Coke and watch Jeff Roberts unsnap the clasps on his banjo case. It makes a reassuring sound like a loud click, like the sound of released tension, and I wait for the inevitable banjo chord. It is not long in coming. When the band takes the stage, Missy Werner kicks off a bluegrass chestnut on the mandolin. "I'm on My Way Back to the Old Home," they sing and with Eddie, Jeff, and Missy singing harmony, the band sounds as good as any bluegrass band I've heard. The dobro rakes a rhythm in the background, and the instruments respond to flat picks with deep resonant sound. Eddie fiddles a solo, or a "break" as it is called in bluegrass, and I can hear gasps from the audience as the excitement builds.

Eddie radiates warmth, congeniality, and his own brand of self-assurance. Certainly he has succeeded in putting together, and keeping together, a band which is a reflection of himself, of what he values musically, what he needs to hear to feel satisfied.

"Ed Cunningham was a one-man bluegrass revival for Cincinnati," says Larry Nager, a music historian and anthropologist who lives now in Nashville, Tennessee. "Ed came along as the great 1970s Circle/Dueling Banjos boom was trailing off and with sheer force of will kept the Tristate bluegrass scene going. He was musically ambitious, always singing great and playing anything with strings, but he never was in it for the ego stuff. If I were still doing the CAMMY's he'd have gotten a Lifetime Achievement Award years ago."

Larry's quote goes right to the heart of Eddie Cunningham: hard work, and an ear for excellence. He augmented his own talent with a backbreaking schedule. Between his day job with the City of Cincinnati (he worked in the housing inspector's office) and building a musical brand, he did the kind of heavy lifting that young musicians seem sometimes unable to grasp.

He started with Jeff Roberts on banjo in a band they called the Ohio Valley Rounders, playing traditional bluegrass with the same sure footing that they bring to the Comet Band. A band named Kentucky 31 came next with Trina Emig on banjo and the late Terri Boswell on guitar.

The Comet Band is basically a spin-off of the Ohio Valley Rounders with a more sophisticated repertoire and style. They have recorded extensively, and delighted audiences at clubs like the Comet on Sunday nights for nearly twenty years. They have played with the Cincinnati Pops Orchestra maybe a dozen times; and they are old enough to have acquired some polish and some exposure to other kinds of music. When the set winds down the musicians take their first break, setting their instruments aside and walking energetically toward the bar to pick up diet sarsaparilla or whatever musicians drink nowadays.

Eddie takes a seat beside me, and I can't help remembering when I first met him. Maybe in the early '80s when he was about twenty years old, skinny as an adolescent and so good at everything he tried he was already a prodigy.

He sang with a rich baritone voice, his notes pure and clear, his guitar playing already excellent.

"My grandmother," he says now, "used to say anyone who had been given so many gifts owed a debt." That has bothered him. "What kind of debt," he wondered, how long would he owe it, how much did he owe. It's a rare insight into Eddie's thinking, for despite his sensitivity to music and art (he is an excellent painter), he is an enigma.

Eddie's large Irish Catholic family was musical. His brother, Jimmy, taught himself to play blues guitar in the style of Mississippi John Hurt. Another grandmother gave him piano lessons. His uncle was a singer named King Fox who performed regularly at taverns around town. Another of Eddie's older brothers, Billy, used to work at Arnold's where he was a very popular bartender. When he wasn't mixing beverages, he could be coaxed into sitting in with the band and singing in his thick, gravelly voice, "Lulu's Back in Town." He was a dynamite singer, but he only knew two songs: besides "Lulu," he could knock it out of the park with "Good Night, Irene." I'd say, "Billy, you'll never amount to much if you don't learn at least one other tune."

"Don't need another song," he'd say deep in his chest, "I've said all I got to say with those two songs."

When I heard Eddie all those years ago, I hired him to play guitar on an album I was making at the time, and he did the gig. The record was never released, but Eddie and I continued to work together now and then. We wrote music, did the score for two plays for Children's Theater, and wrote several songs we liked, a couple of which have been recorded by other artists. Eddie used to show up at my apartment on Main Street with plenty of yellow legal pads, pens, a rhyming dictionary and *Roget's Thesaurus*.

He never gossiped nor spoke a negative word about anyone. He was drawn to songs that told a story, to songs about the poor and downtrodden. He was drawn to music that told the stories of the unfortunate. But I had to piece that out for myself; he never mentioned it.

When Eddie's nephew, David Cunningham, bought the Comet in 1995, Ed asked him what night of the week they might need a band. "Sunday afternoons," David replied, and so the Comet Bluegrass All Stars were born. With a steady once-a-week engagement, the band was able to grow. Its repertoire expanded and its collection of hot licks and hot songs began to take shape. The cardinal rule was that no matter what bookings came through, attendance at the Comet was required, and like the Blue Wisp Big Band, which became popular for playing every Wednesday night at the Blue Wisp, the venue and the band reinforced each other's reputation. You might say they rubbed off on one another.

I was on the first CD he produced, *Sunday Nights Live at the Comet,* a double CD which included many of his favorite players in Cincinnati traditional music. He put out one limited edition recording of the Ohio Valley Rounders with some excellent Jimmie Rodgers material on it, as well as Stephen Foster's "Hard Times" and "My Old Kentucky Home."

Missy Werner, the Comet singer who also plays mandolin, and I found time for a short talk during a break. She has her own "spin-off" band with which she performs in addition to the Comet Band, as well as other "jam" bands. The Missy Werner Band is cheerful, and upbeat, and after talking to her I realize that she is sensible and down to earth about her career, much like Eddie. She holds a full-time day job, yet has managed to release a few CDs, one of which was recorded in Nashville. She is up for awards from the International Bluegrass Music Association, which will be presented when the IBMA convention takes place in September in North Carolina, and she has been selected to be part of a showcase for up and coming new bands at the same convention.

When I ask her about Eddie, she tells me his success is due to the fact that he has a versatile voice. "He isn't stuck in any particular niche," she said. "He can sort of do everything." Missy gives me a wry smile. "I like that he chooses original material to record. For our last CD, thirteen of the songs were written by band members. Listen to *House of Dread,*" she says. "The last CD. It's my favorite. The songs are stories."

"What I like about Eddie as a bandleader is that we never rehearse," she says and laughs. "We are all just too busy. We may get together at a gig early and run over some material we've been wanting to take onstage, then we just get up and play it. Eddie has gone so far as to put a chord chart in front of my feet sometimes so that everybody can look down and get an idea what the next section of the song should sound like. We're at the point where we don't need to practice as much. We have grown together."

As twilight slides into darkness, the lights in the bar fall on the players and elevate them. Onstage again, it is as if Cinderella's fairy godmother has changed them into a fancy band like the Rolling Stones wearing silken shirts and tall boots. They are already running overtime, so they won't have time for a full set, but Eddie is likely to go on longer if the spirit moves him.

Paul Patterson and Sylvia Mitchell have joined the audience. Both of them are violinists in the Cincinnati Symphony Orchestra and the Pops Orchestra, and both of them drop in occasionally to play with bands like the Faux Frenchmen or the Comet Band or just to sit outside in the Comet's garden and eat burritos. In fact, the Comet Band played with the Cincinnati Pops this past Christmas when they were joined by Roseann Cash, Over the Rhine, and other musical guests for a festive three-night celebration of the holiday.

Brad Meinerding, who plays with the band, Over the Rhine, comes in to claim his old place on guitar, joined by Paul Patterson on violin. The band plays an instrumental which has fire and flash, then go on to challenge themselves with less familiar material. It is when the guest musicians sit down, though, that the band hits its sweet spot. Eddie calls "The Train Carrying Jimmie Rodgers Home" and the harmony that Jeff Roberts and Missy Warner add to the chorus is as delicate as antique lace. The audience falls silent until it is over, and then they give up a huge ovation. Another couple of gospel songs, each better than the last, and the band begins to case their instruments and head towards the bar.

"I love that song about the train and Jimmie Rodgers," I tell him.

"I like the start of the song," Eddie says. "It's where the father holds his little son up to see the train. He wants his son to see it because it is a piece of history, because the songs and the singer will go on forever. It seems so … so American."

Jimmie Rodgers was the first country music singer to record back in the 1920s, and his records sold like hotcakes, making him a star during the early Depression. "He had tuberculosis," Ed tells me, "and died when he was pretty young.

"Stephen Foster lived in Cincinnati for a while. He wrote 'O Susanna' here. Somebody told me that when he died—he had TB—he was penniless, the man who wrote 'Camptown Races' and 'Beautiful Dreamer.' When they found him in a room in a hotel he had something like twenty-six cents in his pocket and a scrap of paper on which he had written 'Dear Friends and Gentle Hearts.' Maybe he had started another song." Eddie stops and takes a breath. "He didn't even live to be thirty."

Maybe that was the price he paid for his "gift," as Eddie's grandmother called it. Maybe not. Guitars and banjos and fiddles are back in their cases now, the clasps locked.

I watch the bass player, Artie Werner, take each microphone from its stand and place it in a special carrying case, then wrap the microphone cords around his other hand and lay them gently into their case. There are shouted "good-nights" as the band members file out the door into the summer night, the near horizon luminous with fireflies, the air still alive with music.

THE QUEEN OF DIXIE'S

Back in the late 1970s, May Stidham, called "Daisy May" by her many friends and admirers, was a powerful presence on Short Vine, or Corryville, as it used to be called. You could usually find her perched on a

Naugahyde bar stool at a now-defunct joint called Dixie's Bar up on Short Vine back in the mid-1970s. Dixie's was the last of the working class bars in that old blue-collar neighborhood, and like such places, it was its own little world.

Daisy May liked the bluegrass music my band played. "Fiddle me that 'Sally Goodin'," she'd rasp, and she'd get up and do a grotesque little dance, her body stiff and fragile like one of the wooden dancing dolls you see for sale at the Appalachian Festival. She was a tiny old woman, a crone really, with hair the color of coal dust and a face patchy with rouge. But if the map of eastern Kentucky was written on her face, she kept herself well groomed. I can see her there now, sipping her highball slowly, her soft hands carefully manicured, the fingernails painted bright red.

She said she was sixty-eight, but Julian the bartender said, "I've tended bar here thirty years, and she was here when I came. I swear that old dame's 105." Julian, no spring chicken himself, was slender and white-haired and wore his white bar apron tucked in his belt. He was speaking softly so that Daisy couldn't hear him. "And she ain't aged a day. She's a survivor!"

Dixie's, where Daisy May spent most of her time, was one of those fern bars so prevalent back in the '70s. When I first started playing there on Thursday nights, it had a low ceiling and cheap signs advertising J.T.S. Brown and Pabst Blue Ribbon beer; when the city began to spruce up the parking on Short Vine, a new owner took out the dropped ceiling to reveal a pressed tin one (an acoustic nightmare). Then he hung a lot of potted plants around the room and put in a menu which was heavy on avocado and sprouts. The old regulars bore all this change with a minimum of complaint and continued to gather in the dark, womb-like belly of Dixie's for their afternoon libations, ignoring the University of Cincinnati college students who had overtaken the neighborhood.

Corryville was on the cutting edge then: hippies selling incense and hand-made sandals (and probably marijuana). Paraphernalia stores sprang up, and a used record store displayed albums by the likes of Jimi Hendrix and Janis Joplin. Daisy May didn't like their looks. "That boy needs

Daisy May Stidham held forth on a Short Vine bar stool for years. That's Daisy on the left at the end of a New Year's celebration which seemed to have died early.

a haircut," she'd say. Rock music didn't play her kind of dance tunes. I don't know if she ever knew anything about The Cupboard, which sold pornographic sex toys and marijuana pipes, but I'm fairly sure she never ate any of the pizza that seemed to follow college students everywhere they went. The Firehouse on the northwest corner of Short Vine became a high-tech restaurant with exotic dishes like sun-dried tomatoes. Chefs were becoming glamorous.

The patrons of Dixie's had little to do with these temporary residents. These drinkers were people from "the old neighborhood," and Dixie's was their stronghold. Many of them had known each other for thirty years, and taxicabs had stopped daily at Dixie's for their inebriated clientele. They were like members of a country club, only shabbier.

Daisy liked to talk about politics. "That durned Ronald Rayburn, or whatever his name is, a-cuttin' folks's checks back. Did you ever hear of sich a thing?" Daisy said. She pointed her finger at the man on the corner bar

GREAT BARS

stool. "I'm a'gonna write him a letter." Her voice, pitched low in her chest, rose to high levels at the end of sentences.

The man on the corner bar stool had been slumped there for some time, invisible, but he came to life now. Like most everyone else in Dixie's, he was over fifty and from the old neighborhood.

"Aw Daisy, save your breath," he said roughly. "President Reagan won't never get no letter that you write."

"He might," said another man sitting near the pool table.

"I could finish it tomorra. Harold's got to take me to the doctor," she said firmly.

The man who was asleep at the end of the bar stirred suddenly, and said, "That's all women ever does is go to the durn doctor. I'll tell you what doctors wanta see. Doctors wanta see the Long Green." He rubbed the fingertips of one hand together in a "gimme, gimme," fashion.

"That Ronald Raeburn is the worst of the lot," Daisy said, fumbling for a cigarette and sipping on her drink, a Seven & Seven.

Somebody put a dollar in the juke box, and at the loud downbeat, Daisy got startled and dropped her cigarette. "I'll be durned," she said, her hair somewhat tousled by all this unexpected activity.

I miss the Appalachian population in Cincinnati. They laughed and danced and sang mournful songs. They migrated to Cincinnati in the late '40s and '50s because it was easy to get here; they stayed because it wasn't as bad as most cities. I knew Joe Jones who was born in Over-the-Rhine and became known as "Mr. Spoons." He'd dance through bars on Main Steet, selling tacky plastic corsages, and playing a little pattern on your head with the spoons he carried in his back pocket, their handles wrapped in adhesive tape. I remember Caldonia, too, a black tap dancer who started out dancing on the street corner in Louisville for the coins people tossed in her direction.

Appalachians—or "hillbillies" as they are still called by comedians on late-night television—had never really assimilated themselves into the mainstream. Like Daisy May, they were able to keep their identities intact through their music and their story telling. When Over-the-Rhine was taken over by social service agencies, they packed up their rich culture and moved to Norwood and started opening "country-cooking" establishments that featured pinto beans and cornbread, and biscuits and sawmill gravy. I hope folks let them alone out there. I know they're having a big time.

SALUTE TO A BASS PLAYER

I went to hear Cal Collins play with the Phil DeGreg Trio at the Blue Wisp on Garfield Place, and the audience was elegant: miniskirts and Armani tuxes; young, glamorous people listening, by candlelight, to jazz.

Bob Bodley was playing bass, and I was momentarily transfixed, listening to him lay down a foundation of notes, followed by deep, silent spaces. Years ago, when I first sang on that stage with this trio, I could have sworn I felt electricity pass through Bodley to the piano player, then on to drummer Art Gore. "The bass is the earth," he said to me one night.

Bodley, now in his prime as a musician, is one of the "first-call" bass players in town. He spent fourteen years working and living in New York, playing with some of the seminal figures in the music business, but he came back home in 1990. The transition, he said, was easy. "Nothing much had changed," he said, laughing. He started playing with Ed Moss and Steve Schmidt and Jim Connerly, but he settled in with the Blue Wisp trio as soon as he could.

Bob was a tall man, slender with a face like an Indian's: high cheekbones and a full head of light brown hair, cut like that Dutch boy's on the paint can. His complexion was ruddy, like a countryman's. He had callused fingers, but before he quit smoking he could still roll a cigarette one-handed. Bob wasn't only cool—he was Clint Eastwood material.

"You dig?" he always said, and we did.

The pianist Steve Schmidt said of him, "Bob Bodley is a great bass player. He understands music from the bottom to the top. He understands the right bass note to play against the soloist, and he understands the middle voices as well as the melody."

Schmidt laughed a little. "I can be on a gig with him and forget the exact melody, and Bob is the only bass player I know who can sing it or play it for me. And you can hear it in his solo playing. When it's time for him to step up, he is a melodic soloist."

"I was a kid in the 1950s," Bodley told me. "These guys would come around and give you an accordion if you paid for and finished twenty lessons. You paid for the lessons, and if you learned to play the instrument, you got to keep it."

He did both. Just as he learned the E-flat lap tuba, a Dixieland horn, at Moeller High School. It was there—in fact, in the band room—that he picked up a discarded Kay upright bass, with only two strings, "put some new wires on it," as we say in bluegrass, adjusted the bridge, cleaned it up a little, and started playing gigs.

"I played my first gig when I was fifteen, and I just never stopped," he says. "You dig?" I nodded. "I was playin' bass, doing weddings, club dates, but I was still just 'two-fingering' it, really. Then I met Dee Garrett when Dee Felice was playing at the Buccaneer. He turned me on to jazz, to the repertoire, the changes, and concurrently I took some bass lessons. Eventually I met Ed Moss and started to hang there at the Golden Triangle. That was a six-night-a-week gig, too."

Bodley eventually moved to New York. He found work, sublet a loft, and figured he'd better try it while he could. He ended up working there for fourteen years. "The best thing about New York," he said, after a pause, "was that somebody like Miles Davis could be your neighbor."

He worked with Woody Herman's band, toured and recorded with Art Farmer, toured with Lionel Hampton, and worked with pianists Dave Friedman, Horace Silver, and Mose Alison. In the 1980s, he said, the scene in New York started drying up and for a while New York was dangerous. When his wife, Cynthia, inherited her father's house in Lawrenceburg, Indiana, in 1990, they moved and simply continued their interests and friendships.

I couldn't help thinking about how utterly confident he had been when he accepted that original accordion. "But how did you *know* you could learn it?"

"Just did," Bodley says. "Those little black buttons on the side? They represent the circle of fifths and extensions to the circle of fifths. It's cool. I liked playing the accordion. Anyway, that was the deal," he added. "You gotta pay for the hang. You dig?"

Epilogue: Bob Bodley died on Christmas Day of 2006, of cancer, and the lights at the Blue Wisp were a little dimmer that weekend. He had been a gift to us all and demonstrated how to live richly and honor our own gifts as artists and musicians. Phil DeGreg, who had become close to Bob over the fifteen years of their gig at The Wisp wrote a eulogy for Bob's memorial service. "He approached music with a combination of skill and humility," Phil said, "and being an extraordinary musician he always served the music. Everything Bob did enhanced the music, allowing it to grow organically rather than forcing it or controlling it."

Goodbye, Bob. We'll miss you.

SWINGIN' AT THE DEE FELICE CAFÉ

On Tuesday night I went back to the Dee Felice Café for the first time in many years. It was a damp and rainy January night; the fog was rising off the Ohio River and the lights of the restaurant twinkled, rising out of the northern Kentucky night like the bubbles in a glass of champagne. The sounds of the Dee Felice Swing Band leaked through the double doors, the rhythm, syncopated, the mood, jazzy, the tempo, upbeat. They were playing a classy big-band arrangement of Stephen Foster's "Way Down Upon the Swanee River," in their unusual perch over the bar.

Bill Gemmer and his long-time friend, Clarence Pawn, makes up the trombone section. Gary Winters plays lead trumpet, fortified by Jeff Folkens and John Zappa (the young trumpet player who founded the wonderful Rich Uncle Skeleton Band in the late '90s). The rhythm section of the Dee Felice Swing Band consists of Pat Kelly on piano, Carl Grasham on drums, and Mike Sharfe on bass. Mike, with his long salt-and-pepper hair tied in the back and a lanky scarf layered around his neck, looks like he might be a model in an Italian fashion ad. The reed section consists of Larry Dixon on baritone sax (the biggest horn, the one you can't possibly miss); Brian Hogg alternates on tenor, alto and clarinet, Jim Sherrick on alto saxophone, and Joe Gaudio on tenor. The night was beginning to feel a little less fragmented, the air a bit more settled, and Bill Gemmer counted off "Strike Up the Band," arranged in '30s-style swing, so infectious it could have been coming from a scratchy old record, yet positively full of life.

Bill Gemmer has always been obsessed with swing, with big bands, with vintage, or classic jazz. The sounds he lusts after were laid down by Jack Teagarden and Tommy Dorsey, Louis Armstrong, and Duke Ellington. When he was in fifth grade in Grandview Elementary School, he wanted to join the band. He came from a musical family and his brother took alto sax, prompting his father to prod the boys into emulating the Dorsey Brothers. "All the kids were playing trumpet and clarinet, so I messed around with them, but when the man put a trombone in my hands, that was it. That was what I wanted to play."

He attended Berklee School of Music in Boston briefly, then the University of Kentucky, playing and studying until he began to tour with the likes of the Hugo Winterhalter Orchestra in 1970, the Glen Miller Band in 1974, and finally the Tommy Dorsey Band with Buddy Miller directing. Tommy Dorsey was half of Bill's heart—the other was Texan Jack Teagarden. From those two, and the people they played with, Bill got the pitch, the grind, the slide, the bark. All those things he does with the horn are informed by his own artistic integrity, his own standard of excellence.

He invited the audience to dance with his own gorgeous version of "Getting Sentimental Over You," Dorsey's theme song. Arranger Al Kiger copied the chart from an old record, complete with the rich saxophone quartet which evokes the era so beautifully. Those aching intervals are filled with a desperate yearning, and the dancers take to the floor, melting into their partners like butter into a baked potato. It isn't easy to find bands that play the easy, rocking, rhythm of swing. That's because everybody gets tired of playing "I Got Rhythm" eventually, and one of the ways they keep it interesting is to burn it—play it fast and swing it hard. It keeps the players on their toes. Unfortunately, those attempts to break the sonic barrier are not as danceable. When Billy G's band is playing, you can feel the rhythm in the soles of your feet.

Larry Dixon sat down at the table for a minute between tunes. "What's different about this band," he said, "is that we concentrate on older music, the late '20s to the '30s, picking up sometime again in the '40s. Bill Gemmer is a superb player," he said. "His enthusiasm for that era powers the band."

Bill plays "I'll Never Smile Again," the Tommy Dorsey song which made Frank Sinatra a teen-age idol, with control and perfect pitch (if you're going to be a trombone player, you may as well reconcile yourself to high standards where pitch is concerned.) John Zappa sang Duke's "Love You Madly," and played one of his own charts, "Chestnut Ramble." Larry Dixon's version of the Fats Waller tune, "I Believe in Miracles," was fun and unexpected. The band followed it up with a mambo version of "Tequila," and finished the set with Count Basie's "Two O'Clock Jump," a barn burner.

In an era when our popular culture flickers in our peripheral vision like a computer game, big band music is still compelling. A young hip-hop friend of mine who is an artist, puts it this way. "Man, it just comes at you, right in your face," he says. "I love the sound of all that brass. It makes you feel like there are a lot of possibilities."

The Dee Felice Swing Band is one of those guilty pleasures you shouldn't even try to resist. The musicianship, the authentic harmony and power of the arrangements makes the music more than the sum of its parts. On nights like tonight, it can be transcendent.

GREAT BARS

HE'S FUNNY THAT WAY

It has been a slow, stormy spring, one where the trees shake and shimmy and their branches touch the earth. Thunder rumbles more than it has in years. Back in 1989, in just this kind of sultry weather, my roommate was killed, hit by one of the lightning bolts which struck every few seconds on that wild day.

I couldn't afford to live alone, so I got someone to share my apartment right away. A middle-aged trumpet player named Alan Kiger had just moved to Cincinnati from Muncie, Indiana, and was looking for digs close to the club scene. When I met Kiger for the first time at the old Blue Wisp in O'Bryonville, I had no premonition that we would become friends. He was in his fifties, a prime age for an artist of any kind. He had a broad, open face and abundant salt-and-pepper hair and beard. His eyes were the color of river water. Everybody called him "Kiger," and I did, too.

The other players looked up to him; I could tell by how many of them wanted to sit with him at intermission. He was a jazz man all the way, sometimes dressed up in a worn but fancy tuxedo, other times clad in corduroy pants, dirty Rockport walking shoes, and a worn tweed jacket. He had come to town to play with Dee Felice's band, and to write arrangements for—and sometimes play with—the Blue Wisp Big Band.

I was "gigging around"—singing at Arnold's two nights a week, doing private parties, even touring. With the extra room in my downtown apartment, the musicians thought I was an answered prayer. Kiger was reluctant, but everybody told him to give it a try, so he moved in, carrying a couple of flimsy cardboard boxes, his record player, and the large jar of garlic he took with him everywhere. It looked like one of those glass containers you'd see by the cash register at a tavern, only instead of boiled eggs, it was full of garlic bulbs.

He wore reading glasses down on his nose and had a way of shaking his head when he laughed. ("What do you want for Christmas?" I asked him once. "A Mr. Potato Head and a reason for living," he replied, stroking his beard with his fingers.) He had a deep well of words, each one perfectly picked to suit the occasion, dropped neatly into place like grace notes. He struck fast with his zingers. My friend Barbara said of Kiger, "He was lightning in a bottle."

Weeknights, if we weren't working, we'd eat supper together, whatever we could dig up. I was hopeless at cooking, and so was Kiger, so we'd bring home food from the restaurants where we played and split it up. It wasn't bad liberally doctored with spices, but, boy, I really hated that jar of garlic. When Kiger finally left my apartment, he forgot his precious garlic, and I made him come back and get it. Then, as luck would have it, the rental manager of his new "pad" wouldn't allow the jar of garlic either. None of us could figure out how to dispose of it, so Kiger buried it in a saxophone player's backyard. We all pretended to see the earth bubbling and smoking, as if we had buried nuclear waste.

*

Life with Kiger settled into a routine: A light supper together if we felt like it, then if we were both at loose ends by 9 p.m., he would get out his jazz records, and we would settle into the dining room for a couple hours of intense listening. We sat facing each other at the small dining room table. Mostly we looked out the window at the brick-paved lane that ran past my apartment. There was a lilac bush flat against the wall, and an ugly green garden hose hanging in a round coil beside it. Kiger had an old-fashioned stereo, the kind of record player that had an arm on top of a stack of records. He only had about eleven vinyl records, all of them laced with static, but everything about them was fascinating. I loved to watch the records going around, spinning faster and faster, and I loved the crackle and pop of the static.

Kiger was proud of his meager supply of records. "I may not have many, but the ones I've got are choice," he said, laughing at his little joke. And he was right. He had a couple of records by the trumpeter Bobby Hackett, his playing so thick and lush, so full of yearning intervals you never wanted it to end. Then there was Jack Teagarden, the trombone player who was best known for his work with Benny Goodman and his duets with Louis Armstrong. It was a unique collection, and one that could not be replicated. I took every opportunity to listen. Often, around 9:30, the devil came out. Kiger would open a can of beer from a twelve-pack, and by the time we played Billie Holiday (I always begged for "He's Funny That Way"), he was on his third.

He taught me how to listen to music. Always know who the composer is and something about his life. Get to know the back-up players. Who's playing piano, and who did he play with before this record? A couple more beers, and he dug out my favorite, Zoot Sims. Zoot was a tenor saxophone player who gigged with the likes of Stan Getz and Al Cohn.

The first couple of cuts of Zoot's LP were standards from the American popular songbook, like "Whispering," recorded by bandleader Paul Whiteman in 1920. Some thirty years later, trumpeter Dizzy Gillespie jazzed it up, turned the chords inside out, and bequeathed a new bebop incarnation retitled "Groovin' High." The last song on the first side of the record was a real beauty, an ancient Sigmund Romberg melody called "Little Gypsy Sweetheart." The first couple of lines went: "Slumber on, my little gypsy sweetheart … "

"Little Gypsy Sweetheart" quickly became the closer for our listening sessions. By then, Kiger had finished half of the twelve-pack and was beginning to get "toasty," so I drifted off to bed, closing the door behind me, leaving him to get out his hard-core bebop tunes, what I called the "pornographic jazz collection." That's what it sounded like to me: a drum playing loudly with dips and dweebs and a soprano sax—toots and squeaks and squeals splattered here and there like a Jackson Pollock painting. I preferred to go to sleep to the last chorus of "Little Gypsy Sweetheart" while Kiger sat in my living room and turned from Dr. Jekyll into Mr. Hyde.

He didn't sleep much. By the next morning he'd be up and out of the house way before I was dressed and ready for the day. He walked to a small café for breakfast and coffee, and by the time he got home I was out for lunch with a friend or running errands or at rehearsal for some upcoming event.

Our rooms were at separate ends of the house, and we seldom saw each other in the daytime. I was surprised one afternoon when I came in to find him napping on the living room couch, his golden trumpet an arm's length away. He had been writing arrangements with the staff paper clipped to a hard-surfaced book, and every ten or fifteen minutes he'd pick up the trumpet and play a few arpeggios, "just to keep my lip strong." Brass players have to worry about their *embouchure*, which is what the puckering muscles of the mouth form. The lips, tongue, and teeth make up the *embouchure*. Proper mouth formation can make the difference in a strong or a weak sound.

That afternoon was bright and spring-like and warm, and I took off my coat and threw my purse aside onto an upholstered chair. "What have you been doing all afternoon?" I asked, aware that I was on the verge of turning the conversation into something personal, and that was forbidden territory. But Kiger fooled me.

"I've just been lying here listening to all your crazy neurotic girlfriends," he said.

Sure enough, there were nine or ten messages on my answering machine from women friends in varying states of emotional distress, and they had all called me for "support."

All of us were reading self-help books in those days, and we were all familiar with concepts of "intimacy." We used the word "syndrome" a lot. When I had finished listening to the messages, Kiger gave me one of his Barry Fitzgerald looks, an errant lock of hair at the forehead, and I slunk off, my tail between my legs, to get ready to go to work.

Just shy of his PhD in music from Indiana University, Kiger was highly regarded for the chord charts he wrote for singers and horn players and for his arrangements for big bands, most notably the Blue Wisp Big Band. You could recognize his penmanship anywhere. His beautifully formed notes and his elaborate treble and bass clefs were in black, Gothic, like the printing on a fancy wedding invitation.

"They were more than charts," trombone player Bill Gemmer said. "They were works of art."

Kiger had started out playing with the Cincinnati-born saxophonist and composer George Russell in what was a hot New York City jazz band, and he had some early success in that group, both playing and writing arrangements and copying parts for a whole section, one part for each horn and each rhythm instrument. If the band was sixteen or seventeen pieces, he wrote out sixteen or seventeen charts. As he aged, his writing hand grew more arthritic and he had to learn to use a computer to write. He bought one, but he resisted using it. When I asked him how his computer education was coming along, he said, "I walk past it on the way to the kitchen, and it hisses at me."

He didn't talk much about his early years on the road with George Russell. It may not have been the gig he wanted, but he was getting exposure and polish on his solos, and he was learning to "play well with others." Not all of Kiger's gigs were sophisticated, though. He loved to tell the story of a Romany funeral he played one day in Indiana for the King of the Gypsies. "They put us in the back of a wagon and glared at us and said, 'All we want is three songs: "Sweet Sue," "Autumn Leaves," and "Indiana."'"

Kiger looked pained and sat quietly, fingering his cornet mute. "We rode around playing 'Sweet Sue,' 'Autumn Leaves,' and 'Indiana.' About the fourth time we went around, the saxophone player yelled, in the direction of one of the headstones, 'Hey, Paulie, I've still got the Plymouth.' It was the strangest gig I've ever played."

Kiger's employment with Russell didn't last, and in a fit of pique one moonlit night he buried his trumpet in the back yard, digging the grave himself about three feet down. Marjean Wisby got the news on the telephone behind the bar at the Blue Wisp, and it went all around the club, whispered behind hands, "Kiger's buried his trumpet."

For awhile he existed on what money he could make writing arrangements and chord charts, but the urge to play was too strong to ignore, and so he dug up his instrument and began to drive back and forth to Indiana from Cincinnati, playing with bandleader and composer Henry Mancini and working tours with Johnny Mathis and Elvis Presley. No, he never met Presley, but it was a "notch" in his résumé. He traveled to California with the Blue Wisp Big Band when they did a short tour of the West Coast.

In the best times, when he was sober and playing well, he had an on-again off-again relationship with a woman named Susan, who had a soft, freckly face and carroty curls. She was chic and slender and close to his age. As much as he was capable of loving, he loved her, at least "for a minute" as he might say. He started each episode with her wholeheartedly, but each episode ended badly, and he ended up drinking like a country song, nearly destroying himself time after time.

Susan was worth it. She dressed in dramatic cocktail outfits and high heels, and they'd sweep into the nightclubs and restaurants, beaming and sophisticated. The evening would start out great—they'd order food and wine and the talk would flow. But once the eating and drinking were over, Kiger's eyes and ears were glued to the stage. He listened intently to every note and nuance, how each chord change was built. There were lots of ways to stack those chords, and that, along with the impeccable swing of a really rhythmic head—the basic melody of the song is referred to as the head—could sell a tune to a big band. A seventeen-piece big band was like a hungry maw. *Feed me more notes!* it seemed to cry.

Nothing pleased Kiger more than a new arrangement to be worked out, but it made him a bad date. Like many musicians, he was conflicted: miserable when he played and miserable when he didn't, and he and Susan eventually parted. As my grandfather used to say, "they split the sheets."

Kiger moved back to Indiana in the early '90s, and I lost track of him. I was working a lot, singing almost every night of the week, and I was younger and too self-involved. When Facebook came along, I signed up and was surprised to get a friend request from him. I was delighted, and I wrote a long, effusive message which he probably didn't read. After that I got email messages from him about once a week, messages that were usually about music, pointed and sharp and amazingly witty. Kiger was just plain smarter than the rest of us. He kept up his cyber skills, too. Before long, he had a truly cool page on Facebook. From the musicians he chose to write about to the fonts he chose to display his work, everything was original, warm, informative. He posted his own record collection, one cut at a time, and posted a surprising amount of text about the music.

I didn't hear from Kiger for a long time, and the next thing I heard wasn't good. He had cancer, and it was terminal. Bill Gemmer was able to talk to him. "I don't know what to say," Bill told me he said to Kiger.

"Let it go. Let's talk about music," was Kiger's answer.

I noticed when the jazz postings stopped, but I didn't want an answer so I didn't ask what happened. The loss of his musician's knowledge was like losing an arm or a leg. If you had a song you needed chord changes for or, say, knew a song you thought might have been written by the composer Burton Lane but you couldn't find any reference to it on the internet, you would stamp your foot and long for just one more hour with a man like Alan Kiger. I realize now that I didn't ask the right questions at all, but somehow when it came to Kiger, I always got the right answers.

JOHN VON OHLEN: HE'S GOT RHYTHM

Late on a November night, the trees are bending in the wind while their dried, fallen leaves swirl like eddies in the gutters. The moon is bright and full but the streets of Over-the-Rhine are deserted, possibly because a cold front has moved in and sent people scurrying back into their warm caves. In fact, the only sign of life lies just ahead at a small bar called Japp's, close to the corner of Twelfth and Main. Lights shine from the windows, and the sound of music wafts through the doors every time someone enters or leaves the building. It is an oasis in a dark place, and it draws you like a magnet.

The Blue Wisp Big Band has been playing at Japp's on Wednesday nights ever since the Blue Wisp at Seventh and Race closed, in early summer. It isn't a place you'd associate with a big band, but drummer John Von Ohlen liked Japp's acoustics, and John exerts so much influence that for months now all seventeen pieces of the Big Band have been crowding onto a small stage area, and indeed the acoustics are really good.

The front line of players, the reeds, or the saxophone players (bass saxophone, tenors, alto), read their music charts on stands with small lights attached so the players can see in the darkest of places. The trombones are behind them then a few trumpets. The lead trumpet player, the driving force of the big band, sits in the first chair. The bass and the piano are like knights in a chess game, guarding the trumpet and the drums, the King and Queen.

Drummer John Von Ohlen started the Blue Wisp Big Band back in 1972 when he first came to town and heard "a smokin' trumpet player" named Don Johnson. "Don knew a bunch of heavy horn players, and these cats were playing behind *singers*. Don and I started talking about a big band, because if you get a drummer and a lead trumpet player who can blow the roof off they'll usually start a big band, you know?" He paused and laughed. "They just can't help it."

It helps if the drummer is internationally known, like John Von Ohlen, who made his bones on Woody Herman's Big Band, and was then a featured soloist on Stan Kenton's Orchestra and is included in Wikipedia to boot.

One drummer, Terry Branan says of John in a publication called *Modern Drummer*, "That man is one of my heroes! I was lucky enough to study with him a bit in Cincinnati. He is one of music's unsung heroes for sure. I remember seeing him on a gig with the great Joe Levano, a tenor saxophone player, at the Hyatt Hotel, and my jaw was on the floor. He used to play this ride cymbal with a bite cut out of it—like a quarter of it was missing. Dead as a doornail. In John's hands, though, it sounded incredible."

Listeners tend to speak in superlatives about John. His students are in awe of him—he is the Adjunct Professor of Jazz Drums at CCM Jazz Studies, at the University of Cincinnati, where to the consternation of the faculty,

GREAT BARS

he used to urge his students to quit school and learn their chops on the job. "Go to work," he'd advise.

John doesn't think you can get what he calls "your confidence" out of a book. "It' nice to *have* a book," he'll say, "but it's not really necessary. You need to go out and work. That's where you get it," he says. "On the job. Don't get bound up with licks that aren't natural to you in the name of speed. If you just keep playing, man, you will come up with some *bomb* licks that nobody else can play. *Real* licks, which will have dynamics and shading that you could never get out of a book ... work on mastering your own natural style ... it's a life-long study, finding yourself," but, he added, "it's the only authentic way to live."

⁓

On the stand, John is a visual delight. He is a barrel-chested man with long arms, long legs, and a powerful, natural grace. His drum set is large and surrounds him like an oval, with the big bass drum in front. Cymbals on stands are planted next to a snare, between a high hat and tom-toms. That equipment comes with the territory for a big band drummer. John has said, "You get your time (your rhythm) from the ride cymbal. In jazz, the time used to come from the bass drum. Later, the time moved to the high hat, then to the snare and now it comes from the ride cymbal.

To kick off an upbeat swing number, John will roll drum sticks on the cymbals then switch to brushes on the snares when he wants the sound of a dancer gliding over a gritty wood floor. What he uses on which component, and when he uses it are the mysteries in his bag of tricks, the *"bomb"* licks he has mastered and memorized and now uses intuitively. The trombones add a jerky slide riff, and the trumpets begin to kick in bringing the reed instruments along with them. Steve Schmidt plays a couple of shimmering piano choruses, bringing the band up to the next level.

Now the tension is building. It is time for John's solo, and every eye in the place is on him. He warms up a little on the snare drum and the ride cymbal, throwing in a lick on the bass drum—the bass drum has pedals which he plays with his feet. The emphasis is on beats 2 and 4, if you're playing jazz.

When he picks up the volume, he makes the switch to sticks. The audience doesn't even notice this sleight of hand. Everything is quiet, in anticipation of the climax of the solo, and John doesn't disappoint. He is in total control: the beat runs from one of his long arms to the other, like an electrical current. The sticks are moving so fast they blur; he is breathing hard, his hair whipping from side to side. His head is turned in a profile; his mouth is slack.

He plays a rhythm on the snare. Holds the high hat cymbals together for a muted effect. He swings so powerfully that the audience is shouting even as he brings his solo home, yelling as he counts the beats out for the band so they'll know when to come in. When the trombones slide their way back in on the upbeat, the reeds join them, and the trumpet player climbs high and higher, a ladder of notes, until the audience is on its feet, shouting, by the time he and John drive each other to the high "C" climax together.

While the band takes a break, John continues talking about the formation of the Big Band. "I had a hunch people wanted to hear real big band music," he says, "and they did. We had crowds early on. People could hear big bands that played for dancing, but they weren't real jazz big bands. We blew the roof off the place at the original Blue Wisp in O'Bryonville, but the acoustics were so good it didn't hurt your ears."

John runs a hand through his graying hair, which he wears a little long ("the Prince Valiant look," the Big Band calls it) and takes a deep breath. He props his hand on his knee, stretching slightly. He has an open face, broad and Midwestern. In fact, he is from Indianapolis, and he talks with a bit of an Indiana twang. "My first major job was with the Billy Maxted Manhattan Jazz Band in 1966. It was a great band. "It felt like family," he says of it now, but Woody Herman came calling, and a young drummer would have had to be insane to turn down that chair.

"I played with Woody Herman and his Thundering Herd in 1966–67," he says. It was a band which nurtured such talents as saxophonists Stan Getz, and Zoot Sims, and John was hired after his junior year of high school. He dropped out to return and finish high school, then he was on the road again, this time with Stan Kenton, looking at the world through the windshield of a bus. He didn't have a home until he was thirty-two years old.

"I didn't play well, though," he says. "Hell, I played better in high school than I did on Woody's band. The rhythm section just wasn't happening." John got turned on to yoga master Sivaya Subramuniyaswami. The Beatles were doing it, after all, back in those days.

"My master told me that when I found my natural style, that would be my day of liberation. In other words, when I stopped trying to sound like Buddy Rich or Elvin Jones, I'd begin to work on mastering my natural style, my own way. Finding yourself is a life-long study." And he taught me that if you haven't got your confidence, you haven't got anything."

Stan Kenton, he said, was his idol. "His was the first band I ever saw live. Then Stan folded the band in 1963. I had gotten to know him a little, and I told him that if he ever got the band together again he'd better call me. Desire is everything," he said with a smile. "Sure enough, my desire won out, and in 1970, when I was in Vegas, waiting for a Union Card, I got the call from Stan. When I went with him it was like coming home. Everything was so easy. Where Woody had been a real hard-charger, Stan was easy. I was on an album called *Downtown Blues*, and after that I made something of an international reputation for myself as the featured soloist with the Kenton Band.

"I cut out again in 1972 and went to India. I felt like I was losing myself and I needed a period of study. I stayed with Stan for two years, but the road had worn me out. Stan had a fit. He wanted me to stay or to settle in L.A. and be a big band drummer out there if I couldn't take the road anymore, but I didn't see it that way. I felt like I could start something just as good in Cincinnati. Man, there's good musicians everywhere. Music is, like, *universal*. I rented a cabin in Sunman, Indiana—I still have it—and started playing with some heavy-duty cats in Indianapolis: Steve Allee, composers like Claude Sifferlen.

"I went back to Stan for a brief period when his drummer hurt his ankle. Stan died in 1978. I could never pay him back for what he taught me about music. There are a lot of players, but only a few great players. A good teacher can see through you even if you've built a wall of technique that's actually inhibiting your feeling. A good teacher will strip that down and make you start all over with things more natural for you—more in tune with your nature.

"Anyway," he says, "there I was in my cabin in Sunman, Indiana, and I didn't know anybody. (Guitarist) Cal Collins had heard I was in Indiana, and he called me to play a job at the Buccaneer, in Cincinnati. That was a few years before Cal went with Benny Goodman's band. It was where I met Don Johnson, which takes us back to the beginning of the Blue Wisp Big Band."

"I've always used drum charts in the band. I could probably read better than other drummers because I had spent time studying piano and trombone. Drum parts are the parts arrangers put the least amount of effort into. Especially on jazz tunes. They either give too little or too much, so that you don't know what's up. What you need is a basic road map. Around here, arrangers know I don't like standard drum charts. I ask them to write me the actual line, give me everything the melody player has. That gives me an instinct of whether the melody is going up or down.

"Art is sweat and dreams," he says, and his artistry has drawn celebrities from all over who have traveled to see the Blue Wisp Big Band. The late Vidal Sassoon was a fan, Tony Bennett dropped in when he was in town. The last conductor of the Cincinnati Symphony Orchestra, Paavo Jaarvi, was a regular. Rosemary Clooney, with whom he toured, came in to see him with Nick and Nina Clooney and their son, George. (When John's life partner, Mary Ellen Tanner, died less than a year ago, George Clooney called him to express condolences.)

Steve Schmidt who has played piano with the Big Band since its inception sums John up thoughtfully. "What I love about him is his child-like delight in music. He is simple and sophisticated at the same time. When the band is playing, he is always fully present in the music. There is no separation in him; he does not compartmentalize; he is whole."

Since the last incarnation of the Blue Wisp closed—the club on Seventh and Race—the Big Band has been without a permanent home. They managed to hold out at Japp's until the owners wanted to resume their rock and roll format. They have an open invitation at the York St. Cafe in Newport. If you are interested in John's recordings, *The Baron* and *Rollin' With Von Ohlen*, as well as the Cincinnati Blue Wisp Big Band *Live at Carmello's*, they can be purchased on the internet, though they're not easy to get. And they're all on vinyl and have not been digitized. Still, having an autographed LP of John and the Big Band is well worth the effort. They are already collector's items. Put one on the record player and get ready to swing.

STOP TIME

Fourth Street was alive and hopping. From one door I could hear a ballgame blasting from a cheap radio, and from another the rhythmic chant of the auctioneer in Karp's showroom. "Five, thirty-five, who'll give me thirty-five ... " A middle-aged couple walked out of the door, carrying a table and chairs over their heads to a double-parked van on the corner. A car horn honked loudly; a man swore angrily; and a young woman jogged by in a tight fitness suit, her midriff bared, her shorts tight around her legs. The pianist Steve Schmidt, who was walking right beside me, raised his eyebrows just slightly, then opened the door to the Härth Lounge, which he called his new musical home. "The Härth" is appropriate: it's a cocktail lounge, artfully decorated, dimly lit, outfitted with French provincial chairs and low sofas here and there.

My friendship with Steve goes back many years. We may not see each other often, but then, suddenly, he is everywhere: backstage at a gig wearing a tuxedo, hanging out at a coffee shop in Clifton, or on a piano bench in some unexpected musical dive. I used to listen to him play jazz piano, his hands moving over the keys like magic, his face a study in rapt concentration. His hair, once a premature salt-and-pepper, is silver now, his body a little fuller. Otherwise, he is just the same as the young player I met nearly four decades ago.

When I first saw him he was in his early twenties, maybe twenty-one, and already a star fronting the Steve Schmidt Trio with Lynn Seaton on bass and John Von Ohlen on drums at the original Blue Wisp in O'Bryonville. Lynn Seaton had moved to Cincinnati from Oklahoma just to play in this trio. You couldn't miss Lynn. He was a bear of a young man with a halo of blond curls around his face and really big feet. "In school," he told me once, "they measured my feet and figured I'd grow into the bass." It was a happy choice. He was so at home with the instrument that he rarely showed up anywhere without it.

I listened many nights as Steve and Lynn wove in and out of the music. The grace notes, the arpeggios that linked his chord changes, were rapid-fire, and his blues licks said a lot about his early love of that music. Lynn's tone was deep and low, almost like a growl.

Steve and Lynn were backed up by John Von Ohlen on drums. He had been Stan Kenton's big band drummer. When he quit Kenton, he went to India and studied with an authentic guru just about the same time the Beatles were there. Everybody thought he was cool. That and his reputation as a musical drummer—the only drummer who read the band arrangements and tuned his drums before every gig—made him the most requested player in town.

As for Steve, "I studied piano a couple of years in grade school," he told me once. "In high school, I heard blues bands and began to play the guitar."

But he turned to piano because "the keyboard was laid out logically, not mixed up like guitar ... I started at the Wisp about four years later."

In a relatively short while, the Blue Wisp was *the* jazz bar in Cincinnati. Other musicians drifted in to listen after their own gigs were done. These musicians, many of them fresh from playing a wedding reception or some hotel job, leaned quietly on the bar dressed in tuxedos like so many penguins.

Guests sitting in and jamming with the trio added an extra fillip of excitement to the night. But the band never knew who was going to be playing or what they would play. Steve fed off this contained chaos. "Being able to lay down a foundation to accompany different horn players or singers is a challenge," he told me. "If the rhythm section can get in a groove then you don't need to think so much about it, and you can just let loose and have fun."

The cream of Cincinnati's crop of players came to jam because the Wisp was the place to play bebop, the trio was so good, and you never knew who you'd run into. The result was more than the sum of its parts, and as a consequence, all the music was elevated. It was an authentic "scene."

It was natural that the owners would decide to book national players as added attractions on the weekends. Steve took on that job, his creativity seasoned with a good sense of humor. In those early years, he was able to get musicians like Scott Hamilton and Warren Vache to play with the Blue Wisp Big Band on Wednesday nights, then stay over—usually at Steve's apartment—and play weekends with the trio. He booked a heady mixture of local, national, even international acts.

"The airlines were running $100 round-trip specials to New York City," he says, "and I could get just enough out of the budget to book some quality players. I tried to get a cross-section. We'd have Scott Hamilton, for instance, who was straight ahead swing and bookend him with another guy, like Bennie Wallace." Wallace was an avant garde saxophone player whose instrument pinged like a cell phone.

John Von Ohlen remembers that period. "Steve was the one who made the Blue Wisp a big name nationally," he says. "I came in there because it was a five-night-a-week gig, and that sounded good to me since I was getting tired of the road. Here's this kid who's been playing rock and roll in garage bands, and he was just nailing bebop standards. Everything was hot." John laughs at the memory. "Steve started bringing in old beboppers and giving them what they needed to play."

"Steve is an unusual cat," John adds. "He is an old soul."

When the Blue Wisp moved to Garfield Place downtown, Steve stepped up his booking effort. One of the first bands to play the new club was Sun Ra, a different kind of group whose usual audience were Grateful Dead fans. "His whole band name," says Steve, was "the Cosmo Love Adventure Arkestra, and they represented themselves as a spiritual group, futuristic." Steve told me they had a guy who did yoga stretches on stage while playing the trumpet (he put his foot behind his head) and another player who held a lit torch. The band marched out at the end of the night playing "Zip-a-Dee-Doo-Dah." They were wearing space helmets.

We laugh. "Marjean didn't know what to think," Steve says of Marjean Wisby, the owner of the Wisp.

The years of being around eccentric musicians have made him a good storyteller with an eye for detail. (He wrote his own liner notes on his first long-awaited CD.) Wisby placed a cover charge to help cushion the cost of the bands—cover charges which got as high as $20 for some musicians. It was a fair price to pay for the likes of Lew Tabackin, guitarists Herb Ellis and Tal Farlow, and nobody complained. It was a New York scene in small-town Cincinnati, and free publicity was furnished by writer Dale Stevens of the *Cincinnati Post* and by The Jazz Ark, radio station WNOP. The more they booked great music at the Wisp, the more musicians wanted to come and play there. Musicians like Joe Lovano, Al Cohn, Joe Henderson, and Ira Sullivan—even Ruby Braff—would play at the Blue Wisp, which amazed everyone.

I usually came and caught the last set. One night I even sang a song with Cal Collins and trumpeter Warren Vache. It was an honor to be asked, and I was in a good mood, so my defenses were down when Lynn Seaton pounced. It was a frosty Saturday night, and Lynn wasn't in the mood to go home. He insisted Steve and I go out to breakfast with him. "I know this great place in Newport. It serves killer Mexican food," he said, planting himself squarely in front of me.

"Absolutely not," I said. "It's below zero out there. I'm going straight home and getting under an electric blanket."

Of course the next thing I knew Steve and Lynn and I were crowded into Steve's "jazz car," headed for Newport. The car was an old-model American four-door gas-guzzler with a hole in the muffler and another hole in the floorboard. If you closed the windows you risked asphyxiation, but with the windows open you risked freezing to death. The cold was palpable—like having another passenger in the car.

"Close the window, and let me die with dignity," I whined as we skidded a little on the Brent Spence Bridge. When we got to Newport the Mexican joint was closed.

༄

Before we realized what was happening, Steve was the premier pianist in Cincinnati. Everybody said that. He was living in a one-bedroom apartment in Corryville when Count Basie's band called him to sit in for Basie in Cincinnati when the Count was out sick. Steve grabbed his music and his tuxedo, and his mother made him a sandwich and drove him downtown where the band bus was waiting for him.

"Don't tell anybody you had to drive me to the gig," he told his mom sternly. But the trip was the talk of the town, and word got out. Dale Stevens even wrote an article about it in the newspaper.

It wasn't the last time he was to play with the Basie Band. After Basie died, Cincinnatian Frank Foster ran the group, and one day Steve came home to hear Foster on his answering machine with the job offer of a lifetime.

"I can still quote it," he said. "'Steve, we need you. Could you meet us in Chicago and join the band?'" Steve had two days to think about it. He was finishing his degree in school, he was deeply involved in the running of the Blue Wisp, and as close as he came to saying "yes," the eventual answer was "no."

"We agreed to try it again in a month," he recalls, "but it just never happened." I asked him if he ever regretted that decision.

"It was hard to give it up, but I was so busy and so involved in various things at that time I would have been giving up weekends with players like Joe Lovano and Al Cohn," he told me. "At times I think about it, but it just didn't happen."

It was a loss for the Basie Band, too. One night I watched the Blue Wisp Big Band with Steve at the piano, and they were blowing the roof off the new Blue Wisp on Garfield Place. This band was John Von Ohlen's baby, and they were playing a new arrangement of Duke Ellington's "Sophisticated Lady," a lush chart of difficult changes, unexpected dips and swoops. It was the arranger Alan Kiger who said of that tune, "Many a trumpet player has crashed and burned coming off the bridge of 'Sophisticated Lady.'" I laughed when he said it, imagining horn players lying tangled in parachute cords out in a cornfield somewhere.

The last chorus started with a long solo by Steve. He took a chance, brought the volume and the tempo way down until it was a tender ballad, and you heard the longing in those yearning intervals. It seemed to go on forever, luminous, lovely. By the time Steve brought the band back in, the audience was screaming and clapping wildly. I've heard Steve play that solo a half dozen times over the years, and he's never played it the same way twice.

"Nothing gold can stay," some poet said, and it was true. We drifted in different directions, to different clubs with different musicians. Steve and I kept in touch through the years. We phoned one another now and then, and followed each other's fortunes on Facebook. I heard through the grapevine that he had been seriously ill, and later, that he had married—and divorced.

Then one day he called, and we decided once and for all we were going to have lunch and catch up.

So it was that I found myself walking down West Fourth Street to The Härth, where Steve played on Friday nights—solo—and on Saturday nights with a group. We are both a lot older, but when Steve began to doodle around on the ebony grand piano, I quickly realized he is still the coolest piano player in town. It's something about the tone he gets, as if he strikes every key directly on the sweet spot.

We talked for a while about his recent trip to New York to finish a project with vocalists Amy London, Darmon Meader, Holli Ross, and Dylan Pramuk called the Royal Bopsters. The CD took two years to finish, and the players and singers celebrated with a packed-house week at Birdland in New York City. The CD, devoted to vocalese (the art of singing lyrics to jazz lines), got rave reviews from *DownBeat* and *The Wall Street Journal*. The *Journal* made a short film of the musicians and vocalists performing and put it up on the paper's website. The singers brought the house down every night.

"Who is your favorite piano player?" I ask.

"My inspiration was Ahmad Jamal," he says. "He had a trio around the late '40s and into the '50s, which transcended jazz. I like Herbie Hancock, too, but I'd have to stick with Ahmad Jamal as my favorite. I used to go see them a lot at the original Gilly's, a jazz club in Dayton." He pauses for a moment and looks out the window. "He's still alive," he says. "I think he's about eighty-six, and he's decided not to play concerts anymore, but I'm just happy he's still on the earth."

Steve moved to the piano bench and began picking out some Bach variations, some Ravel. "That guy [Ravel] was one of the first ones to play jazz chords," he told me. He played a little more, and I was mesmerized again by that tone. He coaxed me into singing.

"It's very clear," I started, surprising myself a little. My voice was little more than a whisper.

Steve found the key quickly, laying down some tasty chord changes under me. Inspired by his playing, I pulled myself up and reached for notes I hadn't reached for in years. "In time the Rockies may crumble ... " For a minute I felt a little like Ginger Rogers, and Steve was Fred Astaire, and we were moving over the melody like silk, so easy, so effortless. "Our love is here to stay," I sang, and together we brought home a respectable rendition of the last chorus of that Gershwin tune, looked at each other, and smiled.

8

RADIO:
"MASH THE BUTTONS, WAYNE"

JEFF ROBERTS ON BANJO, JEFF TERFLINGER ON MANDOLIN,
AND BUDDY GRIFFIN ON GUITAR ADDED A TOUCH
OF HUMOR TO THE MUSIC.

RADIO DAYS

The third floor of Landrum Academic Center, where radio station WNKU is located, is dark at 8 o'clock on an early spring night. Just a few minutes ago, there were still traces of daylight, but the night is falling, and by the time my shift starts it will be full on. I like to work in the dark. There are no distractions. There are few students around on Sunday night anyway, but tonight there are none at all. Just the ducks crossing the street the same place they always cross, one parent leading the parade, the baby ducks waddling single-file behind, and the other parent bringing up the rear. They have crossed the busy thoroughfare by the parking lot here for at least twenty years, and as far as I know they have never been hurt. If you approach them from the sidewalk the parents will fight with absolutely no fear. The ducks, like most humans, are possessive about their little patch of land.

I park about five hundred yards from Landrum Academic Center and pass redbud trees and tiny yellow buttercups on my way. My ID opens the door like magic, and I walk quickly to the elevator that will take me to the third floor. At the end of the hallway the production studio is awash with a soft light, illuminating the disc jockey whose shift is almost over. I go in the double doors of the library and begin to take CDs off the shelves to fill up the three hours of my show, *Music from the Hills of Home*. Because my records are mostly bluegrass, the cuts are shorter than the rock records the other DJs play. Bluegrass cuts are about a minute and a half and go by so fast they're over before you really get started playing them.

The music I pick should be varied: different tempos, different moods, different instrumentation, music that will connect to my listener in an almost magic way. I picture the listener thinking, "I used to hear that years ago," or "That reminds me of my mother," and I can feel the connection myself when it happens, as strange as that may sound.

I've always been a little bit addicted to radio. It started when I was a baby in rural Tennessee. My mother said I cried with a high, thin wail that everyone assumed was caused by the colic—until they noticed that the music from the tiny radio in the kitchen miraculously quieted me. I picture three people in rocking chairs taking turns holding me and patting my tiny bottom as they moved me back and forth through the currents until my crying stopped.

Radio became my solace and salvation. As a toddler I stood by the kitchen table and kept time with my hand on the wooden cabinet. I had my favorites: Ernest Tubb and the Texas Troubadours, Eddy Arnold and the Tennessee Plowboys (Eddy was an accomplished yodeler), and of course Red Foley. I loved the girls who sang with the bands, too. All of their names were prefaced with "Pretty Little Miss ... " Norma Jean or Loretta Lynn, or best of all, Dolly Parton, who was my favorite. She sang with Porter Wagoner.

I had a hard time reconciling the voices of my radio heroes with the reality of their earthly appearances. I was surprised to find Ernest Tubb was not at all handsome. Indeed, he was as skinny as a comma. He wore flashy cowboy suits made by designers like Nudie and Manuel, the same tailors who dressed Roy Rogers and Dale Evans in fringed Western outfits. Porter Wagoner, especially, succumbed to lavish displays of gaudy, colored sequins sewed on his suits in the shape of wagon wheels and giant cactus plants.

They wore Stetson hats cocked rakishly over one eye and cowboy boots with sharp pointed toes and metal caps guarding the supple leather tips. I once went to the Grand Ole Opry to meet fiddler Buddy Griffin, who snuck me in the back door. I watched as Bobby Osborne, the high singer on the song "Rocky Top," got out of a van and changed the gray Hush Puppies he was wearing for the white pointy-toed boots of stardom, and as soon as his act was done, I saw him make a bee-line for the car to get to his comfortable Hush Puppies. He swapped those painful boots for the Hush Puppies faster than greased lightning.

RADIO: "MASH THE BUTTONS, WAYNE"

When I had my own band, the Katie Laur Band, we got booked on a public radio station in St. Paul, Minnesota, in the late '70s. Off we went in the green Econoline van we had acquired from the Hutchison Brothers, a bluegrass band from up in northern Ohio, stopping in Milwaukee to make an appearance and limping into Minneapolis at about 4:30 on a Friday morning. The star of the show was a man named Garrison Keillor, someone we'd never heard of. When he called to book us, he graciously offered us the use of his two spare bedrooms. But we couldn't sleep yet. Instead, we unloaded and got ready to do Keillor's 8 a.m. radio show to advertise our appearance on his Saturday Night show, which was called *A Prairie Home Companion*.

I'll never forget my first sight of Keillor. He was a very tall man with thick dark hair and dark-rimmed glasses, and he stood on the back porch in a plaid bathrobe with a cat curled indolently around his neck, both of them watching the proceedings from a distance. Keillor gave directions now and then for suitcase placement and room assignments. He had a deep chest radio voice, which was a little bit scary. "First bedroom on the left," he rumbled, and knocked me off my feet.

Keillor's early morning radio show was a wonderful mix of music: jazz, country, swing, classical. I had never heard anything quite like it, and though I didn't know it then, it would act as a template for what my own radio show would later be, a tapestry of music, woven with care and craft.

A Prairie Home Companion was a radio show with an in-studio audience. A band or entertainer had the good fortune to hear the applause for his performance right then and there. The idea of it, the production values, the sound system, the venue itself were just about perfect. We went through a rehearsal on Friday night, then off to a coffee shop to do another performance (so much for sleep), and we explored Minneapolis a bit on Saturday while Keillor was writing his "sermon" for the night, the message he'd deliver to his audience always including some of the themes he touched on every week: small town values, Minnesota bachelors, and Powder Milk Biscuits, which were so good they'd make "children above average."

On Saturday afternoon, he'd cook large dinners, elaborate feasts of roast beef or seafood. The boys in the Katie Laur Band were not interested in that sort of thing, though, and for the five or six times we traveled to Minnesota to do the show, they'd always run out to McDonald's to eat dinner. I ran across a letter from Keillor a few months ago in which he asked me to pay his respects to the "Fast Food Boys," as he took to calling them. Keillor, who seemed to own only one suit, and that one light khaki, rode over to the theater in St. Paul with us in the van. He took the shotgun seat and invariably got rain water or grease all over his suit coat.

I thought of Keillor when I started doing my own radio show in November of 1989 at WNKU. The previous bluegrass DJ, Ed McDonald, had taken another job—in West Virginia, I think. Ed was blind and had gone back over all his album liner notes with a braille typewriter, which left the letters raised as if they'd been sworn to in an affidavit in front of a notary public. Those first few months of shows were cohosted with Buddy Griffin, who was by then the fiddler in my band and who did everything but swing from the chandeliers. He didn't stay long, and I got my old friend Wayne Clyburn to sit in, and he did just that for about twenty-five years.

Like Keillor did on his early morning show, we used vinyl records. There were only a few CDs in the record library back then. The last night I did the show, in March 2017, the bluegrass section of the library alone contained over a thousand CDs in plastic cases with colorful jackets full of information about the music. All of us complained about them when they began to be popular—they didn't have the "warmth of vinyl" as *The New York Times* accused. Vinyl albums in their cardboard jackets were roomy enough to contain lots of information about the players, pictures, and the music itself. You needed a magnifying glass to retrieve that same information from a CD, but there was no doubt they were easier to play. With albums you had to use headphones and put the needle on the record just so—a few seconds behind the groove before you started to play. It made for dead-air and static and mistakes. After a certain amount of grieving for the old turntables, DJs welcomed CDs. Wayne thumbed his nose at *The New York Times*: "If I had an engineer working for me who still used a slide rule when a computer was available," he said, "I'd fire him."

With the advent of a new affection for public radio ("Radio is the theater of the mind," I heard someone once pronounce), for a brief moment, television took a back seat. Of course it didn't last. Television had attractive stars in well-cut $2,000 suits and radio had strange DJs with outsized egos who existed in parallel universes. They dressed differently: dirty Hawaiian shirts were popular. Personal grooming and niceties like haircuts were scarce, the use of language was different, and they believed their music the best to be heard anywhere. On WNKU, Mr. Rhythm Man's Saturday night show was the hippest of all the programs. Mr. Rhythm Man typically signed on saying he had a "stack of shellacs" which would put some "glide in your stride and some pep in your step."

WNKU was not my first radio station. When the Katie Laur Band was young and full of energy, we played music and did interviews on a lot of important bluegrass radio stations. I remember playing in a used-car lot once where Ray Davis did a popular radio show in Baltimore. Davis was a well-known broadcaster in the '60s and '70s, and his studio was set up in his office above the car lot. He could look outside the glass-enclosed booth and keep up with what was going on in the lot while he did a radio show every day. We appeared several times on *Mountain Stage* from Charleston, West Virginia. I never appeared on the *Wheeling Jamboree* in West Virginia, or the *Louisiana Hayride*, but we visited radio shows that broadcast from somebody's kitchen or a makeshift studio in someone's basement. It was not as glamorous as it had sounded when I listened on the radio.

At the end of March, I did the final broadcast of *Music from the Hills of Home* on WNKU. My cohost, Oakley Scot, put most of it together from titles I listed on the back of my Duke Energy bill. He threw in segments from old recordings he had made and saved from past years. Oakley is what you might call a broadcast hoarder. It was Oakley's nimble technical abilities that enabled me to finish out the radio show at the twenty-seven-and-a-half-year mark.

No doubt we'd still be on the air if the radio station hadn't been sold by Northern Kentucky University to a Christian broadcaster. The night of the final show, we received about two hundred email messages and phone calls. Thanks to the magic of streaming, we could be heard anywhere. We had listeners in far-flung places throughout the United States and in even farther-flung spots like New Zealand.

All of the weekend disc jockeys at WNKU—Mr. Rhythm Man, Oakley Scot, the Real Mary Peale, Pam Temple, Ken Hanes—lost their cherished jobs, and thousands of listeners lost their favorite programs for no good reason that anyone could ascertain. The university and station management had made some bad decisions in past years, but they could have been righted had there been strong leadership, a firm hand. I try not to dwell on old wounds, though.

I was lucky to have done that job as long as I did. I found the feeling of connection when my red "On Air" light was lit to be hard but satisfying work, and I am still sure that the radio frequency is a sort of invisible piece of magic. If you're too far away from the source of the signal when you're trying to tune in your station, you'll only get static. The relationship cannot be forced. You must have the wisdom and the patience to wait for a clear channel. It's like that with humans, too. There is no way to rush reception.

ACCIDENTAL DEEJAY

I started my radio career at WNKU-FM, the public radio station at Northern Kentucky University, on the first Sunday of November, 1989. It was a fairly new station, founded only four years before I arrived. At the time, my bluegrass band was dying a slow, painful death, and frankly, I needed a gig.

Sheila Rue, who was managing the station's programming in those days, asked me to host a weekly bluegrass show on Sundays at noon. At first I said no. I didn't fancy commitment: Take a regular job like this, I thought, and I could see myself yodeling with a diaper and a baby over my shoulder. I wanted to live for art, drown myself in art. Then I remembered the phone

RADIO: "MASH THE BUTTONS, WAYNE"

The Original Katie Laur Band—Jeff Terflinger, Rich Fleig, Katie Laur, Jeff Roberts, and Buddy Griffin.

bill. That's when I snapped out of it, grabbed Sheila's skirt, and said, "Yes, yes, yes."

And so Sheila and I talked turkey. "Now, I'll have to have $100 a show," I explained loftily, "and I think noon is a little early. Do you have anything in a later time slot?"

Sheila grinned, wrinkling her freckled Irish nose, and told me she could get me $30 a show. And the time was non-negotiable.

This was a problem. I was still operating on Musician Standard Time, which meant that in spring I fell forward and in fall I fell forward, too. Noon on Sunday morning might as well have been the crack of dawn. Still, I'd be working with Buddy Griffin, the fiddle player and general genius behind the Katie Laur Band, who would serve as my engineer. That'd be a treat. So I launched my broadcast career—Buddy changing records, me on the microphone.

There was a period of adjustment. Some might call it bumbling around.

"You've just heard J.D. Crowe doing 'The Old Home Place,'" I announced during our first show.

"Ah," Buddy said, "What have they done to the old home place?"

"I already *said* that," I hissed like a goose. Of course I didn't realize Buddy was playing for time, looking for the next record while I fumbled with the cue cards that told me what to say and when to say it. *Remind the listener frequently that they are listening to 89.7 WNKU*, the first card said.

I was pretty sure I could do that. I'd seen that Clint Eastwood movie—the one where he is a jazz DJ, and a listener comes after him with a butcher knife. I had heard Clint make the same kinds of statements as the ones on the card.

"You're listening to 89.7," I said in my sultriest voice. "WNKU."

"Have you got laryngitis, Kate?" Buddy blurted right into the microphone. "Anybody got a thermometer?"

"Buddy," I said, "I don't have a fever. I was trying to sound like Clint Eastwood." I could see that Buddy was still looking for the missing tune. "Let's play something by the Delmore Brothers," I said helpfully. "I've got one of their LPs right here. Alton and Rabon Delmore, from down in north Alabama. I know you like them."

Buddy put on a track that lasted exactly three minutes, tops. "Well, that was a big Delmore Brothers tune," I said when it was over, and checked my watch: only 175 minutes left to go. Where did I get the idea that radio was easy?

Earlier this year, WNKU made a $6.75 million deal to buy two family-owned radio stations—105.9 FM/910 AM (WPFB in Middletown), and 104.1 FM (WPAY, Portsmouth). Now WNKU's signal reaches from north of Dayton to southeast of Charleston, West Virginia. Local listeners who struggled for years to get WNKU on their kitchen radios are amazed the little station can now be heard so far and wide.

Me, I'm still just amazed to be on the air.

In those early days, we were so dreadful people thought we were doing it on purpose—which, I can assure you, we were not.

Still, Buddy made me laugh because there was absolutely no way to predict what he might do next. He especially liked doing his imitation of the

RADIO: "MASH THE BUTTONS, WAYNE"

imaginary WNKU News chopper. He'd climb up on the studio console and thump his chest into the microphone like a gorilla, imitating the sound of the helicopter engine. "Anybody see that little Chevy Nova? Looks like it's stalled on the off-ramp of the Norwood Lateral ... "

Buddy used to call me when he was getting back to town after he'd been in West Virginia for a while. He knew I didn't get up early in the morning, and so he liked to wake me up with a jolt if it was at all possible.

"Madam," he'd say. "This is the Big Money Call. If you can answer my question correctly, you'll win a NEW barbeque grill."

"Where have you been?"

"That's the correct answer. Do you want to keep the grill or do we move on to the next plateau?"

Buddy was the best fiddler I'd heard back then—maybe still—and he loved old radio. His idea of a great job would have been to do sound effects on old radio shows. He was way ahead of Riders in the Sky. What he lacked in sanity, he made up for in pure genius.

He was an enormous influence on me and on the women fiddle players he spent time with. He could play a forward roll on a guitar like Doc Watson and do Earl Scruggs note-for-note on the banjo. He came in one day and grabbed my sterling Revere bowl off the table and put it on his head and pretended he was a knight in battle.

I'd swear I wasn't going out in public with him, and the next thing I knew we'd be going north on I-71 in Buddy's white Vega. He kept his clothes hanging neatly on a pole stretched the width of the back seat. I watched his shirt sleeves moving in the wind, like those old black and white cartoons where a pair of shoes danced without any feet in them. His coffee cup was in a plastic holder between the driver and passenger seats, and there were a couple of cellophane cupcake wrappers wadded up neatly beside it, the remains of Buddy's breakfast. I once suggested he add a green plant to make his car more homey. He lived out of his car for twenty-five years. He might have had an apartment in Glenville or in Charleston, but he still lived out of that white Vega.

When Irmie, as Buddy called his mother, had to have cardiac bypass surgery and go through a strict exercise regimen, Buddy said, "The doctors told Mom to walk five miles a day. We haven't seen her in a week, but we heard she's some distance down the road."

We still worked with vinyl in those days, but a trickle of CDs came in from some of the more progressive record labels. Buddy saw the writing on the wall; his digital prowess went about as far as mashing the buttons on an eight-track tape. He didn't wait for CDs to take his job; he got a great fiddle gig in West Virginia, borrowed $20 (from me), hocked his watch (again, to me), and left town.

I don't remember the names of all the engineers who passed through the show between Buddy and Wayne Clyburn. But one Sunday morning, I slid into my seat at the last minute with a handful of LPs and Wayne was there, and it just seemed like Wayne had always been there, talking about banjo players and whatever else came to mind. The very airwaves seemed to settle down, and the show—*Music From the Hills of Home*—found its groove.

There was still a learning curve. Every Sunday, I'd invariably sign on at noon by saying "Good morning." And every Monday, without fail, Dave Arnold, the station's general manager, would call me and say, "When the big hand and the little hand are straight up, what time is it, Katie?"

"Twelve o'clock," I'd say.

Dave's soft voice would come back over the phone. "And would you call that morning or afternoon?"

"I don't know," I'd say. "It can't be afternoon, strictly speaking, because it's not really after noon. Do you see where I'm coming from?"

According to media experts, people do not want to hear talking when they tune in to a music program; they want to hear music. But Wayne is quite simply one of the best conversationalists I've ever spun a yarn with, and from the first we enjoyed talking about the music we played—and whatever else came up. Whenever we got particularly off-track, the next day the phone would ring.

RADIO: "MASH THE BUTTONS, WAYNE"

"Katie," Dave would say, "what is a Louis Vuitton handbag? And more importantly, what's it doing on the bluegrass show?"

Through the years, it has fascinated me what subjects our listeners were conversant with. One Sunday afternoon we spent a solid two hours discussing the origin of flea markets. Until a caller reached me from a phone booth north of town.

"Hey," he said. "I just wanted you to know that I have driven from Wallace Avenue in Covington, and I timed this. I got all the way to Fairfield, and I STILL HAVE NOT HEARD A NOTE OF MUSIC!"

So I started sailing records through the air at Wayne, we put on something from Ralph Stanley and a couple of songs from women, and after about fifteen minutes of playing some really great music, a listener called and said, "We don't really like bluegrass all that much. When are you going to talk some more?"

You can't please everybody. And I guess you shouldn't try. As a matter of fact, another general manager, Chuck Miller, said, "Don't let anybody sabotage your show or try to take it in another direction. You're behind the mic; it's your responsibility."

Chuck has been my favorite GM so far. Not just because he sticks up for me and Wayne, and whatever musical or conversational side road we go down, but also because he rode out Hurricane Katrina in a bunker in New Orleans eating peanut butter crackers. That gives him street cred in my book.

Early on, Wayne and I picked up two listeners named Effie Bishop and Esther Abrams. They were senior citizens, they were friends, and they loved bluegrass. Effie was blind; she liked "Rocking Alone in an Old Rockin' Chair" because she figured it made her children feel guilty in case they were listening. Esther preferred her country music with a side of lust. Loretta Lynn's "You Ain't Woman Enough" was a favorite.

They'd call in every week with news of Norwood—their neighborhood—and to request songs for each other and for themselves. Like most Appalachians, they enjoyed talking about home. I remember playing "The

L&N Don't Stop Here Anymore" for Esther because the Greyhound Bus had stopped going to Crab Orchard, Kentucky, which was her hometown. That was the most profoundly depressing thing: a town that wasn't even a bus stop anymore.

One week when I didn't hear from them I called Esther, and she said Effie's children were trying to get her in "Oh, one of them places where they assist you."

"Assisted Living?" I said.

"That's what I just said," she countered.

I could understand her children's concern. Effie was legally blind, crippled, and diabetic. But there's a saying in the country: Don't move an old hen off its nest. That was Effie in assisted living. When I went with Esther to see her, she'd "gone down," as the old folks used to say. Her chart made that clear: "Patient is despondent," it read.

Then one day she called WNKU sounding chipper again. "We had activities night last night," she told me cheerily.

"What did you do for your activity?" I asked.

"Why, I took my harmonica out of my skirt pocket and played 'Shortnin' Bread,'" she announced. It wasn't long after that Effie died, her children by her side.

With her friend gone, Esther got out and about and found her way to WLW-TV for the premiere of the Jerry Springer Show. This was in the early 1990s: Springer was taped locally then, and it wasn't the slug-fest that it is now. Before I knew what was happening, Esther had become such a regular part of the studio audience that Springer fixed her up with a new wardrobe and flew her to Chicago for his first national broadcast.

"Jerry thinks I'm his good-luck charm," Esther told me after the trip, with just a touch of world-weariness. Whatever Jerry Springer has done in his life, I have always secretly loved him for that act of kindness. He even sent a limo.

Effie and Esther were not the audience demographic that most radio stations hope for: They were old and they were poor. But Wayne and I didn't have the kind of show where you worried about audience demographics, just like we didn't have producers or planning meetings. We were happy to have any listeners at all. And Effie and Esther were a gift.

Looking back, it seems miraculous that *Music from the Hills of Home* lasted the first year, much less the past twenty-two. For the longest time we barely knew what we were doing; we had dead-air time and we got in actual fights in the studio.

Aaron Sharpe, the station's development director, was producing our fund-raising drive one Sunday when Wayne and I were not in a good mood. Somebody had gotten there ahead of us and eaten all the donuts. Aaron stepped in smoothly and said, "That number to call is 859-572-7897." Then he sent a volunteer out for more donuts. "I've always enjoyed listening to *Music from the Hills of Home*," he said, "especially from the safety of my *own* home."

My father would have liked Aaron. I can remember him saying, when my sister and I went to war in the back seat of the car, "God a'mighty, Suzie"—that was my mother—"pull over and let's feed 'em." All my life, that has turned out to be one of the wisest things anybody's father ever said.

When I was a little girl during WWII, the radio was the beating heart of the house, and the red glow from its dial signaled precious news about the movement of troops and the number of deaths in the faraway places where my father and all my uncles were stationed. And the odd thing is, now I'm on a radio that brings those faraway places to me. *Music from the Hills of Home* has a listener in New Zealand—someone following the show online—who emails us regularly. And then there are the folks who can tune in thanks to WNKU's new listening area—potentially more than two million of them, they tell me. That's a whole lot of VFW Halls and nursing homes for old friend Pester Flatt to play.

It was E.B. White who told the story of the pig, Wilbur, and his great friend and very good writer, Charlotte, the spider who spun herself to death detailing Wilbur's attributes in her web. All of the people who have participated in *Music from the Hills of Home* over the past twenty-two years have made the program what it is. They've given something of themselves and by doing so entertained us and each other. I hope we've entertained them, too.

CORNBREAD NATION

On a recent Sunday night episode of *Music from the Hills of Home*, the radio show I host with Wayne Clyburn on WNKU, a listener brought up an interesting and timely question, "How do you season an iron skillet?" The question came from a young man who told me he'd just moved into a "new" historic house and the morning of his first breakfast the fried eggs he'd been craving stuck to his black iron skillet like glue. His heart had been set on "over light," but he got scrambled instead.

"Where did I go wrong?" he wondered.

Neither Wayne nor I knew the answer to the question, but we talked about it for a few minutes, just to kill some time, then we turned to the more knowledgeable out there in Radio Land, semi-professional cooks like Shantyboat Mike, the Paul Prudhomme of Rabbit Hash.

According to him, "Washing a cast-iron skillet in soap and water is a hanging crime. It will rust your skillet and render it scrap iron within ten minutes."

The calls just kept on coming. It was obvious that we had struck a nerve in our listeners.

"Where can you buy the basic pan?" people asked.

"Flea markets," said Shantyboat Mike. "The stuff they're putting into cast-iron skillets just isn't as good as it used to be. However," he continued, "a new skillet will come with written instructions for the initial seasoning. If you read at a basic level, you should pass the initial phase."

Mike went on to say he always hopes that lard will be used in the seasoning. Lard is the 10W-40 of seasoning oils. "Lard won't get sticky like oil does when it oxidizes," Mike says, "but in an urban environment, lard is hard to come by unless you've just killed pigs and rendered the fat."

RADIO: "MASH THE BUTTONS, WAYNE"

(Have you ever seen a hog butchered? The farmers hang the fattened porkers up by their hind legs from a strong tree branch and slit their throats quickly with a knife. Their blood gushes into a big pan and simmers there. If you listen carefully, somewhere in the distance you might hear a ghostly fiddle and banjo, and the sound of the fiddle, and the blood gushing into the pan fit together as perfectly as a man and a woman.)

Now you're ready to make some of Ma Crow's Depression cornbread, or "ho cake," as it is more properly called. She makes it the old way, without milk or eggs, and she cooks it in a cast-iron skillet, on top of the stove—like a pancake. She combines self-rising corn meal and self-rising flour and enough water to give the mixture the consistency of batter. At first she covers the skillet with a lid until it begins to bubble on the sides, then she turns it like a pancake and uncovers it to brown the crust.

She said she learned how to make the cornbread from her mother in Norma Mountain, Tennessee. "You have to get the self-rising corn meal, but it can't be corn meal mix," she told me firmly. One night Ma Crow taught poet Melissa Mosby how to make this cornmeal delicacy, and Melissa added some new twists: she makes her skillet cakes thinner and actually flips them in the air like an Army cook turning flapjacks. Her cakes turn out flakier, brown and crusty, and small enough that you can carry one in a paper towel, like a toasted pop-tart.

I took one to Lee Hay at WVXU, and she bit into it with obvious zest. "Ummm ... ," she said in a low voice. Lee, from Eastern Kentucky, still eats Vienna sausages and drinks Ale-8. When she bit into it, she said, in her quiet, soothing voice. "Well." Just that one word, but when she says it, it's so absurdly comforting it's like going home.

I wonder if that's what all of us want in these hard times: just to go home and be wrapped in the arms of our childhood again, to hear a mother's voice or see an aunt's red hair, thick and crackling with static when she brushed it.

This has been a chilling season. Mob violence killed an employee at a Walmart's up east before Christmas. Investment bankers reached a new level of greed, even as they foreclosed on their customers' houses. Most of my friends lost money in their pension plans. Are we becoming a Third World nation? I don't know; I don't understand any of it.

The winter has been bitter. My dog, Sister, and I walk a lot, roaming around Vine Street, seeing the skeletal branches of the trees, the freshly fallen snow curved like dunes in the empty parking lots downtown.

I miss the cardinals we used to see in the playground of the School for the Creative and Performing Arts. I loved to watch them take off from the branches of the old trees on Fourteenth and Sycamore, so red against the bright blue sky. I seldom walk down there anymore, so I don't see many birds. Sister is getting older, and though she still enjoys the icy air and the cold wind, she doesn't have as much stamina as she used to when we roamed the streets of Over-the-Rhine, and when I look into her faithful brown eyes, I see myself.

My new apartment on Court Street has only three functional electrical outlets. I like the southern exposure, though, and being close to the YWCA and the library, so I have stowed the microwave, the toaster, the George Foreman grill my sister sent me for Christmas, *and* the blender. To plug in my crock pot, I'd have to sacrifice the refrigerator. I used to pop frozen dinners in the toaster oven. Nowadays, I make chili and cornbread and vegetable soup on top of the stove.

I've gone to ground; I'm in deep cover, waiting for times to get better, for hearts to get lighter, for people to be kinder. I keep my skillet good and greasy, like the song says, and I feel like I still have a fighting chance.

A DULCIMER SCANDAL

The Appalachian Festival has been held on the second weekend of May for over thirty years now, and it never rolls around without my remembering the Year of the Revenge of the Dulcimer Players. It was a quiet Sunday evening, and Wayne Clyburn and I were hosting our radio show, *Music from the Hills of Home*, on WNKU in northern Kentucky. We were reading promotional copy for the Festival, and part of that copy concerned the Dulcimer Society, a group of people devoted to an instrument called the "lap dulcimer." This instrument, which is thought to be the very embodiment of eastern Kentucky culture, has very little volume and is plucked with the sharp end of a quill. If you're in a good jam session at a bluegrass festival, it can be annoying to have a dulcimer player come running up and want to play a solo. Real bluegrass people hold the dulcimer in about as high esteem as they do contra dancers: they're suspicious of the relevance of both, at least to bluegrass culture.

To add insult to injury, a bureaucrat in Frankfort had gotten a bunch of names on a petition, and before anybody could get their shotguns loaded, the dulcimer had been named the "State Instrument of Kentucky." What happened to the fiddle and banjo? What about "Blue Moon of Kentucky?"

With this bad blood in play, I read from the Appalachian Festival announcement, "The dulcimers will be located in one central area under one tent." If only I hadn't paused there. I did, though, and I looked at Wayne impishly and said, "Well, that's good. It will be easier to bomb them that way."

The remark might have gone unnoticed had it not been for a busload of dulcimer players who were on their way to their monthly meeting. They were tuned to WNKU and listening to *Music from the Hills of Home*. When I made my unfortunate remark, their mob caps began to bob around, and they got hot under the collars of their linsey-woolsey shirts.

The next day, all hell broke loose. Letters and e-mails called for our immediate dismissal. People who had pledged money to our small public radio station demanded their money be refunded. Bags of mail arrived at the station asking whether in this climate of terror we really ought to talk about bombing dulcimer players. Did we know how it felt to be bombed? We were aghast.

I had to appear before the station manager and explain myself, and of course I apologized on the air. To this day, I can't understand why I said such a thing, except that for a split second I didn't pay attention. For a split second, I wasn't civil. Of course, I had no desire to see any dulcimer player hurt under any circumstance, but when you're in front of a microphone, you have to be disciplined enough to remember at all times that people are really listening.

Interestingly enough, because I always play the good guy on the radio show, everyone remembered Wayne as being the one who made the remark. Wayne was, after all, the curmudgeon; Wayne, the guy who made fun of Bob Dylan when WNKU still played folk music. (The folk music people and the bluegrass people are a lot like the Sunnis and Shiites. You either believe in Pete Seeger or Earl Scruggs, and as the old saying goes, "You don't mess with Mister in between.")

We didn't get suspended, but a curious thing happened: our ratings went up! The handwriting was on the wall: if you want an audience, be controversial. I couldn't play that game. I would have been too uncomfortable about hurting people's feelings, and I couldn't have withstood the disapproval.

We are lucky to live in a country where we have the right to be ourselves and to follow our own consciences, and I have a venue where I can do that as long as I pay my own way at fund-raising time and mind my manners. I am happy enough to slide along under the radar and watch the entertainment world swell with money like a mushroom cloud somewhere over my head, out of my reach. I like the little things in life: local shows on public radio, a good jazz trio at the bar down the street, the small, fragile art openings in Over-the-Rhine on Final Friday, a really good library book. I am not high-maintenance. I do not demand that my spinach be shipped in from California, or my sushi from Vietnam.

I don't listen to Bill Cunningham, and I don't get up early enough to see Don Imus. If I get in a taxi with someone who's listening to Rush Limbaugh, I've been known to get out and walk the rest of the way (after paying, of course). Too much loud talking gives me a headache. Once I heard a man say that if he could get really good and mad, the energy would keep him going for a few days, maybe even a week. That scares me; you never know where that kind of floating rage might land. Still, it would never occur to me to want these people silenced.

Don Imus said a bad thing, an ugly thing, about the young women at Rutgers, and people reacted viscerally because they were innocent girls who had done something wonderful. It felt like their honor was besmirched and, too, the remark went right to the quick of our national guilt about African Americans. According to the clips I saw in the week following his fall from grace, Imus had said a lot of other shocking things, things that would have peeled back the ears on a hound dog, yet nobody much cared then. He was attracting huge ratings and making lots of money for his sponsors. I wonder if his sponsors weren't paying attention or whether they just didn't really care as long as the cash register was ringing, and the phones weren't.

I can't cast the first stone at anyone after what I said, but I'm glad most of my listeners forgave me (though they're still suspicious of Wayne). The ones who didn't exercised what is every listener's right, no matter how rich or poor, how powerful or powerless.

They simply changed the channel.

WHERE THE HOLLER MEETS THE HARDTOP

"The weatherman's a'runnin' with the dry cows," Moon Mullins used to say on dreary winter afternoons in 1977 and 1978 when the temperatures went to 25 below zero two years in a row. Those were a couple of bad years: tempers were short and batteries dead. Comparing a weatherman to impotent cattle was just the kind of Moon Mullins metaphor which kept us tuning in to his daily afternoon radio show on WPFB in Middletown, Ohio.

He had moved to Middletown from Louisa, Kentucky, with a young family to support, and he brought his rich language and his love of music with him. If you think WEBN's Jelly Pudding was on the cutting edge, then you never heard Moon Mullins. He made Bubba the Love Sponge look mainstream. In fact, so many syndicated shows brag about "radio that breaks the rules," it makes me happy to think back on the glory days at WPFB when Moon didn't even *know* the rules. He started working as a bluegrass disc jockey before the era of being politically correct, and he enjoyed a cult status in the Ohio valley, a region which has enjoyed any number of colorful radio personalities.

In the winter of 1977, my good friend Joe Brashear and I spent a lot of our time plotting for new and better ways to pull up WPFB on the radio. When I was desperate for a fix of Moon's astringent conversation, I had to drive clear up to the Cincinnati-Dayton Road to get the show on the car radio. Joe, on the other hand, had an office downtown, and was in the catbird seat. He had rigged his radio antenna to where he could get WPFB daily. Joe was an architect, but he was also a transplanted "briar hopper," which is what Moon called folks from eastern Kentucky. Joe was, like many people from that part of the world, self-sufficient and proud of it. Joe described himself as "necky—a redneck with a low boiling point."

The central conflict of most Appalachians, the paradox which has eluded sociologists for years, is the conflict about "home." If you're there, you want to be somewhere else, and if you're somewhere else, you're so homesick you can't do anything. In fact, most of us want what we can't have, and in that we aren't much different from the country boys from Powell County, Kentucky, who made up Moon Mullins' audience. He was torn between needing a job in a city and longing for "home," where he was accepted for who he was, where he knew everybody, and they knew him and treated him with respect. Yet Moon knew the siren song of the city, and he took that conflict and amped it up until it was high art.

Tuning in to WPFB was a lot like trying to pick up the Grand Ole Opry on the radio. Two hundred miles from Nashville you got a lot of stat-

RADIO: "MASH THE BUTTONS, WAYNE"

ic with only a little sound coming through. Another hundred miles could give just enough clarity to keep you hooked until finally the warm sounds of Webb Pierce singing, "I Got $5 And It's Saturday Night." That dark warmth in the car, the cheerful sound of audiences clapping, the music itself banished loneliness.

Moon played music from home or about home, and he played what he thought you should hear rather than what you wanted to hear. He was always right. "That's good," he used to say if he liked something. "That'll hold water."

Moon Mullins started his own brand of bluegrass and classic country broadcasting in Louisa, Kentucky, and moved his family to Middletown to be the headline disc jockey for WPFB. WPFB already had a formidable reputation for country and bluegrass music. Even Hank Williams played at WPFB's outdoor tent shows in the '50s. During Moon's tenure, the "position statement" was direct and simple: "We play music for briars," he'd say, and everybody knew exactly what that meant.

"You boys ridin' around with pasteboard in your cozy windows, are ye?" he'd ask brightly, never softening his Eastern Kentucky accent.

"You better get on over to Bill and Ernie Sloan's Texaco and get it fixed 'cause the weatherman says it's a'fixin' to get cold as the back side of a witch's lap."

After listening to the second solo on an Earl Scruggs recording of "Saro Jane," he said, "That sounds like a dominecker hen peckin' corn off the bottom of a No. 2 washtub."

If he didn't like a record, he'd just stop the turntable and say, "That'll be enough of that," and he didn't play it anymore. If the record offended him enough, he'd break it and throw it in the trash. Of course, that was before Clear Channel made programming a soul-less enterprise. I didn't always agree with what he liked or didn't like, but I knew one thing: he loved the music, and he respected the artists, and because he played fiddle himself, he had some insight into musicians' lives.

Moon's colorful idiomatic expressions made for great advertising copy. For instance, a marital spat could be fixed with one of those diamond-chipped dinner rings, a "Kentucky cluster," as Moon called it. He recommended it on behalf of Rogers Jewelry. "Then, if your old lady's threatenin' to sack up her other dress and leave, why you can cut off her finger and take it with you."

He raved about Betty's Drive-In in Franklin for their brown bombers (pinto beans) which Betty served with a big onion and a pone of cornbread until "way into the night." He thought "My Rough and Rowdy Ways" was the "identical" song for Merle Haggard. One of his regular advertisers was Charlie Elam at Elam's Furniture. They were perpetually overstocked, Moon said. Then he added, deadpan, "Charlie said he has to have a search warrant to find Evelyn."

Moon nailed his fellow briars' schism, their longing for acceptance. In our own country, we were kings. In the city, who we had been or who we came from didn't matter. You could hear it when he advertised Don House's "House of Drugs." "They'll treat you just like you git treated in one of them country stores down in Powell County," he'd say, a little wistfully, "Or Menifee County or Montgomery County ... right there where the holler hits the hardtop."

⁂

Epilogue: Moon Mullins, born in the mountains of Kentucky, died in 2008 at the age of 71, of Parkinson's Disease. He died in a nursing facility, probably a hospice facility and was buried in Middletown. To the end of his broadcasting career, he was still testifying for the soft-drink beverage Ale-8. You had to go nearly to Corbin to buy it in those days, I don't know why. To Moon, it was the elixir of home, the taste of water out of an old-fashioned, untreated faucet, and the low of cattle headed back to the barn for dinner.

He fell in love with bluegrass at an early age, and learned to play the fiddle, which he did with many groups in Ohio and Kentucky. I think the thing Moon was proudest of was his son, Joe, a master banjo player with a sweet tenor voice. Joe grew up with the best musicians in his house. He might find Bobby Osborne on his couch asleep. He had no choice but to learn to play; he hadn't heard of computer games, and a variety of musical instruments was easily available to him. Moon and Joe played in a group called "Traditional Grass" sometime in the '80s, and it was just what Moon wanted. Flatt and Scruggs, Reno and Smiley, and old Dolly Parton songs were in their repertoire. Joe's banjo playing is smooth as satin, unhurried, utterly tasteful, and his tenor singing is just what anybody would want: high, thin, and clear.

Moon was beloved by so many musicians. He played their records, and he'd say his criticism right out. There was no "geein' and hawin'" in Moon's world. He plowed a straight row, or he didn't plow at all.

Here are some of Moon's Moonerisms. All of his metaphors were for farmers, musicians, who he considered real people, all attuned to the natural world.

MOONERISMS

If your vessel needs tunin', or your saw needs filin', or your tom cat needs thrashin' go to Homer Grosses' Phillips 66 Station. We'll thrash your cat without using any profanity, make your car sound like a mouse chewin' on a piece of cornbread, set your saw or upset your ax—whatever you need done.

Don't mess up a hundred-dollar drunk with a twenty-cent sandwich.

These Uniroyal steel belt radials are good as long as your engine'll run and your axle ain't a'draggin'.

After reading umpteen school closings and event cancellations due to weather, Moon said, "The Ohio River's only runnin' three days a week now.

There ain't enough people here to start a fight on the Fourth of July with a fifth of whiskey.

I was here ten minutes before my hind end ever got here ... no, that's how bad hit's a'draggin' today ... I'd a been as well off to not put the bridle on the mule ... shoulda just left him on the hill. I ain't a'doin' no good a'tall today ... I needed to come to work today about like a hog needs a songbook.

On Charlie Elam's furniture store in South Lebanon ... Git you one them RCA color consoles ... that's the ones that's got the wood all the way to the floor.

PESTER FLATT AND THE MAGIC OF GOOD WRITING

When the first letter appeared in my mailbox at WNKU radio, I was amused. But I read it and chuckled. The writer signed himself "Pester Flatt." (If you don't know Bluegrass music, Pester's name was an obvious riff on Lester Flatt of Flatt and Scruggs, known best to American audiences for their music on *Beverly Hillbillies*.)

I assumed the letter came from some traveling band playing a joke. On the second page of the typed letter was a brown ring where Pester had obviously rested his coffee cup. "Sorry about the coffee stain," he always said.

His hook was that he had a bluegrass band, and that was the reason he wrote me that first time. He wanted me to announce a name change for the band. Their original name, Pester Flatt and the Lefties, had hurt their bookings at VFWs and Knights of Columbus functions, and so they'd adopted a name change to Pester Flatt and the Rarely Paid. Pester quickly found work playing for organizations like SQUID (the Society Questioning Underlying Intelligent Design), eating at his favorite Waffle House restaurants and living at the E-Z Sleep Motor Court in his hometown of Tepid Springs, Kentucky.

As weeks went on, he continued to write. He had a snappy letterhead showing a band of left-handed pickers with the name PESTER FLATT and THE RARELY PAID. I learned about their manager, Wesley Fatchance, of Better Bookings By and By who owned the E-Z Sleep where Pester lived. Remarkably, the rooms still had rotary dial phones, and outside his window a neon light animated a little saw that moved back and forth across a picture of a log.

I learned the names of his band members gradually: on banjo, Ford Maddox Ford; Acme Ruehlman on mandolin; Stinky Ashcroft on fiddle; and Little Max played bass and drove the bus. (Little Max has since been busted for taking human growth hormone.)

All that first summer Pester wrote me about the festivals he was playing: He had dates for the Flotsam County Fair, the Boysenberry Festival, and his hometown gig at the Woodbine Twineth Retirement Home. He wrote that he had gotten hung up in Eastern Europe on the ever-popular Still Tryin' to Get Down from the Mountain Tour. Another time, he was captured by extraterrestrials and woke up in a Tod Oldham Barcalounger with little space creatures probing his brain. He didn't forget his mother on Mother's Day, either: he had a seat reserved for her at the Waffle House and paid for the whole thing, minus tax, tip and service.

One of the best letters Pester ever wrote is now in the possession of the Bill Monroe Foundation, and it contains the inside story of the "Shroud of Rosine." Rosine, Kentucky, was where Monroe was born, of course. In fact, it's true that someone broke into Monroe's house and smashed his legendary Gibson F-5 mandolin.

What we didn't know—but Pester did—is that Monroe fashioned a makeshift bag out of a linen handkerchief, put the remains of the mandolin in it and took it to Gibson to see if it could be repaired. "Recognizing it as an almost holy relic," Pester wrote, the technician, Charles Derrington, spent four months sorting and gluing five hundred tiny splinters of wood back together.

"They say the great man wept," Pester wrote of Monroe when they returned his restored F-5. "What they don't tell you is that Derrington neglected to return the linen handkerchief."

He had cast it aside until one day he was using it as a polishing cloth and observed the faint image of the shattered F-5. Pester wrote that Derrington vanished under mysterious circumstances and the "Shroud of Rosine" (as it has come to be known) has resurfaced only periodically over the years, once in the Lincoln Bedroom during the Clinton administration. Pester and the boys promptly had tee shirts made with the shroud on one side and Mel Gibson on the back.

The truth is, after over a year's worth of letters, I still have no idea who Pester is. I have Googled him of course, with no luck. Wayne has been checking the Country Blogosphere—ditto. His letters arrive in my mailbox sometime during the week. At first, Wayne and I handled them with tweezers and plastic bags, hoping we could dust for fingerprints or get DNA off the saliva used to seal the envelope. But the magic of Pester's writing, the wonderful way he illumined our Sunday night world, gradually began to work its magic, and we have come around to thinking that whoever Pester is, he has been a gift to us, as good writing always is (and Pester is a very good writer), and it might be best not to ask too many questions.

In *Charlotte's Web*, E.B. White's book about a writer who happened to be a spider, the barnyard animals looked far and wide for just the right word for Charlotte to spin into her web, and she saved her friend's life at the expense of her own. Sometimes writing is like that: it can transform and transcend, inspire, and entertain. Words define us, elevate us. They "fix" us like flies in amber and sometimes tumble out of our mouths with the skill of acrobats.

Join us some Sunday night, why don't you? We're working on an intervention for Little Max (the one who's addicted to human growth hormone).

By the way, if Pester should happen to read this, sorry I don't have a coffee stain—Kaldi's is closed.

RADIO: "MASH THE BUTTONS, WAYNE"

O PESTER, WHO ART THOU?

I opened my first letter from Pester Flatt on a winter night in 2004, toward the end of my shift on WNKU's bluegrass radio show, *Music From the Hills of Home*. Wayne Clyburn, my cohost, and I were in our usual end-of-show rush to get logs signed and CDs re-filed when we noticed the envelope. I opened it and began reading—first to myself, then aloud to our listeners. The writer called himself "Pester Flatt," a take-off on popular bluegrass singer Lester Flatt. He told me his band's name—Pester Flatt and the Lefties—was costing them bookings at VFW and American Legion Halls, and he felt a new, fresh band name might lead to better bookings.

I was intrigued. The letters kept coming and over the next few years, our curiosity at the boil, Wayne and I searched for Pester's true identity. Our search waned, though, as soon as we realized our good fortune in having such "an excellent writer," as E.B. White would have called him. Pester was (and still is) pure entertainment. He was so popular that we learned to read his letters at 7:30 p.m., because listeners wanted to know when to tune in to hear them. That is, if there was a letter. Pester would leave us twisting on the rotisserie for weeks at a time, then the letters would pour in again with news of the band's doings—country star Arf Starley's latest outrage, say, or the time Pester was abducted by aliens, or the latest turn in his romance with girl singer Dessie Belle.

I was proud that Pester chose us to write to. I came to value his fine intelligence, the quality of his character, and his wonderful sense of humor. When I reached out, Pester surprised me by suggesting instead that we conduct an interview and relive some of the highlights of his lengthy correspondence. So I made the drive down to his hometown of Tepid Spring, Kentucky, a place best known for being, as the Bureau of Tepid Tourism declares, "Not Real Far North of Nashville." We met for dinner at Pester's favorite breakfast joint, a greasy spoon called The Broke Yolk where the owner, Ivy Gabbard, seated us in a corner booth. I didn't waste any time getting to my questions.

Katie: What's up with these menus?

Pester: Ivy discovered that ever' time Apple releases another innovation, she has better sales if she puts an "i" in front of somethin' on the menu. She started with the breakfast items when she introduced Biscuits with Red iGravy. Turnin' her attention to lunch and dinner, she added the Rib iSteak (with Delmonico Potatoes), and the ever-popular Eight-Ounce Cod Log is now known as the iCod. She's tryin' to figure out a way to apply this concept to her Carrot Ambrosia, so if you have any ideas there's a free meal in it for you.

Katie: While we're waiting for a server, tell me, when did you realize you wanted to be a musician?

Pester: First time I saw Vivian Della Chiesa sing. I told my daddy that I wanted to be like the lady on the TV and right quick he shipped me off to military school. That's where I learned to pick guitar and first sang in front of an audience.

Katie: How old were you?

Pester: I was in my early thirties. After graduation, I got my first job playin' comb and wax paper with Mad Anthony Wayne Clyburn and the Cynical Mountain Boys. It was tougher training than the academy, but I learned from the great man and 'fore long I started my own string band—The Lactose Intolerant Four. We did a morning radio show just before Farm Report. There was a contract dispute with the sponsor and we soon became The Sunny Boys of Civil Litigation.

Katie: Your manager, Wesley Fatchance, is considered the Colonel Tom Parker of bluegrass. How did you two team up?

Pester: He was the show sponsor, CEO of Fatchance Talent & Literary Agency and its subsidiary, Better Bookings By and By. He offered to drop the lawsuit if we let him manage the band. The first posters he printed had our image backwards, so it looked like me and the Boys were playin' left-handed.

Wesley—or Mr. Fatchance, as I am obliged to call him—thought this'd be a great "hook." We liked the idea 'til we had to learn to play our instruments th' other way 'round.

Katie: But it seems that any interest generated by an all left-handed band was offset by another marketing decision, the band's name.

Pester: Yeah. He billed us as Pester Flatt and the Lefties and we started losing our regular gigs at Knights of Columbus and VFW halls all over Flotsam County. That's when we settled on Pester Flatt and the Rarely Paid. Been playin' bluegrass festivals and workin' steady ever since, though most of that steady work is my day job over to the Restaurant Supply Warehouse. I'm Associate Sharpener in the Cutlery Division.

Katie: You mentioned Better Bookings By and By. They're the folks behind the Better Bookings By and By Bluegrass Music Association, or the B5MA, as we say in the biz. In 1986, they honored you with the "Song of the Year" award for what they called your "gut-wrenching rendition" of "Wipin' My Eyes with Your Tissue of Lies."

Pester: That's a true song. I wrote that when Larva, the first Mrs. Flatt, left me. She was my muse and, after she split, the songs stopped comin'. I s'pose I was seekin' that same inspiration when I married four more women.

Katie: I didn't know that was legal in Kentucky.

Pester: Not all at once. But four more divorces didn't help, neither. I wrote "Will There Be Any Porch Ducks in Heaven?" I wrote "Mother's Not Dead, She's Only Sleepin' It Off." I wrote some awful sad songs and I wrote some awful songs, but none as true as "Wipin' My Eyes with Your Tissue of Lies."

Katie: But in these last few years, you have found true love with, of all people, the girl singer in your band. Who also happens to be the only person, of any gender, to play bluegrass sousaphone.

Pester: You're talkin' 'bout Dessie Belle.

Katie: Well, of course I'm talking about Dessie Belle. And you know what they say: "Love is lovelier the sixth time around." Might we hear the sound of wedding bells yet again?

Pester: I don't think so. I've written enough songs.

Katie: Are you on good terms with your ex-wives?

Pester: Unless I need a scented candle, I don't see 'em much. Laurel, Lutie, Levitra, and Beverly-Ann all went into business with Juanita Fatchance, Wesley's sister. They relocated Juanita's thriving craft boutique into an old, abandoned service station. They took advantage of the service bay—the one with a door at each end—to create what is purportedly the only drive-thru craft mall in the Commonwealth.

Katie: And what about Larva?

Pester: She's the mother of my children, so I keep in touch with Larva. 'Course, I can't call her. Have to wait for her to call me on account of that restraining order. But we're friendly. In fact, we recently celebrated our Silver Anniversary.

Katie: I thought you were divorced.

Pester: That's right. It was twenty-five years ago that Larva filed the papers. So, to commemorate the occasion, we had a little ceremony over to the Flotsam County Courthouse where we renewed our divorce vows. All our friends and family was there as we affirmed our commitment to not stay married. It was very emotional and, for a minute, I thought even Larva was cryin'. Turned out it was just that tattooed tear under her left eye.

My only regret was that my oldest boy, Bradley Kincaid Flatt, couldn't be there. He was in final rehearsals for their fall series over to the State Route Dinner Theatre.

Katie: He's been called "the John Doyle of Dinner Theatre" because of his modern re-staging of perennial favorites.

Pester: He ain't afraid to tackle the most sensitive subjects. That show brung together our collective longing for immortality with the delicate topic of erectile dysfunction in a production entitled *The Prescription of Dorian Gray*.

Katie: There was high praise from the critics. The online edition of *The Inkwire* said, "This work has been infused with a new relevance, a new immediacy that hasn't been seen in a production since somebody first combined dining and dramatics under one roof."

RADIO: "MASH THE BUTTONS, WAYNE"

Pester: That's how come he's been invited to direct the summer subscription series over to the Fairnuff Center for the Arts. They're hopin' to get one of them Regional Tony Awards.

Katie: And now father and son are working together on perhaps the biggest annual event in Tepid Spring, Kentucky. How did that come about?

Pester: Ever' year the holiday crowds just get bigger and bigger. The Tepid Interfaith Council decided to employ more than one venue to accommodate the overflow. Festivities will begin at Our Lady of the Dixie Highway, move on to the Temple Pam and finish up at the Sheet Rock Baptist Church. That's how come this year's event will be billed as Tepid Spring's First Annual Church Crawl (with horse-drawn carriage rides and regular shuttle service between the venues). They chose to end the evening at the Sheet Rock on account of their big, open plan and unobstructed views. There will be a marathon performance of a new work entitled *Away in Some Manger*, written and directed by my son B.K. and produced by the good folks over to the State Route Dinner Theatre.

Like I said, he's been a-studyin' John Doyle's version of *Sweeney Todd and Company*, where the actors accompany theirselves on musical instruments. That's how come he casted me and my band members in the thing. *The Inkwire's* drama critic attended the final dress rehearsal and though she complained about the sponsorship logos on the manger and the fact that Joseph wears a feed-cap, she had nothin' but nice things to say about the rest of the show.

Katie: Indeed! I have a copy of the review right here: "Pester Flatt, Acme Reuhlman, and Ford Maddox Ford appear as the Three Wise Men. Their journey is energized by the cheerfully haunting number 'Oh Dem Swaddlin' Clothes' in a minor key. Then, upon discovering the manger, they seamlessly segue into a rapturous rendition of 'Savior in the Straw.' And though the Good Book says 'Thou shalt not,' the venerable Shecky McReynolds steals the show as the curmudgeonly innkeeper who, for no apparent reason, affects an Italian accent in his only musical number, 'The Inn, She Has No Rooms.'

"Little Max Wasserstein brings an infantile worldliness to the role of 'The Baby' and by accompanying himself on a large upright bass not only exudes a resonant profundity but dramatically accentuates his smallness among the rest of the players. The closing number reflects the director's modernist musings when the ensemble performs 'Shotgun Shells Over Galilee.' And you'll be 'Breakin' Up Christmas' when they start breaking down the fourth wall as the barn animals descend from the stage and assume seats in the house—a moment that even the most devout will find disquieting. In short, *Away in Some Manger* is the feel-good hit of what used to be called 'the Christmas Season.'"

Pester: Yeah, but if the folks up to Cincinnati hear that, we won't have enough motel rooms to hold the crowd!

Katie: I understand this year's celebration almost didn't happen.

Pester: That's right. Mahatma Gaither—new owner of the Chester Arthur Motel—agreed to chair this year's festival on account of last-year's cochairs purchased a timeshare on the Gulf Coast and will be winterin' in Venice, Florida. They abdicated just in time to avoid the committee meetin' before things got ugly. There was a big to-do about the fact that the event was not inclusive or diverse enough. The Wiccans in our community complained that we was helpin' ourselves to pagan decorations—the wreath, the holly, mistletoe, and the tree—but not includin' them in the namin' rights or givin' 'em proper credit. Bill O'Reilly—no relation to the famous Bill O'Reilly but an equally bitter man—declared this to be the latest battle in the "War on Christmas." He brung a buncha folks with him to the meetin' and refused to give up the microphone once he got started. After some forty minutes of this, Rebecca Nurse, chair of the Wiccan subcommittee, mumbled somethin' and turned Mr. O'Reilly into a plastic lawn ornament—a light-up snowman, to be precise—just long enough to hear from some other folks and conclude the meetin'. You'd think that would humble a fella, but when she reversed the spell he seemed just as angry as before. Though that could be 'cause an electrical cord remained attached to the backside of his trousers. He got even more agitated when somebody tried to plug him in. The committee briefly considered a motion to rename the event with all faiths and denominations, but there ain't enough room on the rental sign for all them letters. And, while last year's name—The Winter Solstice Celebration—was very big with the Wiccans, it alienated many of the Fundamentals. But "propensity is the mother of convention" and the new name revealed itself as we worked out the particulars.

Katie: On my way into town, I saw the Voluntary Fire Department out with the ladder truck hanging wreaths and bows on the streetlights. I was reminded that each year Tepid Spring recognizes the best decorated home with a Beautification Award. The whole town appears to be decorated. It's a city of lights, like Paris.

Pester: Paris, Kentucky, maybe. But you're right, there's lotsa lights out there—good thing we're in coal country. Most folks favor the white lights, although one family has wrapped the small tree out front with a million itty-bitty red ones. It is alarmingly beautiful. And for the hundredth year in a row, Old Man Latham has adorned the shrubs and the porch with those big blue bulbs that he bought during the Eisenhower administration. It is out of time and out of place and it'd be garish if it wasn't so stirring—all that blue light in the dark night.

Katie: So did one of those folks win the award?

Pester: Well, this year's award has been held up in committee, not because they couldn't come to agreement but 'cause they didn't know how to explain the decision. And it was a shocker. The honors went to Uncle Dewey Pasternak. He's not any kin of mine, just ever'body calls him "Uncle" Dewey.

Katie: Why did that shock people?

Pester: The reason the decision was so controversial was that he didn't hang but one bulb on his whole house and no other kinda decorations either. But you have to see it to understand how come they give him the award. If you can imagine a little bungalow with one tiny bulb so perfectly placed that it gives you a lump in your throat and makes you smile at the same time. I mean, at other houses there's light-up figures and animated Disney characters and chaser lights and sound effects and cars pull up and people point at stuff and laugh and hop back into their cars and they're off to the next place. But here, folks stop talkin' and ever'one just stares at the little bulb on the little house. Stand there for the longest time. And folks don't say g'bye when they part. They just put a hand on a shoulder and simply smile and nod 'cause they don't wanna break the perfect stillness. And if you go for coffee afterwards, you notice folks tryin' to talk about it, but don't none of 'em know how.

Katie: That'd be worthy of its own article.

Pester: The Inkwire decided to do just that under the title, "This Little Light of Mine." Uncle Dewey told 'em if they ran it under that headline, he wasn't gonna grant an interview. *The Inkwire*'s field reporter asked him if he could put into words the statement he was tryin' to make by decoratin' his house with just one bulb. Uncle Dewey replied that if he could say it with words, he wouldn't have bothered to hang the bulb. You should drive by on your way outta town. It'll put you in right smart of the spirit. Makes ever'thing seem more special. Even the tire-chains on the big salt trucks sound like sleigh bells.

Katie: That's a lovely note to end on. Before I head back to the "Upland South," is there anything you'd like to ask me?

Pester: Yeah. If you're not gonna finish that iCod, can I have a bite?

LETTER TO PESTER

Dear Pester,

Though I don't know who you are or where you are, I feel compelled to write to you and tell you how much your letters have meant to me, a plain, simple bluegrass DJ in the heart of northern Kentucky. When a star like yourself takes time out from his busy schedule to write to an ordinary person like myself, well, sometimes lightning strikes. I can imagine you sitting at the Waffle House right now, pouring yourself a "cup of ambition" as Dolly Parton would say, with all your worries about Dessie Belle (from a woman who's had a career a lot like Dessie Belle's; listen to me, Pester, she is cheating on you) and Mr. Wesley Fatchance (as you are obliged to call him) at Better Bookings By and By, that you'd take time out to write to me and the guy who plays Wayne means you've got that something special it takes to make it in this dog-eat-dog business.

I'm glad that the prom season is over, as you'll be able to rest better at the E-Z Sleep Motel. I used to know a fiddle player named Buddy Griffin who lived at a motel. It was in Batavia, and it was eventually razed to the ground by the man who runs that Crystal Palace religious organization down south somewhere.

Living at a motel can be bad for your nerves and your digestion and can end up making you fidgety. If you love me, and I know you do, give up Dessie Belle and her flighty ways and get yourself a good woman who will fix you a nice cube steak of an evening and make sure you get your shirts ironed before your gigs. This fiddle player who lived in the motel I was telling you about had to leave his laundry out in Milford, Ohio, and pick it up on the way to a personal appearance and trust that his buttons were sewn on and his blue jeans properly pressed. Nobody can do this as well as a good woman, Pester, and you can find one if you just set your head to it.

Your friends and devoted admirers,
Katie Laur and the guy who plays Wayne

9
FRIENDS

APPEARING AT IRMA LAZARUS'S BIRTHDAY CELEBRATION: JIM HUEY ON DOBRO; JEFF ROBERTS ON BANJO; TOM CAHALL ON BASS; KATIE LAUR; AND BUDDY GRIFFIN ON FIDDLE.

AFTERNOONS WITH IRMA

On hot, muggy Cincinnati summer days, I drive my old Ford up the elegantly curved blacktop lane to the Lazarus house, past the patch of watercress that Irma planted many years ago in a cool stream of water that trickles from the top of the hill. When I park and walk through the gate, into the shade of the massive oak tree, the temperature seems to drop ten degrees. Suddenly, the Springer spaniels are upon me, jumping and whimpering with excitement, their whole bodies wagging along with their tails. The male, Sean, has a green tennis ball in his mouth and his big brown eyes are shining and hopeful, but I am firm and walk down the stairs to the terrace.

Irma lies stretched out in her Brown Jordan *chaise longue* under a modern-styled canopy, the famous Lazarus Lizards darting across the hot bricks into rocky crevices. Over the tops of the trees behind her, I can see the river and the skyscraper of downtown Cincinnati, the city which Irma Lazarus helped to shape as surely as any politician or public figure in the history of the city.

"Hello, darling," she says, looking up from the book she is reading, which is wrapped in a yellow Mercantile Library dust cover, and gives me a smile. I take her hand and give it a light squeeze.

"How are you today?" I ask, for she has been ill a while now.

"Not good," she replies, in a matter of fact way, and changes the subject.

"You know," she says, "I love looking at my trees now. They're like the marks you put on the door to measure yourself when you're a child; I can tell my age from them."

She points to a large tree of a pale green, almost yellow, standing with the other trees that line the drive.

"That's a raintree," she says. "I don't think there's really a Raintree County in Indiana, but years ago, when that movie came out, I planted the tree as a sapling. Now look how big it has grown. It's almost luminous, don't you think?"

She is right. Once I notice it, my eyes return to it again and again.

※

The north end of the Hyde Park grounds surrounding her house are thick with wild flowers and a few dogwood and redbud trees that bloom sweetly in the spring. Everything is quiet here, like a nature preserve. Before she was ill, Irma was an avid gardener, and on the summer days when I came to swim, she'd be pulling weeds like a driven women. I might find an entire theater company in the pool, or as I did one day, Mikhail Baryshnikov poised on the diving board in a leopard-skin bikini, the tiny ballerinas in his troupe sitting in lounge chairs on the terrace, stitching their pink satin toe shoes like fairies.

"I bought this land for $3,000 while Fred was in France in World War II," she says, waving her hand over her domain, "and everybody told me I was crazy. Fred's brother told me I would not like my neighbors. Everyone else said it was simply not the 'in' neighborhood. I bought it anyway," she says, pausing to take a swat at Sybil who is pawing at her legs.

"I'm impressed with how much better disciplined these dogs are since Ashley Stephenson's first visit," I say, my tongue in my cheek.

Irma laughs happily at the mention of his name. "Wasn't he simply wonderful," Irma says.

Ashley Stephenson was the Queen's Royal Horticulturist, and he came from London a few years ago to judge the Cincinnati Flower and Garden Show. Sean and Sybil had been pups then and completely out of control. On the last Sunday of his visit, the weekend of the Kentucky Derby, Fred made mint juleps so potent that after drinking just one, the Queen's Royal Horticulturist stopped talking about the Latin names for plants and loosened up enough to share with us his favorite recipe for Spotted Dick.

"Let me show you how I discipline the Queen's dogs," he said. He stood, Sean and Sybil jumped on him, and he took the two fingers of his right hand and brought them down sharply on their noses. The dogs sat down instantly and looked surprised; discipline was an altogether new concept for them. "You see," Stephenson said, "you just give them a thwack."

FRIENDS

We were all on our second mint juleps by then, and Irma and I were so amused by the word "thwack" that, later, whenever one of us said it, both of us would giggle uncontrollably. A few days later the whole affair was just a dim memory to Sean and Sybil, and they were worse than ever.

"Once I bought the land," Irma says, talking about her house, "I had an aerial photograph taken and sent to Fred—he was stationed in France—and he was enthusiastic about it. He consulted a number of European artisans, and we began to plan the house. My sister Eleanor's husband, Carl Strauss, designed it."

She looks happily at her house, a weathered modern-looking Bauhaus kind of structure, sitting at the end of the driveway. It is unpretentious, with a glassed-in room on the lowest level and a long patio on the second level, connected by a stone stairway, lined with tall cactus plants. "Did you notice the clematis this spring" she asks, and I nod enthusiastically. It curled around the trellis by the driveway, its blossoms vivid purple.

She sits up, away from the back support of the lounge, takes off her straw hat and pulls her white hair into a pin high on her head. At 81, she still wears the dramatic dark glasses, the Irma Lazarus eyelashes. Nobody in Cincinnati can pull off glamour as well as she does.

First of all, it's the company she keeps: her friends are captains of industry, prominent politicians, and the cream of the arts world. Then, for all her public persona, she has always been a private, occasionally inaccessible person for whom the telephone is anathema. Another component of her glamour is her daring sense of fashion. When someone complimented her on her outfit at a gala one night, she said she had her dressmaker whip it up out of the late Thomas Schippers' white eyelet curtains. According to Fred, she once had an evening coat made from a brightly covered shawl she bought at a Goodwill store, and she wore it to a symphony function in New York City. In the *Times* the next day, there was a picture of three society women: Mrs. So-and-So in her Oscar de la Renta, Mrs. Such-and-Such in her Givenchy, and Mrs. Fred Lazarus III whose outfit came from Goodwill.

She wore miniskirts and black fishnet stockings in the '70s and boogalooed at discos until the wee hours of the morning; then the next day she'd be up and on the road by 6:30 a.m., stumping for the Ohio Arts Council—which she and Fred nurtured through its infancy—or driving somewhere giving speeches to promote the orchestra. During this time (when she was also raising five children), she hosted her own television show on the arts on WCET, called *Conversations with Irma*, on the air for more than thirty-five years.

Once a week she interviewed notables such as her dear friends, Leonard Bernstein, Beverly Sills, Aaron Copland, Carol Channing, and Roberta Peters. She has said that her most fascinating interview was with conductor Wagner's grandson, who talked about skinheads and anti-Semitism. Of the Copland interview, "I wish Channel 48 hadn't destroyed it—or reused it, whatever they did—because it was his 75th birthday, and he said something surprising to me. He said that as he aged, ideas still bubbled up inside him as much as they ever had, but that he felt less urgent about them. I'd have expected just the opposite."

Irma raises herself from her chair and walks slowly towards the pool. "It's time for my exercises," she says cheerfully. "A therapist came to the house and prescribed them to strengthen my arms and legs." She wades into the cold water and begins to lift one leg slowly and painfully against the weight of the water.

She talks while she does her movements. "I knew twelve conductors well in my lifetime; they stayed at my house from time to time. One Thanksgiving, Eric Leinsdorf and his wife cooked Thanksgiving dinner for Fred and me and Michael Gielen and Bernie Rubenstein. Having three of them at the same time was a bit risky naturally—we could all hear Leinsdorf ordering his wife about in the kitchen—but it turned out fine, and we had a great dinner.

"Of course, my favorite was Lenny," she says smiling, speaking of Leonard Bernstein, whose career she guided and nurtured. "Lenny always used to say that praising an artist was like pouring sugar through a sieve; they can't get enough of it."

"How wonderful it must have been to know him," I say and she nods her head.

"He threw himself into everything. All his energy, all his passion, he brought to everything he did. But he could get carried away with himself sometimes, and his wife, Felicia, was quite good for him. She'd prick his balloons." Irma laughs and begins to stretch her arms. "There is a famous story about a conductor who died while waving his baton about, and Lenny got quite emotional and said that he simply couldn't think of a better way to go. Felicia thought about it a while and said, 'I think I'd rather go at Bloomingdale's.'"

"I met Lenny here in Cincinnati when he came to audition for a job which he didn't get, and then later, Fred and I were at Aspen. And Lenny was staying there as well, trying to be incognito, which was ridiculous. Absolutely everybody knew it was him. I wrote him a note saying that Fred and I were staying at the same hotel and asking him to ring us. He did and he said, 'Irma, you have to teach me to ski.' I said I had never taught anybody, but his instructor kept following him around, wanting to talk about his own interpretation of Brahms, so I agreed to do it. I went to the gift shop and bought a very small replica of the Norse Snow God for him. As we climbed higher on the lift, I thought: *what if he can't even get down the slope*. But I needn't have worried. He was a wild, reckless skier, and when he started down the slope, people just scattered in every direction, getting out of his way. He was absolutely fearless."

The spaniels are tugging relentlessly at Irma's arm. When she finally throws the tennis ball into the swimming pool, the dogs run as fast as they can, each of them trying to reach the ball first. It is Sybil who plunges into the pool and climbs out with it grasped tightly in her jaws. Sean is waiting, and with a growl and a bit of bullying, takes the ball away from her and trots proudly back to his mistress with it.

Irma shakes her head. "She does all the work," she said, "and he gets all the glory. It's still a man's world. I was working at the symphony with a man I admired a lot, and he came to me one day and said, 'Irma, you really ought to be chairman of the board of the symphony but, of course, that's impossible. You're a woman. The chairman of the board has to be a man.' I told him he was right of course, with my fingers crossed behind my back.

"When I was a young volunteer, I was quite outspoken. I didn't like the conductor, and there were a number of other things I felt were needed to make this a first-class orchestra. One day I got a call from the president of the symphony asking for an appointment to meet with me, and I thought 'Uh-oh, I'm going to get told to keep my mouth shut.' Instead, he wanted to ask me to head up the woman's committee, because, as he put it, 'we've never had a Jewish woman do that.'"

Irma pulls herself cautiously out of the pool, smiling at the ironies of a world she has already begun to shut out.

"But why did you do it all?" I blurt. "And where did you get the energy?" It is something I have always wanted to ask.

"Well, darling," she says slowly, "I was born privileged, and to tell the truth, I have always felt a little guilty about it. My twin sister, Eleanor, and I were born after my parents had been married seven years. They wanted children badly, and all of a sudden they got twin girls. We had a German fraulein, which was the thing in those days, and my father would walk behind her when she was strolling us down the avenue so that he could overhear the oohs and ahhs and 'Aren't they precious' comments from other people as they passed us on the sidewalk. He was so proud of us.

"Then, too," she says, lowering herself carefully into her chair on the terrace, "my mother was a classical singer. She gave recitals and sang professionally, really, and of course they went regularly to the opera, so I grew up loving music. When I was at Smith College, the emphasis was on involvement, working to make the world a better place, that sort of thing. But in the end," she says, finally stretched out again on the lounge chair, "volunteering is simply a way of life in Cincinnati, more than any other place I've ever been."

*

We are both quiet for a while, and I see she has nodded off for her afternoon nap. I slide quietly into the cool water and begin my laps, but my mind is crowded with memories of Irma and Fred, the color and excitement they have always brought to everyday events. I remember swimming here late one night after performing in one-hundred-degree heat at a bluegrass festival at Stone Valley. I was tired and grumpy at the festival, and suddenly Irma and Fred and a group of Spanish expatriates they had befriended, pulled into the festival grounds in Fred's black Mercedes.

Irma has always been at her best in the unbearable heat, and she had brought a picnic basket with her. I had told her that most folks did this at bluegrass festivals as they can sit in the shade listening to the music as long as they wanted. But I was dismayed at the contents of her basket. Instead of fried chicken or ham sandwiches, she brought pâté and wafer-thin water biscuits, a plate of sliced tomatoes dressed in oil and fresh basil, a chocolate bundt cake, and of course a couple of excellent white wines from Fred's cellar instead of a six-pack of Pabst Blue Ribbon. I laughed and told her she hadn't got it quite right, but all of us sat under a shade tree and ate happily, and my cross mood dissolved instantly.

I stop swimming at the end of the pool and shake the wet hair out of my eyes. When I look up, a shaft of sunlight is illuminating Irma's raintree. It is a moment of pure enchantment, and suddenly my mind calls up my loveliest memory of Irma and Fred.

It all happened on an otherwise dull night at Arnold's downtown, where I used to sing on Tuesday nights with a swingy jazz band called the Rhythm Rangers. Fred and Irma came in with a group of friends after a playhouse performance. Irma was dressed in Thomas Schippers' curtains that night, as I remember, and she looked as beautiful as I had ever seen her, her salt-and-pepper hair freshly coiffed, her smile radiant.

She danced for a while with Maurice Jacobs, her favorite partner in those days, and they looked to me like something out of a movie. I sang "Mean to Me" for her, and as the room became more crowded, she and Morrie danced themselves out the back door and onto the sidewalk. The band was playing "Rose Room" and Irma and Morrie were whirling around the sidewalk like Fred Astaire and Ginger Rogers. I watched them through the window, and presently Fred went outside and tapped Morrie on the shoulder and cut in.

I walked quietly out the door to watch them. The moon was nearly full, and the fruit trees in front of Arnold's were just beginning to blossom. Fred gathered Irma into his arms quite naturally and said to her in a sort of sexy way, "Irma, I don't think you're allowed to dance on the sidewalks." They danced together cheek-to-cheek, down the sidewalk, away from me, but I could see them as they passed beneath the streetlights, and the notes of the clarinetist, playing "Rose Room" wafted sweetly on the night air.

CRUISIN' DOWN THE RIVER

On Highway 52, going east from Cincinnati, you pass the dun-colored horse stables at River Downs, looking like tracks of rabbit warrens, thick with mud. Used Christmas tree signs dot the horizon, leftover from the holiday, along with a toppled, tattered sign saying "Donald Trump for President," which has been abandoned like the "Sparkle Maid for Hire" sign. This is conservative country we are entering.

"It's hard not to take it personally," my friend, Nicky, says, about the rusted-out scenery. We are taking a drive today, east to Georgetown, Ohio, and we are in a light-hearted mood. For one thing, we are riding in style in Nicky's dark plum Cadillac, the one he bought when he was in Hollywood working in big-time show business. Since he's moved back to Ohio, the car seems a little frivolous, but it is oh-so comfortable we could ride forever like a male/female version of Thelma and Louise. I turn the car stereo up, and we listen to Ella Fitzgerald singing George Gershwin, and we drive on past the dreariness, past the silos at Moscow churning out clouds of white smoke, and a tattered Confederate flag nailed to a billboard.

Once we leave the detritus and dreariness behind, the Ohio River comes into view, shining, metallic, its currents standing out on the surface of the water like the ruffles on an evening gown. Two boys stand on the bank skipping stones across the water, their small faces and hands red and chapped from the biting wind. On this winter's day, the sun hits the Ohio River just right to make the water sparkle and dance. Tree trunks lean slightly towards the current as we drive alongside on Route 52. It is cold; it is January.

A long, slow barge comes into view, floating majestically. Nicky laughs and says that barges offend him. He has lived in California for so long he is put off by anything slow and deliberate. "Get out of my way," Nicky says, flinging his head back just like Franklin D. Roosevelt as we pass a Mail Pouch tobacco barn.

Like Nicky, I have lived close to the Ohio River for most of my life. I could see the river from the window of the first apartment I lived in when I came to Cincinnati in 1966, and I suspect the river itself has become part of my DNA. So many things I've done have been directly related to the river. In fact, it is hard to imagine anything important happening in Cincinnati without the Ohio River as a backdrop.

Back in the days when settlers drifted down the Erie Canal from New England farms with their lives and their belongings loaded onto wagons, the Ohio River was their goal. The first Europeans to see the river were the French explorers in birch bark canoes who called it *La Belle Rivière* (Beautiful River) as they paddled past the rich countryside, loaded with game. It was much later that the settlers came.

Around Pittsburgh, they strapped everything they owned, including the parlor piano, on flat boats, and let the river take them into Ohio. It was a little like taking a roller coaster ride, braving the currents and the white water rapids. The ones who survived it got oxen to pull the flat boats on dry land, or else simply bought teams of horses and covered wagons to take them into Cincinnati. Those who could afford it bought passage on the gaily painted steamboats sailing up and down the River. Some were headed for St. Louis, some for California, others were gone prospecting for gold.

Nicky and I were still listening to the radio in the Cadillac and prowling down the backroads of little towns like Ripley and Higginsport. All of these villages were about the same size: population 1,600, stone houses lining the streets, large maple trees, the branches bare and colorless now. Before long it will be time to tap the sugar and boil it down to make maple syrup. The river is more than an address; it is a way of life.

Years ago, I was engaged to marry a young man from Higginsport. His father had pitched on the Higginsport softball team, and Tom and his family had lived on the floor over the Higginsport Post Office. Tom loved the river and learned to swim holding on to the tail of his collie dog, Rex. After he was grown, Tom still had a great dog-paddle stroke, his head out of the water (he wore glasses while he swam), his arms and legs paddling stoutly underneath the surface of the water.

For a few charmed years, Tom and I hiked the Nature Center in Hillsboro with our dog, Hoosier. Nights, we played with an old-time jazz band on the patio at Arnold's with the stars overhead. Then on a hot summer day in 1989, Tom was killed instantly by a bolt of lightning at King's Island after a gig. He was buried in his family's plot in the cemetery in Georgetown. The funeral was crowded and, as such things can sometimes be, almost festive. Most of the river-town people were there, the women dressed in wide-brimmed straw hats and flowered silk dresses. Musicians and friends from Cincinnati came as well, dressed a little more casually.

After that, on Sundays, I would drive to Georgetown, just a little ways short of Ripley, to sit with Tom's widowed father, Perry Cahall. I'd watch a baseball game with him, talk to him about music (he had been a tuba player). One Sunday, right where I turned off of 52 to go to Georgetown, my previously non-functioning car radio suddenly came on and Hazel Dickens was singing "Hills of Home," as country as only Hazel could sing it.

Quick tears came to my eyes, and after my visit to Tom's father I went home and found my old records and played them. A week later, Sheila Rue, who was the general manager of public radio's WNKU, approached me at

Arnold's about doing a radio show on Sundays on that station. Did I have any ideas?

Luckily, I did. "How about a bluegrass show called *Music from the Hills of Home*? I said, and they liked it and hired me with a minimum of fuss. With Tom gone, I needed the gig. I held onto it for twenty-seven years.

Brown County is full of Cahalls and Tarbells, and Jim Tarbell tells a story I may have told before. (At our age, Jim and I are apt to repeat stories, though we enjoy them just as much the tenth time around.) In one branch of the family, several men with the name of "Perry" were so easily confused that they had to be given nicknames. "Hog" Perry raised pigs, "Sheriff" Perry tended to the law, and that left "Jerry Perry" about whom I know nothing at all. "Sheriff" Perry was Jim Tarbell's great-grandfather, and it may have been that "Hog" Perry was Tom's great-grandfather (he and Jim were cousins). In any case, one day "Hog" Perry drove his pigs down to the river around Ripley and started walking home with a fat purse full of silver. He was set upon by robbers who killed him and stole his money. As for "Sheriff" Perry, Jim swears that Val Lewis in Georgetown insists "Sheriff" Perry's ghost is still up on the third floor of the courthouse and haunts the inhabitants to this day.

Jim even has a romantic riverboat pilot ancestor named William Tarbell. William Tarbell came here by way of the West Indies, Jim says, then on up to the Ohio River Valley through New Orleans. He became a riverboat captain, got a job on a steamboat, stopped one day to save a young woman from a flood, and married her.

Eventually, someone started noticing the river for the asset it was, and starting in 1988 Cincinnati decided to produce an event dedicated to the river and the steamboats. It was to be called Tall Stacks, and Rick Griewe recruited me to work on the entertainment committee. I found a magician in Atlanta who did an old-fashioned act: he sawed his wife in half by gaslight. I found actors to play Abraham Lincoln and Frederick Douglas, and string bands to play "Bonnie Blue Flag" and "Lorena." It was immediately Cincinnati's most popular celebration, and I watched steamboats of all sizes float into the harbor from home ports as far away as California.

After that, every four years in October, the Cincinnati and northern Kentucky riverbanks were transformed into another century, another time, and women dressed in antebellum gowns strolled from boat to boat while banjos and fiddles played Stephen Foster songs. All of it filled the air like a dream, and for those four days Cincinnatians worshipped the river, took countless prize-winning pictures of it, and memorized statistics about the old days of riverboat races and colorful riverboat captains. Men in khaki pants and walking shoes with binoculars around their necks, hiked for blocks just to see the sun rise on the river, the shanty boats and yachts that floated upriver for the event slipped out of their watery parking places for an early, unobstructed view of the bend in the Ohio. I think there were nine or ten steamboats that first year, from Minneapolis, St. Louis, and of course the *Belle of Louisville*, arch rival of Cincinnati's *Delta Queen*.

The event was spread over the riverbanks in Cincinnati and Northern Kentucky, and my bluegrass band ended up playing in the rain under a yellow tent with ten other musicians who were rained out as well. We took seats in the tent and began to play old fiddle tunes and equally old bluegrass songs, mostly led by John Hartford who became the unequivocal King of Tall Stacks that first year. In his Victorian shirt and vest, his string tie and his bowler hat, he tap-danced into the audience's heart. He had written dozens of river songs, played the fiddle and the banjo, and could call out the names of the steamboats with his back turned to them, just by listening to their whistles.

The festival went on every four years, until 2000. By then the steamboats had mostly become gambling boats and getting them to steam all the way to Cincinnati and forego all that income became out of the question. All that was left of the event was cheap souvenirs and a ghostly sound of a calliope playing "Cruisin' Down the River" when you passed a certain point on the Serpentine Wall.

Nicky and I stopped at the Front Street Café in New Richmond and had a cup of coffee. It was pleasant to sit in the small café and watch the Ohio out of the large window. Despite the cold, some brave souls wearing heavy coats sat outside on benches built for just such viewing. Despite Nicky's caustic comments, it was a wonderful day. There was a light lift of steam where the warmer water met the cold air.

In the deep purple Cadillac again, we headed for Point Pleasant, and we were rewarded with a historical marker that said, "President Grant's birthplace," and smelling adventure, we turned in there hoping to see historic rooms, museums full of historic things from Grant's boyhood. Naturally it was closed. "Open from 1 until 4:00 p.m.," the signs said, but even though it was only 2 p.m., we were out of luck. We drove around the circle in the small town to Grant's schoolhouse, but that, too, was closed.

"On to Ripley," we shouted, fists to the sky; Ripley, the tobacco capital of Ohio, home of the Ohio Tobacco Festival. On a warm afternoon I had seen booths and stands offering tobacco candy and other goodies with pamphlets on the history of Brown County spread out on the top shelf of a display case. But there was no such luck today, either in Ripley or at the Brown County Fairgrounds which were padlocked shut. I had played at the first Brown County Bluegrass Festival many years before and was awed with the demonstrations of farm machinery, both contemporary and antique. I saw a gas-operated threshing machine, an old-time tractor pull, and all the behemoth machines looking like they had just come from a Thomas Hardy novel with a heroine like Tess d'Urbervilles peeking out of the fairground bleachers.

In the entertainment world, fireworks on the river is a pretty easy sell. When WEBN came up with the WEBN Labor Day Fireworks, nobody was prepared for how enormous it would be, but by noon on Labor Day the curved concrete Serpentine Wall by the river stage was beginning to fill with people. Families in shorts and sneakers and alligator tee shirts were strolling towards the river with picnic baskets and blankets. Bands were lazily setting up sound systems on stage, musicians tossing microphone cords at each other in the heat, then setting up mic stands and amplifiers.

The speakers from WEBN blared out '70s rock and roll with the kind of volume that made your heart beat fast and hard, and in the background the "ribbit ... ribbit" sound of the WEBN's mascot frog chirped like a loud cricket.

"Born to be wi-i-ld, born to be wi-i-ld," the radio blasted, and suddenly it was dusk and the pace was beginning to pick up like a rock and roll festival. People on the Serpentine Wall were trying to save seats for latecomers, but incoming audience members just sat down anyway. The first explosion came at 9:30. The riverfront was packed; every blanket was full, hippies wandered here and there aimlessly drinking beer, while families sat in folding chairs and looked on disapprovingly. But with that first ear-splitting crack, with that first rocket that lit up the sky, the audience was one, and they "oohed" and "aahed" until the last burst of awesome colored magic gunpowder died out, and the last streaks of smoke floated from the sky.

THE FUNERAL OF JOHN HARTFORD (2001)

In the spring of 2001, the news of John Hartford's impending death spread up and down the river like a whisper. By May, the buzz on the internet was constant; his final illness hit with the suddenness of bad news. Young musicians from Nashville and from the southeastern mountains who knew his work played old-time country music outside the window of his house in Madison, Tennessee. They played quietly out in the yard, cleaned up after themselves and left, giving John's dying an almost mythical quality. With the last of his strength, John summoned Earl Scruggs to come and play "Earl's Breakdown" and "Home Sweet Home" close to his ear, then he sighed and whispered, "That was perfect."

Of any performer, John's slender build and craggy face were most familiar to river lovers, and sometimes the river lovers came to like bluegrass.

FRIENDS

The saddest of occasions—When John Hartford died, even the river people mourned his passing. From the captain's deck at his house, he could see his own mile marker, the first one named for a living riverboat pilot—the John Hartford marker.

When the *Delta Queen* steamboat was still headquartered in Cincinnati, he put in his hours and got his steamboat license. He could sit for hours with weathered river men and talk currents and eddies; he was heartsick when his friend, Captain Fred Way, died. At the same time, John had won important awards in the commercial world: Golden Globes, Grammys—for the songs he wrote and performed about the river.

I met John Hartford in 1975 at Betty Blake's house in Mt. Adams. Betty had tirelessly collected enough signatures to persuade Congress to change its position on overnight steam travel. The *Delta Queen* was still in Cincinnati, and Betty was golden. The party was a celebration for her son's birthday, and John had planned a fifteen-musician show, a bluegrass cruise on the *Delta Queen* as a tribute to Betty.

John and I sat down and started singing old-time country music. John was no ordinary "song catcher," and I was hard put to keep up with him. He had just finished up his Grammy-winning record, *Mark Twang*, but I was young and in good voice and sang some songs that interested him, and as a result I was asked to join his band of merry musicians on the *Delta Queen*.

I flew from Cincinnati to St. Louis and boarded the boat as it came downriver from Minnesota. It was the Road Trip from Heaven and a watershed time for me. I knew after a couple days I didn't ever want to go back to the old times, working in an office or with another band. From dinnertime on, sometimes all night until breakfast, all we talked about was music, and when we weren't talking, all we did was play music.

Doug Dillard, tall and skinny with long hair the color of a lion's mane, was the banjo player, an old friend of John's from his early days in St. Louis when he had spent a lot of time with Douglas's family, the Dillards, playing square dances and weddings at resorts in the Ozarks, their stomping ground. Douglas didn't start playing until about 10 at night, and when it came time to quit, his fingers had swollen around the ends of his picks and he couldn't get them off. So he just kept playing. The passengers who showed up for the early breakfast shift (I am talking "dawn" here) thought we had gotten up extra early for their amusement and were so impressed.

"It's not easy for musicians to get up this early, Syd," one woman explained to her husband, who was already drinking Bloody Marys. The truth was, we just hadn't gone to bed. We ran on coffee and adrenaline in those days, and it worked just fine. Once we'd played through the first breakfast shift, we went right on to lunch, a tray of food behind us on the piano, cigarettes stubbed out in scrambled eggs in a most unappetizing fashion.

*

Sometime during those all-night conversations I heard John say his first job was with the Bray Brothers in Missouri. When he heard Earl Scruggs, he said, it was as if he'd been struck by lightning, a primitive feeling of having been "saved." When he was just a teenager he had hooked up with the Dillards (remembered by fans of the *Andy Griffith Show* as the "Darling Family"). Eventually, out in Hollyweird, as John called it, he joined Glenn

FRIENDS

Campbell as a banjo player and fiddle player on his television show, then became a writer for the Smothers Brothers.

When Glenn Campbell recorded a song John wrote called "Gentle on My Mind," it caused a sensation for which John was not prepared. It had a folk quality to it, a Beatles feeling. The song was eventually recorded by more than a hundred artists, including Frank Sinatra, who sang it with a slightly altered lyric: "gently on my mind." It became, in those years, the second most-recorded song in history, right behind Paul McCartney's "Yesterday." It received millions of hours of airplay in one form or another. Suddenly, John was a household name.

"What could I do to follow that?" he said mournfully.

He never allowed "Gentle on My Mind" to be recorded for any commercial purposes; instead, with the royalties, he moved back to Nashville to continue performing as a singer/songwriter. His music, played with fiddles and banjos, sometimes included unusual sound effects like playing his face on "Good Old Electric Washing Machine," or his high-pitched tones on "Hey Baby Wanna Boogie." The album he produced and played on for fiddle great Benny Martin is one of my all-time favorites. He learned to tap dance on an electrified board at the same time he was fiddling.

He recorded riverboat pilots from his short-wave radio and added them to his music. He was like a child, unleashed with the latest electronic wizardry. As he grew older, though, he moved back to the bluegrass he had grown up loving, and towards the end of his life he set out to preserve the fiddle tunes he had learned from old players. That's what won him fiddler Dave Edmundson's respect. Edmundson, who is as knowledgeable an authority as we have in this city on old-time music, explained it this way: "What John did for old-time fiddle music—by transcribing these obscure fiddle tunes, bringing them out of obscurity and preserving this very important body of American music—was of incalculable value. John was miles ahead of the rest of us. I figure the rest of my life I'll try to play a fiddle tune every night just for John."

Once I went to meet John backstage at the Appalachian Festival at Old Coney Island. We walked along the Licking River, up the hill, through dappled green maple leaves, and it was as if we were walking through pools of light and shadow, through a great canyon of years. He had already showed me his new system for carrying three musical instruments and his garment bag at the same time. We took a taxi to my house, because John had several hours between shows and wanted to unwind. I remember he tap-danced in my kitchen while I poached an egg. The sun shone just so on the yellow kitchen, on the yellow yolk of the egg.

"I've learned this system from a dance teacher," John said, and he showed me how he could take off and put on his shoes standing on one leg. "Don't ever sit down to put on your shoes. Always stand up."

One Christmas I drove down to Nashville to interview him. I had gotten some grant money, so I rented a car and got a motel room instead of sleeping on somebody's floor. There was just a little skift of snow on the ground. It was chilly, and I could smell the woodsmoke burning, as pungent and natural in Tennessee as sage in New Mexico. John had bought Sonny Osborne's Cadillac, antlers and all, and we drove it to his regular Thursday night pickin' session at Larry Perkins' house.

The next day, John came after me to show me the top floor of his house. It was an exact replica of a captain's deck on a steamboat, with a large round steering wheel, river journals bound into volumes of matching leather. He had a short-wave radio, so that all the riverboats and tugs that passed his house could radio him. When pilots were headed his way, they'd radio him, and he could listen to the river talk which comforted and centered him. I could also see his famous mile marker from that spot, the first one named for a living riverboat pilot—the John Hartford marker.

He often spoke of his friendships with the river people, and his pleasure in them never wavered. "It'll be late at night," he told me once, "and it's cold and damp and dark, and maybe the captain will have a nip, or everybody will be drinking coffee, and the stories start." He said, "It feels like you're in an old Dutch painting."

FRIENDS

The last time I saw John was on a Thursday at the beginning of March, 2001. His bus, formerly owned by Waylon Jennings, was parked in the lot at Union Terminal, and he was in town to entertain at a meeting of the Propeller Club, one of those traditional river meetings John always liked so he could see old friends from the Coast Guard and other riverboat pilots.

"Sorry it's such short notice," he said when he called. "But come and eat dinner with us." I did, leaving my dog and catching a ride over to Cincinnati's West End. John looked tired and slightly puffy from a recent dose of steroids. He was sick again, of lymphoma, after many years in remission. He told me he couldn't touch strangers anymore or shake hands; his immune system was so compromised a virus could kill him.

He was sitting on the orange lounge chair on his bus, and I sat down across from him. He was dressed in denim overalls, a red-checked hunting shirt, and a cardigan sweater. He was so thin he could hug himself, his cheeks and nose were pink with patchy skin. He had a deerstalker cap on his head and those half-moon-shaped reading glasses perched on his nose, like Barry Fitzgerald.

"Sherlock Holmes," he said, and we were off in a conversational flow that was like being in the same current on the same river, as if we'd spoken only yesterday.

When our food came, we ate it without much real attention, though it was good. The band was playing on the new *Belle of Cincinnati*, and they were a little on edge about getting set up. John started telling me about writing "Gentle on My Mind," a song he almost never talked about.

"I wrote it after seeing Dr. Zhivago," he told me. "I was writing all the time then, writing while I tied my shoes, writing while I ate. I had Julie Christie's face in front of me while I was writing the first two lines. After it was a hit, I was on an airplane with her, and I sent her a note telling her I had written those two lines with her in mind, and I signed my name. I sent the message to her by the stewardess, and the stewardess came back and told me Miss Christie would like me to sit with her."

"Was she as beautiful as you thought she'd be?" I asked.

"Yes," he said, "she was ... "

He smiled a lot, that last time I saw him, goofing around with facial expressions, crossing his eyes.

⌒

After the band got set up, John told me as we walked to the stage that he had a system for playing the gig. "I haven't got much strength left in my hand, so when I get to the hard parts these guys—he indicated the band—"will jump in and cover up for me."

The band was ready to go, sitting down this time, around an open mic. They started with "Squirrel Hunters," chanted by John—"Squir-rrr-el hunters, let her go boys"—and it was so much like the old-timey fiddlers of my childhood that it raised goose bumps along my spine.

Back at the table, an old river captain came and sat with us. He said, "I know you cain't talk, and you cain't shake hands."

"But I can touch your elbow with mine," John said, and he did.

The old man sat a while, his face reddened from the sun, peeling in places like a farmer's. His hands were swollen and callused, victims of his own passion for the river.

Starting in 1988, John lent his credibility—as a riverboat pilot and musician—to Tall Stacks. At the festival in 1992, John was everywhere at once, doing instructional films on boat safety for the Coast Guard and also doing music videos, one of him singing an Uncle Dave Macon song called "I'm Goin' Back to Dixie." It's still one of my all-time favorite Hartford performances.

At one Tall Stacks event, I remember riding a water ferry across the Ohio with John. He liked to smell the October air and watch the currents. Up close, his eyes were the color of river water. That night everything was lit up—the bridges, the buildings, the boats. The river rocked us gently, and around us, the world was like a shiny carrousel, up and down; the music never stopped. "This is wonderful," he said.

He didn't love calliopes but he could tell all steam whistles apart, and sometimes, onstage at Tall Stacks, while the band vamped, he'd chant into the microphone, "I can hear the *Belle of Louisville*, and I can hear the *Delta Queen*." He knew the voices of the boats as well as he knew the voices of Bill Monroe and Ralph Stanley.

"Listen to them," he once told me, just as one of the boats came down hard on a note, and the sustained quality of it simply overwhelmed any other sound anything else could make. "That's the real music of the river," John said.

It was hot when I went to Nashville for his funeral, that suffocating heat that smothers you and makes you look hollowed out and pale. John's house sat right in the bend of the Cumberland River, and in the circular driveway were six of the whitest stretch limos I ever saw, a reminder of the six white horses in the old blues songs. John was laid out in the parlor. I stood a few moments alone beside his body. I kept hoping he'd wink at me and tell me he had a system for beating this whole death thing. He didn't, of course; I hadn't really expected that he would.

The funeral consisted of many musicians performing John's songs. I sat with them in chairs in the back, by the swimming pool, under a shade tree. I saw Vince Gill and Marty Stuart. I heard Earl Scruggs. I saw Sam Bush, Tut Taylor, and Vassar Clements got together with some of the other musicians to do "Steam-Powered Aereo Plane." Emmylou Harris, Gillian Welch, and David Rawlings sang "Long Journey." After they were done, Gillian turned away from the crowd and sobbed, and Emmylou took tissues out of her purse and passed them out like a veteran. I brought a proclamation from the City of Cincinnati signed by the mayor, saying that June 7, 2001, was officially John Hartford Day in Cincinnati.

In the last years, we called and emailed each other regularly, and I sometimes sent him poems. The first one was called "Chromo" and I found it in a volume of Carl Sandburg. It was a short, one-stanza verse about a river town, and John wrote me back immediately, a little miffed that Sandburg had just got started on a "perfectly good poem and didn't finish it."

"I've got to have chemo. Send me a poem," he'd write, and I could read the urgency in his message. When I'd exhausted my own store of poems, he sent me his own verses, shaped like hourglasses and figure-eights on the page. I loved those poems but after his death, it hurt to look at them.

It all seemed surreal to me; I could not believe he would let go of life. John had a bow he liked to make at the end of the show. He'd tip the crown of his derby hat with his nimble fingers and let it roll down his arm until he caught it. Then he'd put it on his head and leave the stage.

I only wish that I could clap hard enough to make him come back for an encore.

SISTER: DIGGING UP BONES

Somehow when I think of my dog, Sister, it is always autumn, and the red and yellow sugar maples blend with the golden color of her coat as if some New York designer had had her dyed to blend and "pop," as they say nowadays in the fashion magazines. Sister was that beautiful.

Sister and I lived together in Over-the-Rhine for roughly twelve or thirteen years, until we moved to Klotter. She was fourteen when she died, a good, long life for a dog, anyone would be quick to tell you. She was smart: a medium-sized mixture of border collie and golden retriever, and her coat was red and thick, and if she was your dog, fourteen years wasn't long at all. It was the blink of an eye.

In those short years I came to know her to be a fierce competitor, a devoted protector. "Ask yourself," I could almost hear her say, "Do you feel lucky?" Then she'd growl deep in her throat where only I could hear it, and I felt safe and not alone in the quagmire that was Over-the-Rhine in the '90s.

FRIENDS

Sister was the only dog I ever had who was a born athlete. I lived near the School for Creative and Performing Arts between Sycamore and Broadway, and at evening time, I would walk Sister to the playground and watch her run. She would stretch out, low to the ground and give it her all.

"Run," I'd yell, carried away by her elegance, and her legs would move like pistons. I wasn't the only one who admired her. At least two young men walking pit bulls offered to buy her.

"That's a good dog, lady," they'd say. "That dog can run."

I wasn't looking for a dog when we met. Lisa Mullins, a young woman who ran an organization on Main Street called "Enjoy the Arts" had rescued a big red dog when she found it running along Scott Street in Covington, a rope, which had been deliberately cut, tied around its neck. The red dog was threading through traffic at rush hour as if she were herding cars, barking constantly.

"I can't keep her right now," Lisa said (she was a sucker for a lost dog) when she brought her to my apartment on Main Street. "I've got workmen in the house, and I'm afraid she'd freak out and bite someone."

My own dog, Hoosier, had died a few months earlier, and I was determined not to take in another dog. "I promised myself no new dogs," I said, "but if you want to leave her with me for a couple of days while the workmen are there, I can do that."

"I'll bet we can find her a great home," I said to Lisa earnestly when I returned Sister to her two days later.

"I've got a lead on somebody who has a farm, somebody associated with the Symphony … "

"Great," I said. "Maybe some culture would calm her down."

Lisa laughed and took Sister's leash. I felt a little twinge, but I ignored it. By the end of the weekend, Sister was back at Lisa's house.

"She was restless and just wouldn't stay on that farm," Lisa told me on the phone. "And I've got three carpenters at my house I've been trying to nail down for months. I had to bring her to the office," she added.

As soon as I agreed to a couple more days of dog-sitting, this new, strange dog took off, pulling Lisa down the street at full speed, sniffing out my apartment as if she were Rin Tin Tin. When she came in and saw me, she was ecstatic.

If you've never experienced a dog who is overjoyed to see you, you've missed one of life's great experiences. Sister jumped up and put her paws on my shoulder. She wagged her whole body, as if she were doing the shimmy. She licked my hands; she sniffed me and finally she quieted down and sat, every inch of her quivering with her desire to please me.

Lisa laughed. "Too bad you're not in the market for a dog. She's already picked you out for sure."

During the next couple of days, the dog and I went everywhere together. She was a good walker once I reined her in, and she'd stay on my right side, looking up into my face to see if this pleased me.

"Good dog," I said.

Sister had a couple more weekend jaunts, but none of them worked, and Lisa and I kept up our visitations with her. I suspected I was going to keep her when I decided to name her. We were at the School for Performing Arts again. I was deep in thought. "Ginger," I said, thinking out loud, but she didn't slow down, so I kept trying: "Penny?" Nothing. "Foxy, Molly, Lilly … "

Suddenly, a name popped into my head. "Sister!" I said, and she looked up at me and gave a short bark. "Sister." I said it again, a little louder this time. In the south, Sister is a perfectly logical first name, and I had been reading a magazine article about a woman named Sister Parrish. The name stuck.

"Sister!" I shouted.

Out of nowhere a nun appeared, walking through the trees on the east end of the playground.

"Were you calling me? Did you need help?" she said.

A nun! I hadn't even known there were any nuns in Over-the-Rhine.

"I'm so sorry," I said. "I didn't mean to be rude."

"Well," she said, "I heard you calling Sister … "

"Oh," I said laughing. "Well, I was calling the dog," I said. Now why had I said that? "I didn't mean to be sacrilegious," I said, digging the hole a little deeper, my face turning a deeper shade of red.

FRIENDS

"My name is Sister Monica," the nun said, and she was laughing, too. "We have a charter house of nuns on Main Street. None of the sisters will believe this story."

Sister looked at Monica and sniffed disdainfully. She was ready to go home. With me. And that's where she ended up staying for the rest of her life.

*

During that time we took over 1,500 walks, ranging through Over-the-Rhine, even downtown. We covered most of Liberty Street and Central Parkway, Piatt Park. The people at Fifth Third didn't allow me to bring her in that building when I went to do business, so I tied her around the telephone pole by her leash, went inside and held my breath, scared she wouldn't be there when I got through my transactions. Later, on Court Street, I found U.S. Bank, and they allowed Sister to come in, as if she were a "Fat Cat" businesswoman. She would lie down beside the visitor's chair and take a nap while I made my transactions.

We became a couple, you could say. Sister knew what I was thinking: if she picked up food vibrations, she followed me to the kitchen, but she was no chowhound. She was selective about what she ate; she wanted to keep her figure. If I went anywhere near the leash, she scrambled to go with me, sure that we were ready for a walk. If I was sad, she stayed quiet, within petting distance, ready to soothe my cares and worries with a dog grin or a well-placed kiss. And in exchange for my giving her a home, she was a considerate roommate: she was fully housebroken. If she had to get up in the night and go outside, she'd stand at the edge of my bed and bark two or three times until I screamed for mercy, got dressed at 4 a.m., and grabbed the leash. Better that than the alternative.

Sister understood ball games in a way few humans do. One day at the playground, I heard, "Lady, get your dog!!" and when I looked up, there was Sister on the playground playing soccer with the physical education class. Somehow she understood soccer as soon as she saw it. She understood that it was her job to keep the ball away from anybody else and to steal it back if someone else got it. As I watched in horror, her leash in my hand, Sister was holding the soccer ball in her mouth. She was stretched out low, running for all she was worth, holding the ball in her mouth her head high, all the way to the end of the field. Behind her, both teams were chasing her, screaming. When I got her collared she was panting happily, dozens of little hands patting her.

"She's great," one little girl said.

"I'm so sorry she ruined your game," I said.

"No problem. I'd rather practice with her than any humans. She can really keep the ball away, just pushes it with her nose or her paw."

Living in Over-the-Rhine as we did, Sister and I became art critics, visiting studios and drinking coffee at Kaldi's with sullen, paint-smeared men and talented women. The artists in Over-the-Rhine had their favorite memories of Sister, for she was as familiar to them as I was. We'd stop in Base Gallery on the day of Final Friday. I loved to watch the artists hanging their work for their exhibits. They were excited, nervous, like thoroughbreds on race day, sure of a big sale this month, rarely getting it. (By Saturday they were singing the artists' blues: "Why doesn't anybody want to buy my picture?")

Final Friday was the night the artists' galleries stayed open late. It was festive. Lights were hung and new work displayed for people who came into the neighborhood once a month to see the spectacle. Even Kaldi's was hung with art: Alan Sauer's great pen drawings of humans who looked almost like robots with lightning flashing out of their eyes, Jim Wainscott's exquisite nudes, the skin tones like peaches warmed by pink and gold. The giraffes and elephants Kelly Wenstrup carved stood in the window of Kaldi's like a great jungle safari.

One Friday Sister and I watched all day as some artists from Alaska hung a huge native-influenced calendar in the window. However the sun hit it caused it to move in some miraculous way. Sister wasn't allowed in Kaldi's unless it was late at night, and I was singing. Then sometimes she would meander in and lay at my feet while I rocked out with a progressive bluegrass band. Those were halcyon days, of art, music and poetry readings. The readings were unlike anything I'd ever seen. The poets called them "slams," and when they spoke their work they hammered with their bodies and no words were off limits.

However, the artists, models, musicians and poets, all of us, perhaps, remember Sister best for her participation in the Bockfest Parade the first year we moved there. Bockfest was an Over-the-Rhine institution, held in the dead of winter every year, probably to get people drinking beer through Lent. The tradition celebrated the Bock Beer, which was a kind of beer heavy with grains monks used to drink during Lent so they wouldn't pass out from fasting. Each year a giant festival commemorated the arrival of Lent and, looking further, "the coming of spring." It started with a parade, led by a goat-drawn wagon carrying a keg of the first Bock beer and a group of men dressed as old-school monks with braided sashes tied around their rough woolen robes.

The parade formed at Arnold's Bar and Grill at 210 East Eighth Street on the designated Friday, turned right on Main and followed Main to Kaldi's where the marchers would halt for speeches by dignitaries wearing lederhosen or tights and medieval get-up if you were a man. Women wore the Rhine maiden dirndl skirts and laced bodices with small circlets of spring flowers in their hair and bands of flowers around the sleeves of their blouses. One or two women were always chosen to be the Queen of Sausages, and she carried a tray of Avril's best brats and metts at the head of the parade, waving at the admiring throngs while the VIPs rode in a horse-drawn carriage, also waving at the crowds, everyone having a great time until they got to St. Mary's Church where the priest would bless the beer.

To understand Bockfest, and what motivated its participants, you had to take into account the planning and preparation that went into it. It was like the Macy's parade—they started working on the event a year ahead and the committees, sub-committees, publicity, beer, printing, posters, even renting the goat and cart each year—all that was planned in minute detail. I was really looking forward to it the year that I moved to Over-the-Rhine. That year the planners had decided to add the "Bocking Dogs" contingent to the parade, and about sixteen purebred dogs of all sizes, perfectly groomed and exquisitely behaved, stood at attention in front of Arnold's, their owners beside them just like that movie *Best of Show*.

When the parade got to Kaldi's, they stopped again to make proclamations or whatever. Jim Tarbell had on an elaborate hat and costume and was taking low bows. Inside, Sister was restless. Of course I hadn't mentioned a word about the parade to her; still, she knew there was something going on, and every time I opened the apartment door to check on my laundry, she paced back and forth, back and forth in front of the door. I wasn't even aware of the Bocking Dogs until they stopped in front of Kaldi's, but Sister must have heard something far off or smelled a scent, because the next time I went out the door, she was out herself and down the stairs, just as some new tenants decided it would be good to move into the building during the Bockfest Parade. They propped open the locked front door and before I could get the wash in the basket, Sister was out the door, with me in hot pursuit.

She raced through the outer doors and into the assembled "bocking" dogs, all of whom forgot their training and turned into a pack of snarling canines. Handlers were snapping leashes on collars and trying to restore order, but it was chaos. Someone yelled, "Get that damn dog out of here," but Sister had left the apartment without her collar on, so there was no way anybody could grab her. The parade watchers lined up on the sidewalk, and the artists watching out the window on the bar side of Kaldi's were laughing hysterically, yelling, "Go, Sister." One tiny white poodle in a little embroidered dress was so upset she walked over to the side of the street and squatted down and peed right on the skirt of her outfit.

The whole thing didn't last ten minutes, but it seemed like an hour to me. I was mortified. Someone eventually grabbed Sister by her mane of red hair and got her out of the street and back in the door of my apartment building. The artists thought it was the best Bock Parade ever, but I received formal notice that Sister was permanently banned from future parades in Over-the-Rhine.

Sister and I lived a long time in that apartment, until the axe fell and the landlord decided to turn our apartment building into condos. We were the last tenants there. Some of the artists made a mini-documentary of our departure, and then everybody picked up something and good-naturedly put it on the truck.

Sister and I had moved to Race Street and then to Klotter in Lower Clifton, as I call it, before she died. I had noticed about Christmas that she was more listless than usual, but everything appeared to be all right. Her coat was still shiny red; she still wagged her tail when I came in. I thought maybe she was a little down because we were in a new neighborhood. About February, though, I noticed her breathing becoming ragged, short, and our walks were shorter than they used to be. I took her to Dr. Mike, the veterinarian, who x-rayed her and informed me she had a tumor on her lungs. "She's not uncomfortable," he said in his gentle way, "but bring her back next Saturday and we'll decide what's to be done."

"You mean how we'll get her well?" I corrected him.

"Well," Dr. Mike said, "she's fourteen years old now. Let's see how she is next week."

I didn't have to wait a week; Sister died soon after we saw Dr. Mike. She behaved uncharacteristically, wanting out at early in the morning while it was still dark, racing to the top of the green hill across the street and eating grass to make herself throw up. The tumor was making it hard for her to breathe, and she wanted it out of there. Finally, she came back down and laid herself on the ground and let me pet and soothe her until I could get her back in the house. I wrapped her in a warm towel, put a sheet down, and laid her in my bed, holding her, talking to her, petting her. I must have dozed off, because around 6 a.m., she nudged my chin firmly with her nose, looked up towards the sky and breathed her last breath.

The people in Over-the-Rhine mourned her. The artist Alan Sauer said that seeing her in the Bockfest Parade was the best thing that ever happened to him. "I almost didn't go, and then I laughed harder than I have ever laughed at anything."

"It seems odd to see you without Sister," someone will say, and I smile and say "Yes," and tell them quickly that she died peacefully, at home, in bed. It is the street people who show their feelings. I ran into an old acquaintance at Washington Park who looked at me with rheumy eyes and said, "I knowed your dog must be dead by now, but I just had to ask. I thought there might a'been a miracle, and she'd still be alive. She was sure some dog," he said, laughing a little.

"Yes," I said, "She was sure some dog."

A SOPHISTICATED LADY (2012)

Phyllis Weston was waiting for me at her gallery in O'Bryonville on a warm Friday afternoon in mid-autumn. I could see her a half-block away, in her pink designer suit and low-heeled bone-colored shoes. Her hair was twirled up in an elaborate French twist—a swirl that added a centimeter or two to her height. Even so, she was tiny, a doll-sized woman. Up close, after hugs and "darlings" and "so glad to see yous" she was the same Phyllis I've known since 1975—older, of course, and frailer, but still possessing the force of a tornado. She has been called the Grande Dame of Art in Cincinnati, and certainly she is that.

There are two things that Phyllis has never been willing to tell me: her age and the recipe for her decadent chocolate cake. Both are wonderful mysteries—the kind that keep you guessing. Is she eighty-five? Does she use heavy cream in the frosting? I know this much. The chocolate cake is unmatched, and Phyllis is at an age at which a lot of other women spend their days tucked up watching reruns of *Murder, She Wrote* and waiting for grandchildren and great-grandchildren to visit.

That is not the life for Phyllis. Here in her lovely gallery, she took the arm of her assistant, Cate Yellig, leaning on her ever so slightly, and her vital juices seemed to bubble over. "The art gives me life," she said simply. Then she handed me a pair of 3D glasses. I had come to the gallery to see a display of works by Cincinnati artists Mark Patsfall and Brian Stuparyk called *Elements of Perception*. But when I put on the glasses and peered at a piece by Stuparyk, I couldn't focus.

Cate suggested I try them with the blue lens over the right eye, and that did the trick. The painting's disjointed images merged immediately into something I could grasp: an octopus overtaking Fountain Square! In the next room, I was thrilled by artist Mark Patsfall's video sculpture. A disciple of Nam June Paik, he had installed a couple of mixed media pieces on silkscreen with lights and video. The stick figure in one of the installations had a mechanical mouth that appeared to be swallowing dollar signs, coins, and bills. I clapped my hands over my mouth, smothering a grin.

"Oh, did you already see it?" Phyllis said when she saw me.

"Isn't it absolutely wonderful?" I said.

She nodded. "It makes you feel like a kid again."

Phyllis once told me that she knew when she was a little girl that she wanted to be involved in art, she just wasn't quite sure how. The how turned out to be as an art dealer. She's been influential in art circles in Cincinnati for more than forty years, much of that time spent at Closson's, when the exclusive furnishings and decor store was downtown and included a gallery. According to Constance Coleman, an octogenarian painter who also refuses to retire, Phyllis was a force in the Contemporary Arts Center in the 1960s when the CAC was presenting works by of-the-moment talents such as Andy Warhol, Claes Oldenburg, and Robert Morris.

"Phyllis gathered contemporary paintings and painters and convinced them to show in this new venue," Coleman says. "She made a significant difference in the success of the CAC. Of course, that's all we thought about in those days: contemporary art. We were driven to show what young artists were doing *right now*, the better to make Cincinnati a part of the national landscape."

It's clear to me that Phyllis still has the same drive today; it's what propelled her to this venture in O'Bryonville. "I worked at Closson's for forty-two years," she told me. "Then I was off a year before I started my own gallery. It's been everything I hoped it would be. Once you decide to do something, well, then do it!" she added, her tiny frame summoning the words she'd lived by for so long. "And don't let anything get in your way."

⸎

If Phyllis has made a living from art, she has also made an art of living. I met her and her husband, Leo, in 1975, on the same hot summer night I met Irma and Fred Lazarus, on Fred's creaky old houseboat with a tiny kitchen belowdecks. They were having what Irma would have called "a gala" for the opera singer Alan Titus, who was the guest of honor that night. He was appearing with Cincinnati Opera that summer in *The Merry Widow*, but a few years before he'd set the world of classical music on fire when he sang in the premiere of Leonard Bernstein's *Mass*, and Bernstein was a favorite of Irma's. I was there as someone's date and was too shy to say much of anything to anyone.

I remember the night was lovely, with sweet breezes and the sounds of the river everywhere. Fred cooked a dinner of steak and salad and apple pie, some of which had been brought aboard in baskets lined with red and blue checked cloth napkins. We ate, floating down the river in the pitch-black night. The farther we got from downtown, the darker the night became, and the deeper our sense of ease with one another. Someone produced a guitar, and Alan Titus began to sing folk songs in a powerful, well-muscled baritone. Fred asked for a particular song, and Alan didn't know it, but I did. I have no idea where I got the nerve (it might have come from one of Fred's martinis), but I suddenly burst into the tune: *I gave my love a cherry/ That had no stone ...*

Everyone on the boat was silent at once, and I finished the old riddle song to thunderous applause. Then Alan Titus jumped in with "The Wabash Cannonball," so loudly I imagined schools of fish at the bottom of the river being jarred from sleep. He was kind enough to declare I had the most beautiful untrained voice of any he had ever heard, and he came into my next gig at the King's Row in Clifton, with Irma, Fred, Phyllis, and Leo in tow and got up to sing "The Wabash Cannonball" with such gusto he scared the band half to death.

It was the beginning of my long friendship with the four of them: Irma, Fred, Leo and Phyllis. I sang at almost all of their parties for many years after that, and they showed up at my local appearances, no matter how shabby the venue. They used to come to Aunt Maudie's in Over-the-Rhine, dressed in formal clothes after the symphony on Saturday nights. *Please don't sit at the front table*, I'd silently pray, because I knew it was infested with roaches. And of course they chose that table almost every time. Miraculously, the enormous, prehistoric roaches never appeared until Phyllis and Irma were on their way out the door. But I lost ten years of my life on those nights.

Phyllis's Leo was a handsome man, in a Clark Gable kind of way, with dark hair waved back from his face and thick bushy eyebrows. He smoked unfiltered cigarettes back in those innocent days when a halo of cigarette smoke was just the slightest bit romantic. Leo had graduated from Harvard and although he had a private income he was the first real pack rat I ever knew. Once, when he and Phyllis were in Boston staying with their older son, Todd, Phyllis called to tell me they were coming home early, adding (under her breath), "I have to get Leo out of Nob Hill before the next trash collection."

While Leo sat atop his collection of recovered treasures, Phyllis's career as the director of Closson's art gallery flourished. Her shows at Closson's were sellouts; her energy, her resourcefulness continued to astonish. She gave a number of people their first shows, among them the nature artist John Ruthven. Phyllis's desk was in the thick of things, right out on the floor—she got more customers that way—and she liked to chat if there were no prospective buyers around. At the first hint of interest in a particular picture, though, she was on the scent, like a setter pointing a pheasant.

As her Rolodex grew, so did her influence with artists and buyers. In 1981, when she was selected to put together a group of paintings for Procter

& Gamble's executive wing, it made her reputation. I remember how she slaved over that project; I'd find corrected galleys for the catalogue all over her desk upstairs for what seemed like an endless amount of time. But when she finished it, she won instant stardom in the art world, and P&G had a selection of paintings to make any corporate headquarters proud.

In 1996, Leo was diagnosed with lung cancer. Phyllis was stricken; there would never be another Leo—or "Lay-oh," as Irma called him, pronouncing his name in the European manner. My friend, Don Parker, who was a math professor, worked advanced math problems with him for hours. I took bluegrass musicians by while he was sick, and we played for him on what was to be his last day outside the house before the cancer overcame him.

Phyllis was close to quitting but "Leo made me promise I'd go on," she told me. "I kept going in to work, because it was his wish for me that I would continue working." It was probably the best decision they could have made, she says. "The art has given me an identity, and the kids [the artists] keep me young."

The Closson family eventually sold the store, and it moved to Montgomery with a plan to feature more "decorative" art. It must have felt like a great loss to Phyllis, after years of building up the store's reputation as a source for serious work. But if Leo's death didn't end her career, she wasn't quitting over this change of affairs either. She had a third act in her, and she started The Phyllis Weston Annie Bolling Gallery in 2006 (it became The Phyllis Weston Gallery in 2010). She got out her bulging Rolodex, called in her markers, and brought the best artists she knew, many of whom she had shown long before any other gallery owner was willing to take a chance on them. And she had the perfect venue for the kind of old-fashioned, elaborate parties that create excitement around an exhibit: her own home.

We called it "the mansion"—Phyllis's antebellum house on the east side. Perched on a high bluff overlooking a bend in the Ohio River, from her living room you could watch the long, slow barges as they glided toward

Louisville. The ancient oak tree in front of the house shaded the grounds in the summer and made a great playground for the energetic gray squirrels when the tree began to shed its leaves. Legend has it that in steamboat days, two huge torches were kept burning on this hill so that the riverboats could see to steer the tricky turn safely.

The house itself was enormous. Its windows reached nearly twelve feet from the floor to the ceiling, gracefully rounded at the top. The first thing you saw when you came in the door from the veranda was the curving staircase with its wide banister of polished hardwood. It's the kind of staircase you'd want to get married from, and in fact, a former Cincinnati resident, Jani Gardner, did exactly that. Jani was a writer, and she had a way with words and a sense of humor. Floating down the stairs in a bridal gown, she winked at Phyllis's son John. "Always a bride," the oft-married Jani quipped, "but never a bridesmaid."

I remember how Phyllis laughed at my oohs and aahs when I first saw her living room. The furniture was all upholstered in white, and with light pouring in through those tall windows it was the most elegant thing I'd seen outside of *Architectural Digest*. "Oh, dear," she said. "I just got old chairs and sofas second-hand and covered them in the same white fabric." Here and there a painting or a piece of sculpture jumped out at you, luring you over for a closer look. The plain white furniture was a perfect backdrop for the art, which, as Phyllis said, "was just the point."

So when her new gallery called for her to bring out her finest, Phyllis had her housekeeper, Yvonne, polish the silver, and she staged a few magnificent parties. She lit the sconces in the dining room, lined the long table with food in cream-colored bone china, then let the candlelight and wine work their magic on artists and customers alike.

I remember attending a party there for Michael Scott, a landscape painter who studied in Cincinnati whom Phyllis had given his first show before he moved to New Mexico. He and his guests and potential buyers arrived laden with antique silver concha belts and turquoise necklaces, some of them dressed in Nudie suits worth a few thousand dollars each. It was one of the most festive evenings I've spent. It paid off in sales and commissions, freeing Phyllis to do more contemporary art, while still selling mainstream paintings on the second floor.

"The Russian painters are collectible now," she told me that day in the gallery. "But they are maddening. You think you have a show with them in February, and they aren't ready by January. It takes a lot of patience to deal with them. Still, they're so worth it when they produce."

I laughed and wondered who would prevail: the Russians or Phyllis. I imagine she's an excellent "prodder" after all these years of shepherding artists. The rest of her foursome—Irma, Fred, Leo—are gone now; only she remains. When you've lost that kind of friendship, what are a few stubborn Russians? If they think they can outlast her, they'll be disappointed. Phyllis shows no signs of giving up.

*

She is one of those people who has become her job, and she tackles it by looking forward, not back. Even so, when I am with her I can't help but remember the old days.

"Do you remember my giving piano lessons to Yvonne?" I asked her, and she laughed.

"Of course I do," she said.

When I house-sat for Phyllis and Leo at the mansion I'd work on "Jesus Loves Me" with the housekeeper, Yvonne, on the out-of-tune grand piano in the living room. I did a double-take one day when Yvonne—my "student"—started the tune in G, rolled into C, and took off as if she were channeling Tina Turner.

"And all the chocolate cakes I baked for you when you house-sat," Phyllis said, musing. We were sitting down now; I had drawn her into my reveries.

"I remember going to Irma's with you for lunch one day, and [the cook] barely served us a cup of shrimp salad because the two of you were on a fearsome diet," I said.

"Discipline," she said, looking at me a little sadly. "Irma was made of steel."

"You know you've been an inspiration to me," I said, laughing a little tearfully. "You never gave up. I won't forget that."

She didn't say anything. She simply put her hand over mine and looked far away, somewhere over my shoulder.

CURTAIN CALL (2011)

The death of a good friend is like the mess that's left in the kitchen after the party's over; like the untidiness of a room once life has left it. Emily Dickinson described it best. In her plain, unaffected way, she reduced Death to a domestic event, something to be swept up and put away for the next time, a room in the heart to be straightened, the trappings returned to a hall closet. Life goes on. Miss Dickinson was a pragmatist in her poetry, and Jim Edgy, my own dear, departed friend, shared her sensibility.

Art began popping up all over the United States during the Kennedy era, when Jacqueline Kennedy invited the cream of America's creative class to perform at the White House. Americans embraced this new style of excellence—a little self-consciously, perhaps, but elegance and beauty were things we had hungered for unconsciously. In any case, Jim Edgy, a young man in Macon, Georgia, was a seeker.

I first became aware of Jim in 1970, when he was hired to run the Kentucky Arts Commission, which eventually got renamed the Kentucky Arts Council. Kentucky is a wide state and he was met with confounding clashes of culture when he moved to Lexington. He faced the challenges with grace and good manners, and most important, respect. For instance, he made a point of seeking out the culture of southeastern Kentucky—the fiddle and banjo tunes of the mountains, the great families who carried songs from Britain and kept them alive in the new land. He also met and befriended the horse people between Lexington and Louisville. Throughout this refining process he attempted to keep music, dance, paintings, and theater on an accessible level everyone could enjoy without any condescension. Like a great dam, the boats rose to higher levels and then were lowered once again on the other side.

"I knew Jean Ritchie," he told me once, when I asked him about the musical Ritchie family who lived outside of Hazard. Jean Ritchie became known as the "Mother of Folk" for such songs as "The L&N Don't Stop Here Anymore" and "My Dear Companion," which she sang with Pete Seeger and the Weavers. "Perhaps more important," he added, "I knew her sister, Edna, who organized the family's song collections and spent many years in Europe tracing the origins of the music."

He paused, thoughtfully. "Did you see the movie *Songcatcher?*" he asked.

I said I had; I loved Maggie Greenwald's film about a straight-laced college professor who fell into a passion with Appalachian music. "I would have loved to see the faces of the people in the Old Country when they heard all the verses of 'Barbara Allen' the way they came to be sung in Kentucky," he said.

By recognizing the importance of the folk arts in Kentucky, he legitimized them, embracing the brilliance of artists like Bill Monroe and the color and resonance of bluegrass music itself. Irma Lazarus, the doyenne of Cincinnati culture from the early '60s till the day she passed away in 1993, eventually flushed Jim out like a prize covey of quail and actively wooed him for the Ohio Arts Council. The arts council was her baby; she'd helped found it in the '60s, and in 1974, she lured Jim to Columbus to serve as its director. Ohio's arts were even more diverse than Kentucky's had been: polka bands, ballet dancers, symphony players, and all manner of singers and actors and visual artists who, as Irma saw it, needed to be carded like woolen strands and knit into one dazzling tapestry representing the state. And in her view, Jim Edgy was the one to do it.

It was the '70s, after all. Anything was possible.

Years after her death, Jim still spoke of Irma Lazarus with amusement. "Irma liked Southerners, Episcopalians, and gays," he recalled, smiling. "And I fit all three categories."

FRIENDS

Jim and Irma would periodically set off in his vintage Volkswagen convertible, bound for the cornfields and rural counties in southeastern Ohio to stump for money and support for the arts, with Irma packing a Thermos of coffee and hard-boiled eggs and Jim drinking Coca-Cola from an old-fashioned green bottle into which he'd dumped a small bag of salted peanuts. "I had never seen anyone drink Coca-Cola for breakfast," she said to me once in horror.

"I had a lot to learn," Jim said, laughing at the memory. "We all did. I remember getting a grant for a symphony performance in a small town. When I showed up for the performance not a soul was there. The symphony was waiting in a bus outside a closed building. That's how I learned about audience development."

Jim Rhodes was Ohio's governor then, a staunch Republican. Rhodes wanted to reward Marge Schott with a state political appointment commensurate with the large amount of money she had contributed. So he gave her a seat on the arts council—an honor to which she responded by sputtering, "Culture? I wanted *agri*culture."

"Marge thought giving money to the ballet was a lot like giving money to a bunch of fairies in tutus," Jim told me, laughing at the memory. "Bless Marge's heart. She always said exactly what was on her mind."

Still, they lived through it all—the excitement, the disappointments, the unbelievable wonder of a time when Ohioans were falling in love with the arts. I have never forgotten driving to Irma's swimming pool on a torrid day in summer. Baryshnikov himself was perched on the diving board wearing leopard print trunks, poised to execute the perfect dive.

It was in the company of Jim and Irma that I got to know the inimitable Freddie Franklin of the Ballet Russe de Monte Carlo, an Englishman who still danced in his eighties and dashed off Sunday *New York Times* crossword puzzles with such alacrity that I used to telephone him in New York when I was absolutely stumped. "Wasn't it cunning how they worked out 118-down?" he'd say to me, and he went on to explain it, as if I already knew anyway, and he was just making conversation.

In the late 1970s, Jim left Ohio for Washington, D.C., to work for Nancy Hanks at the National Endowment for the Arts. His relationship with her was not as close as the one he had with Irma, and within a few years he was back in Ohio, settled in Cincinnati. He was as busy and driven as ever. When he rehabbed a house on Dayton Street in the West End, he built an apartment onto it for visiting artists; I even rented it for a while. Over time, Jim served as the associate director of the Cincinnati Art Museum, the director of the Cincinnati Ballet, then ran the Cincinnati Chamber Orchestra. He ran a couple of restaurants, too, and somewhere in there we drifted apart. I remember he called me once and apologized because he and his partner, Bob Lee, hadn't been in touch. He said he wasn't feeling well. "Bob and I have been planning to have you over," he'd say, "but then I just run out of steam."

Jim learned the reason for the lassitude that had overtaken him, and late last spring, he sat down and wrote a calm and beautiful email to his friends in Cincinnati to tell them, in the kindest possible way, that he had been diagnosed with amyotrophic lateral sclerosis—Lou Gehrig's Disease—and that he had about a year to live. "Many of you won't know how to talk to me," he wrote, "but I'm the same person I always was ... I'm not afraid to die. All of us will die."

He went on to say that he wanted to spend time with all of us, talking about ideas, art, music—the things he had always enjoyed. Nothing could be more dreary, he declared, than talking about his illness, which he had to talk about way too much with doctors and had to live with every day.

Reading this news was like being kicked by a mule; I had to go to bed with ice packs under my lower back. But Jim's resilience straightened me out. He saw his diagnosis as a luxury, giving him time to plan and be with his friends of many years.

And so we began another adventure, this one with our mutual friend Lib Stone instead of Irma. We decided to meet weekly, have lunch, talk about life, and see movies. Some were terrible; others just could not match the drama of our time together, and we eventually drifted toward other activities. I began to look forward to our visits with great enthusiasm. It was draining, and at first we walked on eggshells with each other, but then it was a joy just to be in Jim's house again, so full of art, sculpture, and pottery perfectly hung and placed. As he approached his death, he was cataloguing the paintings, the watercolors, the wonderful ceramics.

"I believe if it were me, I'd just go to bed and let somebody else worry about it," I told him during one of our summer visits, taking a sip of iced tea which Jim served to me in grand Southern style, a wedge of lemon, a frosted glass.

"Oh, no. That wouldn't do," he replied. He told Lib and me about a cat he and Bob had to have euthanized. "I didn't want the cat to spend its last night in a concrete cell at the animal hospital, sick and all alone, so we brought her home with us and spent the night with her and took her in the next day for the procedure. I held her in my arms the last minutes of her life," he said. "I had even paid for the procedure ahead of time, so we wouldn't have to go through that."

I couldn't help rolling my eyes and smiling. "Well," he said, "I hated to have people see two old men bawling their eyes out over a cat."

"You were never old to me," I told him. And he wasn't. At 74, his blue eyes were still as innocent as a child's, and he had the same cowlick in his dusty blond hair that he'd had when we first met—a rooster tail, as we would have called it in the country. And we were both from the country.

I stopped talking for a while and let the water pool in the corners of my eyes. I thought of a very funny story about Irma and Jim, which distracted me for a moment. It happened after Jim had accepted the NEA position. He and Irma put their heads together and settled on a young man named Wayne Lawson to replace Jim. They planned a dazzling dinner party for him and the search committee in Jim's apartment in Columbus, where he was living back then. "I'll do the flowers," Irma said.

It was a two-hour drive from Irma's house in East Walnut Hills to Jim's apartment in Columbus. She never believed in spending money on things like flowers; instead, she picked branches of dogwood and flowering fruit trees from her yard and laid the stems on newspapers in the back seat. What with a hold-up here and there, she was late getting to Jim's, and when he answered the doorbell, she pushed past him.

"I need to get these in the bathtub fast, dahling," she said. They had no time for questions and fell into their own particular shorthand to finish the dining room before the guests' arrival.

Wayne Lawson rang at exactly 7:30, young and nervous, auditioning for the job of a lifetime, and like everyone else, dazzled by the thought of meeting Irma Lazarus.

"Where is she?" he asked Jim, running his finger around the inside of his collar.

Jim looked up at him and squinted. "She's in my bathroom," he said absently, "cleaning out the tub."

The stars must have been aligned precisely, because the dogwood branches made a quick enough recovery to grace the dining room table, and Wayne Lawson went on to run the Ohio Arts Council for thirty years.

On this past Memorial Day, Jim's friends gathered for a picnic at Dr. Tom Partridge's farm in Hillsboro, Ohio. The farm was as green as Ireland, and Jim sat in the log cabin Tom had so carefully and so artfully reconstructed. He was surrounded by people who loved him, in a rural setting like his beloved Georgia. The food was spectacular, the wine extraordinary, and just as Jim had requested, the talk was of ideas, creativity, art, music, and dance. Irma thought almost anything could be resolved by a picnic, and she would have approved of the whole affair.

Few people knew that Jim had been an organist for almost all of his working life, playing at whatever church needed him. Now that his Sunday mornings were his own, he could return to Christ Church Cathedral downtown to worship. Being Jim, he had already planned his funeral service and had selected the organ pieces and the music for the choir. He was proud to have secured the rector to speak at his funeral at Evensong, something reserved for only the most honored church members. Part of his ashes will rest in a niche at Christ Church in the chapel where Evensong is held.

One Sunday morning, not long before his death, I sat beside him on the pew while the rector anointed him quietly with sweet oil, the Balm of Gilead to Jim. I held his hand, and we both cried as the rector's procession moved on, holding the cross before them.

The last story Jim Edgy told me, before he died in November, was about an Armenian rug dealer at Closson's. It was 1974 and Jim was moving from Lexington to Columbus to join the Ohio Arts Council. On the way he'd stopped in Cincinnati to explore—halfway between Lexington and Columbus, in the middle of the old and the new.

Closson's was magnificent in those days: sophisticated, elegant, unmistakably Closson's. They carried fancy china and faïence and only the finest flatware. He said he found himself drawn to the rug department in the back of the store. He was hot, tired, and thirsty, and he sat down on a pile of rugs, amidst patterns of color so rich and deep he was amazed.

"Do you like rugs?" Mr. Markarian, the rug dealer, asked, appearing from nowhere, like a genie from a bottle.

"Why, I don't really know anything about them," Jim said, surprised, "but I think they're beautiful."

Mr. Markarian smiled like Hercule Poirot, Jim said, and within two hours, he had sold Jim three rugs of great value, which Jim rolled up and put in the trunk of his VW bug. For payment, he signed his name and new address in Columbus on the back of an envelope.

The rugs, like the arts, were a wonderful investment for Jim. Indeed, he used those rugs in all the houses he lived in for the next thirty or so years. The colors remained rich and deep and the patterns elegant—just like Jim himself.

PSALM OF PRAISE

I raise you up, O God of my people
On this Great Day in the Morning
I see the orange ball of the sun
Which you have set above us
To warm us and light our way.
The rains which spring from Heaven
In the heat of the day
I hear the humming sound of crickets
And feel the fruitfulness of the Earth.
That enormous pear tree
I saw this morning
Will yield bushels of golden fruit
In the fullness of time
How do we deserve this bounty?
What God conceived the cycles of growth and ripening
Harvest and death and rebirth yet again?
O, Great Day in the Morning
In the luxury of summer
Stay by our sides for what may come to pass
Before the light has faded
And the night comes on.

–Katie Laur

"OH, SWEET MAMA" (FOR KATIE LAUR)

While them menfolks in the band sing one loud chorus
of *oh no you don't*, she edges her way up to that stage,
just a girl from Tennessee trying to hum-ignore
the reverb of *hillbilly* threats distorting her memory.

As if all the Appalachian grit and grime of her migrant climb
stomps through her throat, she closes her watery eyes
to see back in time, song-circled around grandma's radio,
waiting on a war to send home her *oh yes you can* men
who'd fiddle-accompany, mandolin-chop, guitar-strum along
to the living room choir of sisters wrapped in petticoat pride,
airing out the Devil in that hallelujah chorus where
The valleys stand so thick with corn that they laugh and sing.

Her eyes open wide, reminded of the ministry of music
gathered 'round her microphone mouth, and out shouts
oh sweet Mama, mournfully mining Mother Maybelle
and Sara and Hazel and Alice, Aunt Molly and June
and Loretta and Patsy, Rose and Dolly, Ola Belle and Emmy Lou,
so that by the time she arrives at *daddy's got them deep elem blues*,
all them menfolks on the stage suddenly change their tune.

—*Jake Speed,* Cincinnati songwriter and musician